UNIVERSITY OF NORTH CAROLINA
STUDIES IN THE ROMANCE LANGUAGES AND LITERATURES
Number 95

CHARLES NODIER: HIS LIFE AND WORKS
A CRITICAL BIBLIOGRAPHY
1923 - 1967

CHARLES NODIER:
HIS LIFE AND WORKS

A CRITICAL BIBLIOGRAPHY
1923 - 1967

BY

SARAH FORE BELL

CHAPEL HILL
THE UNIVERSITY OF NORTH CAROLINA PRESS

depósito legal: v. 407 - 1971

artes gráficas soler, s. a. - jávea, 28 - valencia (8) - 1971

CONTENTS

	Pages.
PREFACE	9
INTRODUCTION	13
BIBLIOGRAPHY	
Part I: A Critical Bibliography of Nodier Studies, 1923-1967.	45
Part II: A Tentative Bibliography of the Works of Charles Nodier, 1923-1967	137
APPENDIX: Bibliography, by autor, of Nodier studies, 1923-1967	158
INDEX	183
ADDENDUM TO PART II	188

PREFACE

During a preliminary inquiry into the present state of Nodier studies in 1963 I found acute need for a detailed Nodier bibliography. The nineteenth century did not produce a single such study; and the only one in the twentieth century, Jean Larat's *Bibliographie critique des œuvres de Charles Nodier* (3)[1] of 1923 is, of course, long out-of-date.[2] The scholar interested in Nodier has been compelled, then, to search the numerous general bibliographies available, as well as the more specific but very limited bibliographies appended to pertinent works of other scholars. The present investigation was undertaken in the hope of ameliorating this situation by providing adequate coverage of Nodier studies since 1923.

The bibliography is divided into two large sections, the first of which is an introductory essay on the direction Nodier scholarship has taken since 1923. As this period has been found to

---

[1] Numbers in parentheses throughout this study refer to corresponding items in the bibliographies.

[2] Since the manuscript of the present volume went to the printer, a good bibliography of Nodier's original publications has appeared: Edmund J. Bender's *Bibliographie: Charles Nodier; bibliographie des œuvres, des lettres et des manuscrits de Charles Nodier, suivie d'une bibliographie choisie des études sur Charles Nodier, 1840-1966* (Lafayette, Ind.: Purdue University Studies, 1969), v, 83 pp. It is an up-to-date catalogue of Nodier's works, excluding reprintings; letters; and manuscripts, along with a selected, but largely unannotated, list of studies from 1840 to 1966. (Essentially the same bibliographies appear also appended to his dissertation [301].) It rectifies many of the inaccuracies and oversights in Larat but does not supplant him as a reference for material *on* Nodier to 1923. Professor Bender's book provides an excellent companion volume to the present study.

coincide with a change in interpretation of the importance of Nodier, it is a period of unusual interest.

The second section consists of two bibliographies. The first, and primary one, is a critical bibliography of Nodier studies. For the sake of as complete coverage as possible, works in French, English, Italian, Spanish, and German have been included. Miscellaneous works in other languages, when noted, have been added at the end without annotation. No systematic effort has been made to search out the literature in languages other than the five indicated.

As this is intended to be a critical study, it has not been felt necessary to list every reference to Nodier that was found. In general, the bibliography does not encompass literary histories, except for a few of exceptional importance. Selection of items for inclusion was based on relative importance of the material, as well as on the amount of space devoted to Nodier. It should be stated, however, that a few mediocre items have been included for the reason that they appear in other bibliographies and therefore require comment regardless of their critical value.

Because of the significant evolution in Nodier studies during the period covered, a chronological arrangement of material was decided on as the best method of illustrating this change. Entries are numbered consecutively. However, I regret that the late arrival of some material necessitated in several places the use of numbers such as 1-A and 1-B. Each entry has a *précis* of subject matter and, in many cases, a brief critical comment. Most items have been seen; but where they have not, they are indicated as "Not seen." Every effort has been made to give full bibliographical information. Unfortunately, it is in some instances incomplete because of omissions in the original reference or because the material was seen only as a photoreproduction which did not permit complete verification of the citation. Reviews, when known, are noted, following the *précis,* under lower case letters. To facilitate finding the contributions of a given author, an alphabetical arrangement of material by author, without annotations, has been provided in an Appendix. In addition, a number of "See also" references have been used to aid in the location of material on certain subjects, though these point only to the most important material and by no means offer a complete guide. An index provides further aid in finding subject matter.

The second bibliography comprises a tentative list of the works of Nodier republished between 1923 and 1967. As many as possible of these editions have been seen both in France and the United States. But because of the unavailability of a large number of them, major reliance has necessarily been placed on national bibliographies and publishers' catalogues, as well as the printed catalogues of various libraries. For this reason, bibliographical data for many editions have not been verified personally. It is my intention that this part of my study serve merely as a modest starting point for whoever may wish to do further work.

Again, language coverage is French, English, Italian, Spanish, and German, with editions in other languages, when known, added at the end. Separate divisions have been made for complete works, selected works (containing two or more items), and individual works, with a chronological arrangement within each division. Translations are arranged by language following the works in French.

Most of the editions are undistinguished, representing simply republications without critical or scholarly comment. However, this is not always true, and significant editions have been given critical annotation. Prefaces, introductions, and postfaces with specific titles by specific authors have been included in part one of the bibliography (with numerical references from the edition in which they appear), but untitled and anonymous prefaces have been summed up under the edition. As before, where material has not been personally examined, it is labelled "Not seen."

Looking to the future, I plan supplementary studies to keep both bibliographies current. In the meantime, it is hoped that the material presented here may prove of some use to Nodier scholars.

I should like to take this opportunity to acknowledge gratefully a large indebtedness to those who have contributed toward the completion of this work. Mrs. June Smith and Mrs. Donna Fredrickson of the University of North Carolina Inter-library Loan Center provided valuable assistance in obtaining material for my use. The distinguished Nodier scholars, M. Jean Richer of the University of Nice, and M. Marius Dargaud, Adjoint d'Archives at Alençon, were most kind in supplying information and advice. But it is Dr. Alfred G. Engstrom of the University of North Carolina Department of Romance Languages to whom the largest measure of thanks is due for his unstinting interest and judicious counsel from inception to completion of this work. I wish also to thank the Research Council of the University of North Carolina at Greensboro for generous financial assistance toward publication. Finally, I express appreciation to my husband, without whose active support and cooperation this study would not have been possible.

INTRODUCTION

Charles Nodier has never been completely forgotten by his countrymen, as periodic popular re-editions of his *contes* and an examination of the ample bibliography of Jean Larat (3) show. However, his fame suffered a sharp eclipse following his death in 1844. The first years of the twentieth century saw a substantial renewal of interest in Nodier by scholars like Michel Salomon, Léonce Pingaud, Eunice Morgan Schenk, and Antoine Magnin. But that interest was manifested primarily in the man, the host of the "dimanches" at the Arsenal, the disseminator of Romantic ideals, the naturalist, rather than in the literary work. A change in direction in Nodier scholarship, centering increasingly on the work, dates from approximately 1923. It is the purpose of the Introduction to demonstrate the change, as revealed in this bibliography, and show its evolution. Three stages of development can be seen. From 1923 through 1939 there was a growing attention to the works rather than the man. The war years and those immediately following saw a decline in scholarly output, with emphasis primarily on the celebration of the centenary of Nodier's death, but with a perceptible movement in the direction studies would take after 1950. The period from 1950 to the present represents a marked increase of interest in all aspects of Nodier's literary work and thought and at least a partially successful attempt at re-evaluation of his importance. Unfortunately, no significant bibliographical studies of Nodier exist for this period. However, encouragement is taken from the fact that Jean Richer as far back as 1951 (171) called attention to the lack of a bibliography since Larat's, and in 1965 (288) cited the bringing up-to-date of Larat as one of the most urgent tasks for Nodier scholars.

* * *

1923-1939

Larat's two major works, published in 1923, remain the pioneering efforts in their areas of Nodier scholarship. The *Bibliographie critique des œuvres de Charles Nodier* (3) is the only major bibliography devoted to works by and on Nodier.[1] As in the case of many studies which are first in their field, certain gaps have here gradually become evident. But, in spite of growing awareness of its omissions and errors, Larat's bibliography necessarily continues to be an essential reference tool for the period before 1923.

La Tradition et l'exotisme dans l'œuvre de Charles Nodier (4) represents a turning point of even more consequence in Nodier studies. As the first extensive publication devoted largely to the literary work of Nodier, it is of primary significance in the development of present-day trends. Realizing that "la biographie de Nodier était ce qui importe le moins chez lui" and that "l'essentiel était dans ses vastes connaissances littéraires, dans la sensibilité vibrante ... dans son imagination" (p. ii), Larat elected to explore thoroughly Nodier's literary themes.

> N'y a-t-il pas quelque disproportion d'effort à consacrer tout un volume, fût-il excellent, à élucider ses gasconnades, alors que lui-même affirmait sans se lasser que l'exactitude et la réalité ne sont rien, que ses seules joies lui venaient du rêve? Le vrai problème n'était-il pas d'explorer ces rêves plutôt que de les dénoncer? Accuser Nodier de mensonge, n'était-ce pas demeurer à un stade superficiel, alors qu'il eût été essentiel de porter dans l'étude de ses songes ou de sa sensibilité nébuleuse un souci d'analyse qui les élevât à la dignité d'un objet de science? Prendre quelqu'un en délit de mensonge, serait-ce aussi fructueux pour le sociologue que d'examiner les formes du mensonge dans l'ensemble de ces relevés? Bref, il nous semblait qu'en étudiant les thèmes littéraires où Nodier avait cru pouvoir exprimer les aspirations de sa sensibilité, les élans de son imagination, ou même simplement sa soumission à la mode, on passait d'une étude d'intérêt individuel à un problème d'ordre général, à des vues souvent nouvelles sur la formation du romantisme. (p. ii)

---

[1] The publication in 1969 of Edmund J. Bender's *Bibliographie: Charles Nodier* has already been noted in footnote 2 of the Preface.

For Larat, then, a study of Nodier threw light upon the whole Romantic movement, and he neglected no major angle of inquiry into his literary production.

Early in the century scattered interest had been shown in a few of the influences seen in Nodier — for instance the Illyrian. However, the period from 1923 through 1939 was one intensely concerned with the broad themes and influences found in his writings. Much of the interest was doubtless inspired by Larat; but some of the studies were undertaken independently. At the same time that Larat was investigating Illyrian influences in *La Tradition et l'exotisme dans l'œuvre de Charles Nodier* (4), Rudolf Maixner was preparing his thesis in Croatian, *Charles Nodier i Illirija* (297). Although it partially overlapped Larat's study, the publication of fragments of this thesis as "Charles Nodier en Illyrie" (11) in 1924 was an occasion of some importance; for it marked the beginning of a long series of Maixner's studies in French, culminating in the perhaps definitive *Charles Nodier et l'Illyrie* (231) in 1960.

Two other scholars during the same period also made contributions to the knowledge of Nodier in Illyria. The Franc-Comtois, Abel Monnot, in "La Slovénie et Charles Nodier" (13), gave a reliable account of Nodier's stay there, with some good insights into the political situation. But Monnot disapproved of Nodier's use of Slovenian material: "Ce moineau franc de chez nous s'en va pondre ses œufs dans les nids des nocturnes et des vampires!" (p. 211) René Dollot in "Les Romans illyriens de Charles Nodier" (56) did a good, detailed study of the Illyrian influences in *Jean Sbogar* and *Mademoiselle de Marsan* and found more — including authentic local color and fidelity to nature in the landscapes — than had been discovered theretofore.

Other themes and national influences in Nodier were being explored at the same time. Although Walther Mönch's *Charles Nodier und die deutsche und englische Literatur* (64 and 296) is, in general, an overly philosophical treatment of Nodier, in some respects it is excellent. Mönch found that Nodier understood and was at home in English and German literature and gave some of the most specific and detailed examples to be found of the influence of those literatures on his work, as well as a fine comparison of Hoffmann and Nodier. In addition, his consideration of the influence of Nodier's immediate French predecessors is illuminating.

Alice Killen, in her important study of *Le Roman terrifiant ou roman noir de Walpole à Anne Radcliffe* (2), considered a different aspect of English influence on Nodier and found that he was one of the first of the Romanticists to write in the *genre noir*. Reginald Hartland in *Walter Scott et le roman frénétique* (40) called especial attention to Nodier, minimizing the influence of Scott and leaning more heavily on the frenetic influence than did Miss Killen. His work is marred by the inclusion of unnecessary summaries, and comment on works which are not pertinent, but says much that is good.

Margaret Bain's thorough treatment of *Les Voyageurs français en Écosse, 1770-1830* (55) also examined the significance of Scott, and more especially of Scotland, in the work of Nodier, finding that the voyages of the Romantics were more influential in the literary regionalism of authors like Nodier than were the novels of Scott.

The fantastic, magic, diabolism and Satanism, and occultism are other exotic or esoteric themes attracting the attention of Nodier scholars in a wide variety of studies. Maximilian Rudwin, who devoted his efforts almost exclusively to diabolism and Satanism in literature, in "Nodier's fantasticism" (15) found that "Nodier was a fanatic *fantaisiste*. He was obsessed with the phantasmagoric world. Reality was to him, as to Hoffmann, but a pretext for the flight of his imagination" (p. 8). It was Nodier who pioneered the fantastic in French literature, and diabolism was an integral part of his fantastic. Émile Cailliet, in *The Themes of Magic in Nineteenth Century French Fiction* (72), gave a large place to Nodier in the "wonder literature" of the nineteenth century and considered his principal contributions to it. *Le Diable dans la littérature au XIXe siècle* (90) by Claudius Grillet emphasized a different aspect of Nodier's fantasticism — his influence, with specific examples, on the other Romantic writers: Lamartine, Vigny, Hugo, Musset, Balzac, and (through Balzac) Gautier.

A facet of Nodier allied to magic and diabolism, his relations with the Illuminists and various other "exaltés" and their influence on his work, was examined by Auguste Viatte in *Les Sources occultes du romantisme* (44). But Nodier's interest in occultism was a passing one. "Il y a chez Nodier un sceptique, un dilettante incorrigible, qui savoure l'originalité des doctrines les plus oubliées. Ce trait le définirait même" (II, 145). He did not develop any system. Rather, "son œuvre est la première où les croyances des initiés deviennent un ornement littéraire" (II, 161).

Finally, we must cite one excellent work toward the end of the period under consideration, Albert Béguin's *L'Âme romantique et le rêve* (96), which considered, with unusual insight, the role of dream and the unconscious in the work of Nodier, giving special attention to *La Fée aux Miettes*.

To this point we have been concerned with the influences and themes found in Nodier. During this period there was also a beginning of interest in the effect of his literary work on other authors, whereas previously concern with his influence had been confined largely to that of his personality and ideas. Henri Bauer, in *Les "Ballades" de Victor Hugo* (89), found that here Nodier was the most important precursor of Hugo and commented: "Son rôle auprès de l'auteur des *Odes et ballades* est d'une qualité telle que l'esquisse rapide des idées de Charles Nodier constituera l'acheminement direct à la ballade romantique selon Victor Hugo" (p. 33). Nodier exercised all the more influence on Hugo since he was Hugo's best friend during the period of composition of the *Odes et ballades*. Bauer discerned Hugo's debt to specific works of Nodier in ten poems. Claudius Grillet, in *Le Diable dans la littérature au XIXe siècle* (90), pointed out, as we have seen above, the influence of Nodier's fantasticism on the major Romantics. And Mme Henry-Rosier (97) found that if Lamennais did not plagiarize Nodier's *L'Apocalypse du solitaire* in his *Paroles d'un croyant*, at least Nodier preceded him.

This period also marked an awakening of serious interest in the individual works of Nodier with two careful studies by Jules Vodoz. All too many authors at this time felt the necessity of passing in review the body of Nodier's fiction, without making any real contribution toward its interpretation. Vodoz' studies were a definite step forward. The first, and by far the more considerable, was his *La Fée aux Miettes* in 1925 (17). Since his avowed aim here was "d'interpréter ce récit ... en m'aidant des idées de la psychologie analytique" (p. vi), his study would seem to provide a welcome response to Larat's (4) statement that "l'interprétation de ce récit, en apparence destiné aux enfants, exigerait toutes les lumières de la psychanalyse" (p. 321). Excellent in many of its insights, Vodoz' essay is marred by the arbitrary character of much of his symbolism and by an apparently preconceived idea that Nodier's strange tale constitutes his intimate biography. Yet the study raised questions and proposed answers that are still reflected in today's criticism. More importantly, it was a beginning to a long series of differing interpretations of *La Fée aux Miettes* continuing to the present time. In "Zu Charles Nodier's *Moi-même*" (37), Vodoz continued his psychoanalytical approach to Nodier's literary work, finding in this youthful autobiographical novel, which most commentators have refused to take seriously, the key to Nodier's character.

Along with the growth of interest in individual works came increasing attention to previously unpublished material. While much of this is intrinsically unimportant, it adds considerably to our knowledge of Nodier's literary formation. In 1924 Larat published six letters (10) that form a first sketch of *Les Proscrits* and pointed out the difference between the sketch and the published novel. Georges Gazier, a scholar who has made sizeable contributions to Nodier scholarship, in 1928 (39) described another of Nodier's youthful works (untitled, but on the subject of the influence great men have had on the century in which they lived) written in 1807 for the "concours d'éloquence" of the Académie des Sciences, Belles-Lettres et Arts de Besançon. A third work of this early period, the satirical *Parnasse du jour,* was described by Mme Henry-Rosier (61 and 91), who has written extensively on Nodier. Interest in Nodier's unpublished correspondence continued in this period with contributions by Gustave Simon (35),

Richmond-Laurin Hawkins (58), Paul Tisseau (75), and an anonymous contributor (32).

Larat's consideration, in *La Tradition et l'exotisme dans l'œuvre de Charles Nodier* (4), of Nodier's hitherto largely neglected career as a journalist inspired further interest in his critical and journalistic activities; and Thomas Palfrey's "Charles Nodier et *L'Europe Littéraire*" (21) made a sound addition to the work of Larat. Camille Vuillame's brief but concentrated article on "Nodier journaliste" (38) has interesting information on Nodier's journalistic career both as a literary and political writer. Edmond Eggli and Pierre Martino in *Le Débat romantique en France* (77), which covers the years 1813-1816, presented four of the difficult-to-obtain critical articles of Nodier. One of the more important contributions of the period on Nodier's journalistic career was the publication for the first time of his *Statistique illyrienne* (19a), a collection of the articles he and his collaborators wrote on Illyrian subjects for the *Télégraphe Officiel* in 1813.[2] A good assessment of this book by R. Warnier (87) shows that it is important not just as a catalogue of Nodier's Illyrian interests, but as an indication of certain general aspects of his literary formation.

Though Nodier's learned activities and writings have no particular interest or value for today's audience, some of them were still studied occasionally as a carry-over from the preceding period during the years 1923 through 1939. Nodier's activities as a bibliophile, for example, have attracted much attention from other bibliophiles over the years; and Ejnar Munksgaard's "Charles Nodier et son cercle" (42) provides an unusually interesting preface on this subject. Miquel y Planas' good "Vida de bibliófilo Nodier" (12) emphasizes this particular side of Nodier as a man and a writer; and Theodore W. Koch's edition of *Tales for Bibliophiles* (45) has pertinent material in the preface and notes on Nodier.

Some attention has also been given to Nodier as a naturalist. Ch. Broyer and Virgile Brandicourt both had articles in the 1930's on this subject. Broyer, in "Charles Nodier, cryptogamiste" (76),

---

[2] The *Télégraphe Officiel* was a journal published by the French regime et Ljubljana from October 3, 1810, to September 26, 1813. Nodier was its director from the end of 1812 to the retreat of Napoleon's forces in September of the following year.

identified by their modern names some of the mosses, ferns, and lichens described by Nodier in his *Promenade de Dieppe aux montagnes d'Écosse;* and Brandicourt's "Charles Nodier naturaliste" (82) is a condensed sketch of Nodier's works on natural history and his contacts with natural scientists.

A. H. Schutz, as a philologist himself and in answer to those who he felt had given undue place to Nodier as a philologist, examined the problem in "The Nature and Influence of Charles Nodier's Philological Activity" (23) and found that Nodier's feeble works in this field have rightly passed into obscurity. But another author, Robert de Souza, in "À Propos du phonographe" (81) was kinder to Nodier, finding that in the preface to his *Vocabulaire de la langue française* he was the originator of both the word "phonograph" and the idea for the machine. Also concerned with the learned side of Nodier, R. N. Sauvage in "Nodier et les Vaudevires" (68) revealed a minor aspect of his interest in the Middle Ages.

Though the years 1923 through 1939 saw an increase of interest in the literary and critical work of Nodier, this does not mean that Nodier the man was neglected. In fact, the idea of his personal charm and the fame of his salon were still such that numerous otherwise good studies were needlessly burdened with repetitious accounts of his life and evocations of the soirées at the Arsenal. However, a number of valid additions to the knowledge of various aspects of Nodier's life were made during this period. Jean Larat's "Charles Nodier en Alsace" (50) shows some of the violent and picturesque influences on Nodier at the time of his sojourn in Strasbourg during the Revolution at the impressionable age of thirteen. The always informative Georges Gazier again made a contribution with his "Nodier à l'Arsenal, d'après les carnets de voyage de son ami Ch. Weiss" (9), presenting the parts of the *carnets* of the Besançon bibliophile and librarian that furnish intimate glimpses of Nodier during Weiss's visits between 1822 and 1834. Two articles concern the little-known role of Nodier as librarian of the Arsenal. Almost half of Paul Deslandres's historical article, "La Bibliothèque de l'Arsenal, berceau du romantisme et sanctuaire du théâtre" (28), is devoted to Nodier, with whom the Arsenal's fame began. Georges Hartmann, aided by unpublished correspondence, made an important addition to the knowledge of Nodier as librarian in "Charles Nodier et la Garde Nationale à l'Arsenal pendant les journées de juillet 1830" (57). "Charles Nodier et Victor Hugo" (73) by Paul-A. Charles traces the relations of these writers as illuminated by two recently-discovered articles by Nodier on Hugo's *Marion Delorme*.

Only one book-length biography of Nodier was written during this period. Mme Henry-Rosier's *La Vie de Charles Nodier* (62) has a lively style and stimulating presentation of material to recommend it. But it is an undocumented and fictionalized account and, though based on original sources, cannot be relied upon by the scholar.

The descriptions of the *dimanches* at the Arsenal were so frequent during this period as to be trite. However, two items seem worthy of mention on this score. Fernand Baldensperger in "Les Années 1827-1828 en France et au dehors" (24) made one of the best statements available of the real significance of the salon. And Émile Henriot's "Le Salon de Charles Nodier" (30) describes the atmosphere there with less sentimentality than is frequently found.

A considerable amount of the interest shown in Nodier during this period was due to various centenary commemorations of Romanticism between 1927 and 1934. As a part of the celebration the Bibliothèque de l'Arsenal featured an exposition of items connected with Nodier and his family and friends which accounted for three items of interest. A valuable catalogue (33) of the exposition was published; and Frantz Calot in "Le Salon de Charles Nodier et les romantiques" (26) and Émile Henriot in "Le Salon de Charles Nodier" (30), mentioned above, commented on the exhibition. Paul Souday (43) in 1928 published the "discours de réception" of the Romantics (including Nodier) elected to the Académie Française; and in 1934 G. C. in the *Journal des Débats*, for which Nodier once wrote, specifically commemorated Nodier's reception (83). "Un Centenaire romantique: le mariage de Marie Nodier" (47) by Georges Gazier, contributed to knowledge of the relationship of Nodier with his daughter Marie and with his friend Charles Weiss.

It is significant that during this period there is an increasing interest in Nodier by foreign scholars. The work of the Croatian, Rudolf Maixner (11 and 297) and the edition published in Yugoslavia of Nodier's *Statistique illyrienne* (19a) have already been mentioned, as has the work of the German scholar Mönch (64). Two other Germans were also concerned with Nodier. Edouard Blaser in 1927 wrote, in "Um Charles Nodier" (25), a good summary article on Nodier for the German reader. In 1929 Josef Stadelmann did his doctoral dissertation on *Charles Nodier im Urteil seiner Zeitgenossen* (46), which, though it leaves much to be said, is still the only work on the subject. It is perhaps natural that the Yugoslavs, because of Nodier's stay in Illyria, and the Germans, because of the heavy German influence on his work, should be among the first foreigners to study him. But isolated scholars of other nationalities were also becoming aware of Nodier. The Spanish scholar Miquel y Planas early in the period showed an interest in him. "Una Vida de bibliófilo Nodier" (12), already mentioned, preceding a Spanish edition of *Franciscus Columna*, is an excellent life of Nodier for Spanish readers, with the emphasis on Nodier the bibliophile. One American scholar, Francis P. Smith (100), was interested in Nodier through an American edition of *Jean Sbogar* translated by Peter Irving. While these publications are only a modest beginning, indeed, to foreign consideration of Nodier, they do represent a wider interest than had been shown up to this time.

However, it would not be a fair picture of the period if the impression were left that all the critical comment on Nodier was favorable or sympathetic. Even those most desirous of establishing his validity for twentieth-century audiences recognized certain weaknesses in him as a man and as a writer. Some, like Joseph Aynard in "Les Idées et les livres: Charles Nodier" (7) believed that his work is of little consequence today: "Un fantaisiste extraordinairement habile à s'assimiler les idées, qui commence tout et laisse achever aux autres, tel nous apparaît Nodier" (p. 186). His importance lies in his character, his life, and personal influence on the other Romanticists: "... On peut semer beaucoup d'idées précieuses sans rien mener à bien" (p. 187). A few critics, like Émile Henriot in "Courrier littéraire: Charles Nodier ou le mythomane" (59 and 148), seem basically to like Nodier neither as a person nor as a writer; but Henriot definitely represents minority opinion in this respect.

It is illuminating to examine what a few of the outstanding literary histories and encyclopedias, repositories of "standard" opinion, had to say of Nodier during this period. The important *Histoire du romantisme en France* by Maurice Souriau (36), published in 1927, recognized that Nodier was the great literary influence of his time, but through his personality and his erudition as projected in his salon, rather than through his work, "qui est de second ordre" (I, pt. 2, 115) and only a "gagne-pain" (I, pt. 2, 119). Five years later Pierre Moreau in *Le Romantisme* (74) dealt with Nodier much more briefly, and, while admitting his charm, seemed to dismiss him with the word "flâneur" (p. 160). At the same time the *Larousse du XXe siècle* (Paris: Larousse, 1928-33) summed him up with this appreciation: "Nodier, aimable et ingénieux écrivain, n'a guère été qu'un amateur en toutes choses." It is thus evident that histories and encyclopedias had not yet begun to reflect the idea seen in some scholars that the work of Nodier is of real importance.

There remains only to look at the editions published from 1923 through 1939 to see what they reveal of the period. There were approximately two dozen editions of Nodier's selected works, including a few published in England, Spain, Italy, and Germany. At least three editions were adaptations for children. With two or three exceptions, those which we have seen are uniformly undistinguished, being only popular editions. The 1923 *Œuvres choisis* (5a) contains excerpts of a wide selection of Nodier's fiction, memoirs, poetry, correspondence, and his discourse before the Académie Française, and is preceded by a good biography and critical appreciation of Nodier by Albert Cazes. *Statistique illyrienne* (19a) is important as the only collection of Nodier's articles written for the *Télégraphe Officiel*. One other edition might be pointed out for the excellence of its introduction: the 1924 Spanish publication of *Franciscus Columna* and *El Bibliómano,* preceded by "Una Vida de bibliófilo Nodier" by Miquel y Planas (119a), already mentioned.

Approximately forty editions of Nodier's individual works appeared between 1923 and 1939, over a dozen and a half of which were published in the United States, England, Spain, Italy, and Germany. Again, they were almost entirely popular in nature. *L'Histoire du chien de Brisquet* and *Trésor des Fèves et Fleur des Pois* were among the most frequently published of Nodier's writings, indicating that a large number of his printed works were adaptations for children. There were also several editions of *Le Bibliomane* and *Franciscus Columna* because of the interest of bibliophiles in a number of countries; and *Inès de las Sierras* was published four times in Spain, doubtless because of its Spanish setting. It is worthy of note that, in spite of the attention attracted to *La Fée aux Miettes* by Jules Vodoz' study (17), only two individual editions of it were published during these years, and both of these came in the late 1930's.

No comparison can be readily made with previous editions, as this is one of the respects in which Nodier bibliography is most deficient. However, it may be said that Nodier was rather well represented in popular editions during this period, indicating a solid interest by the reading public. Moreover, he was not unknown in foreign countries, especially Spain and Germany. But as yet there was no interest evident in scholarly or critical editions.

The period, then, from 1923 through 1939 was one of increased interest in a growing number of aspects of Nodier scholarship. But most important was the awakening realization that his literary works are more deserving of careful attention than had been previously thought.

* * *

1940-1949

The war years and those just following saw greatly reduced activity in Nodier studies. If it had not been for the publications of Marius Dargaud, as secretary of the Comité des Amis Jurassiens de Charles Nodier, and articles inspired by efforts of Dargaud and the committee in behalf of the centenary celebration in 1944 of the author's death, attention to Nodier would have been scant, indeed. Yet interest in him was maintained, if at a lower level, and showed some inclination in the direction that would be followed after 1950. On the whole, however, the same general aspects of Nodier were studied during this period as during the years 1923 through 1939.

The interest in broad themes and influences, rather thoroughly explored in the preceding period, persisted, though to a lesser extent. Rudolf Maixner continued in two papers his studies of the rapports of Nodier with Illyria. Of these, "L'Élément illyrien dans *Jean Sbogar* de Charles Nodier" (110) looked in detail at Nodier's novel, and examined the question of plagiarism; and "Voyageurs français en Dalmatie réels et imaginaires: Xavier Marmier, Albert Dumont et Francis Levasseur" (126) considered borrowings from Fortis and Nodier by other writers on Illyria, especially in regard to translations of the popular Dalmatian elegy of the *Femme d'Asan-Aga*. One other author was concerned during this period with Illyrian elements in Nodier. Dinko Stambak, in "La Complainte de la noble femme d'Asan-Aga ou l'invitation romantique au voyage illyrien" (149), examined the fifteen French translations of the same elegy, including the two by Nodier, and saw Nodier's personal experience in Yugoslavia as the reason for his pre-eminence in Illyrian matters.

Scotch influence, which was the subject of much comment in the preceding period, accounted for only one paper from 1940 through 1949. R. K. Gordon in "Le Voyage d'Abbotsford (105) gave an amusing relation of Nodier's journey to Scotland, and an estimate of its influence on his work.

The only other preoccupation with themes at this time was with the fantastic. John A. Guischard in *Le Conte fantastique au XIXe siècle* (133) included a mediocre treatment of Nodier. Pierre-Georges Castex, on the other hand, in two good pages in his *Anthologie du conte fantastique français* (144) defined well Nodier's place as a *conteur* of the fantastic without dealing with specific works.

While interest in the themes and influences in Nodier was decreasing, there was greatly increased attention to his specific influence on other authors and to his position as a precursor of later literary modes. Christine Morrow in *Le Roman irréaliste dans les littératures contemporaines de langues française et anglaise* (107) cited Nodier, "qui mêle au réel le féerique, l'ironique et l'hallucination, d'une façon aussi indéchiffrable que la synthèse d'observation et d'intuition qui constitue la vie" (p. 9), as one of the important precursors of the *roman irréaliste* and counted among his successors Virginia Woolf, James Branch Cabell, James Stephens, Alain-Fournier, Jean Giraudoux, and Julien Green. Pierre Martino's *L'Époque romantique en France, 1815-1830* (135) pointed out that Nodier's article "De Quelques Logomachies classiques," of April, 1824, contained ideas that Sainte-Beuve would advance later in his *Pensées de Joseph Delorme*. And three of the men writing in connection with the centenary of Nodier's death considered him a precursor or innovator in various respects. André Thérive (129) called him a precursor of Nerval and Heredia. Frantz Calot (104) felt that in linguistics, as well as literature, he was something of a prophet, foreshadowing Esperanto, and that he raised bibliophily almost to a genre of writing. In "Nodier after a Century" (128) Paul Rosenfeld examined the ways in which Nodier was an innovator and found that in *Jean Sbogar* he introduced the idea of the social revolutionary and thus produced the first socialist novel; that in the *Novena of Candlemas* he introduced the lyrical expression of the peasant spirit; and that in the *Castles of the King of Bohemia* he anticipated Mallarmé, Apollinaire, and Cummings. "... Looking back over the past century, we can perceive the startling results of the new methods and materials which amused his contemporaries; and moreover possess general reasons for seeing in all such inventions 'the seal of genius' " (p. 19).

Some interest in individual works of Nodier was also shown during this period, as in the preceding one. Albert Béguin in "Nodier et Nerval" (114) compared *La Fée aux Miettes* and *Aurélia* and concluded that Nodier's story deserved to be as well-known as Nerval's. This article is important also as a beginning of attention to specific, rather than general, rapprochements between Nodier and Nerval, which will be found to increase in the succeeding period. The other work of Nodier noted individually was *L'Histoire du roi de Bohême*. In 1946 Yanette Delétang-Tardif (138) became acquainted with this rare and delightful fantasy and suggested a new edition, a desire that was fulfilled in 1950 by the Club Français du Livre reprint of the 1830 edition (95a).

Publication of previously unpublished material by Nodier continued with additional, or corrected, letters contributed by Fernand Marc (134) and Marius Dargaud (125-A, 137, and 147). However, several other aspects of Nodier which elicited a certain amount of interest in the preceding period were almost neglected. There was one small contribution to Nodier's career as a critic when Fernand Baldensperger in *La Critique et l'histoire littéraire en France au dix-neuvième et au début du vingtième siècles* (131) presented, with comment, an excerpt from Nodier on Revolutionary oratory, which he had had the opportunity to hear firsthand in Besançon in his youth. Likewise, only one contribution was made to the literature on Nodier's learned works. In volume XII (*L'Époque romantique*, by Charles Bruneau) of the multivolumed *Histoire de la langue française des origines à nos jours* by Ferdinand Brunot (145), Nodier's extraordinary ideas on language were summarized.

An aspect of Nodier's activity which received wide attention in the period 1923 through 1939 — the salon — was accorded almost none during this decade. The only real consideration of it, by R.-N. Raimbault in "Charles Nodier et son temps" (108), was devoted largely to pointing out that most descriptions of the salon had been inexact because they were static, ignoring the evolution in its character.

Continued interest in Nodier's life and elusive personality was manifested, with the fortunate difference that in this period there was less merely repetitious recounting of the known facts. One of the most interesting studies was that of Dr. Benassis, "Essais de clinique romantique: Charles Nodier ou l'onirique" (103), in which the states of Nodier's health throughout his life were examined in relation to the contradictions in his character and to his literary production. "Évidemment, ni onirisme, ni schizoïdie caractérisés en véritables délires ne peuvent s'appliquer à Nodier; mais on peut penser à de simples troubles d'allure onirique ou schizoïde, légers quoique désagréables ..." (1941, p. 55). This mental state was reflected in his work; for example, *Smarra* and *La Fée aux*

Miettes. The attraction of Vampirism for Nodier must also be related to his "onirisme." Dr. Benassis concluded that with this temperament Nodier should have been, and was, one of the first supporters of Romanticism.

Gustave Charlier in *Le Mouvement romantique en Belgique 1815-1850* (146) made an important addition to what is known of Nodier's career, presenting material on his trip to Belgium, and his reception in the Belgian press.

The sole book-length work on Nodier during the entire period was Mariette Held's substantial *Charles Nodier et le romantisme* (153), which, while not strictly biography, is more appropriately considered here than elsewhere. In three parts, it dealt with the historical role of Nodier in the Romantic movement, examined the Romantic elements in his work, and gave an excellent psychological analysis of his character.

By far the most productive year of the whole decade for articles devoted to Nodier was 1944, the centenary anniversary of his death. The efforts of Marius Dargaud and the Comité des Amis Jurassiens de Charles Nodier were directly or indirectly responsible for a large part of this material. Among the items published in connection with their celebration at Lons-le-Saunier were a program (123), a valuable catalogue of the exposition (125) organized for the occasion, and a *Recueil de documents* (127) concerning the event. One journal article by Tancrède de Visan (130), three by R. Aubert (111, 112, and 113), and a series by Dargaud (116, 117, 118, 119, 120, 120-A, 121, 122, 124) concerned the centennial; and a 1946 article by Dargaud (136) related the committee's difficulties in planning the celebration under the Occupation. Three other articles connected with the centennial, but unrelated to the celebration at Lons-le-Saunier, appeared. Frantz Calot in "En 1844 Charles Nodier mourait" (104) recalled Nodier's last moments and regretted the impossibility of a commemoration et Paris. André Thérive in "La Cité des Plumes—Nodier précurseur" (129) also expressed regret that the centenary of Nodier's death passed almost unnoticed in Paris because of the war. And Paul Rosenfeld in "Nodier after a Century" (128) looked back over the hundred years since Nodier's death and saw him primarily as an innovator.

During the period from 1940 through 1949 an important tendency to consider Nodier in new contexts was beginning to develop. Alfred Engstrom in "The French Artistic Short Story before Maupassant" (106) examined the most important of Nodier's *contes* and found that only one, the first part of *Inès de las Sierras,* can be called an artistic short story. In "The Formal Short Story in France and Its Development before 1850" (132) the same critic came to the conclusion that, other than the stories of Balzac, Mérimée, and Gautier, part one of *Inès de las Sierras* is the only first-rate artistic short story to be found in France before 1850.

In regard to another area of Nodier's literary activity, his poetry, which was well regarded in his time but receives little attention today, it is of interest that as recently as 1946 Georges Duhamel included him in his *Anthologie de la poésie lyrique en France* (139), although with the recognition that he is appreciated primarily for his prose. At about the same time Luigi Fontana in "L'Arte di Charles Nodier" (152) analyzed Nodier's fiction, concluding that its special charm lay in its basically poetic character. Such attention to unstudied aspects of Nodier will be seen to increase in the next period.

It is also significant that from 1940 through 1949 there was a definite increase in the proportion of interest shown in Nodier by foreign critics, as may be amply seen in the literature cited in the preceding pages. The increase is all the more notable since almost the entire western world was involved in World War II and its aftermath during this decade. Yet work on Nodier was being published in the United States, Canada, Belgium, and Italy, and continued in French by Rudolf Maixner in Yugoslavia. It might be pointed out, however, that criticism by German scholars, fairly evident in the preceding period, was entirely lacking at this time.

The publication rate of editions of Nodier declined only slightly during the years 1940 through 1949. There were more than fifteen editions of selected works and approximately twenty of individual works, with — besides France — the United States, England, Spain, Italy, and Switzerland being represented. As in the preceding period, the *Histoire du chien de Brisquet* led in number of editions of individual works, with six. It should also be noted that the number of editions of *La Fée aux Miettes* increased to four, as compared to two in the longer period from 1923 through 1939. Again, the editions that I have seen are undistinguished, being largely popular in nature. Yet it may be said that, in view of the circumstances of these years, on the whole the publishing situation with regard to Nodier was reasonably healthy.

Indeed, the entire picture of Nodier scholarship during the period might be looked upon as unexpectedly satisfactory. Continuity with the period from 1923 through 1939 was manifested in the more important aspects of study, while many of the unfortunate repetitious elements were disappearing. At the same time evidence of evolution toward the next period was discerned in other respects.

* * *

1950-1967

The year 1950 marked the beginning of a period — that has continued until today — of greatly increased activity in Nodier scholarship. It has produced almost as many studies of Nodier as the preceding two periods combined and in addition has seen a more definite change in direction of interest than was evidenced during the war years. That change has been especially noticeable in the increasing attention to Nodier's specific influence on other authors; in the number of studies devoted to previously unconsidered aspects of his work; and in the greater attention accorded him by foreign scholars. Furthermore, an increase in the overall quality of scholarship has been noticed, accompanied by an almost total decline in the purely repetitious elements seen previously.

Of course, many writers of the present period have shown that familiar subjects had by no means been exhausted. The broad themes and influences to be found in Nodier continued to draw considerable critical comment. Rudolf Maixner made two contributions to his studies of Nodier and Illyria, the second of which is of primary importance. "Un Article 'illyrisant' posthume de

Charles Nodier" (178) commented on a pertinent fragment Maixner had recently discovered. His book, *Charles Nodier et l'Illyrie* (231), was the culmination of a lifetime of inquiry into the subject. Scholarly and thorough, it may well prove to be the definitive work on Illyrian influences in Nodier.

The fantastic, diabolism, and occultism in Nodier also received further attention. "Nodier et ses rêves" in Pierre-Georges Castex's *Conte fantastique en France de Nodier à Maupassant* (167) is perhaps the best study available of Nodier as one of the masters of the fantastic *conte*. Marcel Schneider in *La Littérature fantastique en France* (275) treated Nodier at much less length, but contributed new ideas, especially as to sources for *La Fée aux Miettes*. *Le Diable dans la littérature française de Cazotte à Baudelaire, 1772-1861* (232) by Max Milner contains good pages on Nodier as a critic and writer of Satanic and diabolic literature and an evaluation of his influence on Aloysius Bertrand. On the little studied influence of occultism in Nodier two items may be cited. Robert Amadou and Robert Kanters' *Anthologie littéraire de l'occultisme* (155) contains a short appreciation of the general nature of Nodier's occultism.

> Des réflexions des théosophes de tous les temps, qu'il connaît bien, il tire en somme une souple vision du monde. ... C'est donc par sa culture et par le "climat" de sa pensée que Nodier ressortit à l'occultisme. Mais que l'influence de celui-ci ait été profonde, on le voit dans certains textes ... (p. 212).

In "Romantiques français devant les sciences occultes" (197) Jean Richer considered occultism in Nodier, Hugo, Balzac, and Nerval and found that Nodier was a precursor in its use for literary purposes.

Besides continued research in the broad themes and influences in Nodier, an entirely new interest was manifested, from the beginning of the present period, in a wide variety of smaller themes and influences. Hella-Henriette Freymann's doctoral dissertation in 1956, "Aspects littéraires des tendances platoniciennes dans la France du XIXe siècle" (201), examined a large part of Nodier's fiction, with emphasis on his idealistic tendencies. Another dissertation, "Vico and French Romanticism" (261) by Arthur Paul Metastasio, sought to establish the Italian philosopher, Vico, as an initiator of French Romanticism and found that Nodier seemed in many cases to represent the most complete amplification of Vico's ideas among the French Romanticists. Two other studies concerned the idea of paradise in Nodier. Albert Béguin in "Charles Nodier ou l'enfance restaurée" (156) concluded that two times, in *Trilby* and *La Fée aux Miettes*, Nodier recreated the paradise of childhood. Winfried Engler studied the subject more at length in "Der Mythos vom verlorenen Paradies bei Charles Nodier" (247). He saw two kinds of paradise in Nodier, the *locus amoenus* and the paradise of childhood, presenting a mixture of the personal and mythical that was influential in the development of the idea of paradise in literature up through Alain-Fournier and Truman Capote. Three other themes in Nodier were focused on by other authors. Gwendolyn Bays in her *Orphic Vision: Seer Poets from Novalis to Rimbaud* (265) looked at the simple, innocent seers that appear in Nodier's *contes*. *Artists and Writers in Paris; the Bohemian Idea, 1803-1867* (268) by Malcolm Easton inquired into Nodier's youthful relations in Paris with a group of painters and examined the depiction of the artist in Nodier's early work. And Jean-Laurent Prévost included in *Le Prêtre, ce héros de roman d'Atala aux Thibault* (180) a study of the Romantic treatment of the priest in Nodier's *Franciscus Columna* as opposed to the more realistic treatment in *Thérèse Aubert*. All of these were completely new inquiries, possibly indicating a tendency to study other new themes in the future.

During the period since 1950, there has been a continued growth of interest in the varied aspects of Nodier's influence on other authors, French and foreign; in his borrowings; and in his position as a precursor. It was during this period that one of Nodier's most important direct influences — that on Nerval — began to be studied to any extent in specific, rather than general, terms. In 1958 Jean Gaulmier in "Nodier manqua d'être Nerval!" (216) remarked with surprise that Nodier was not recognized more widely as a source for Nerval. But Jean Richer had in 1950 already begun studying, in his excellent "Nodier et Nerval" (165), the direct borrowings of Nerval from Nodier and common themes in the two. In "Gérard de Nerval et *Sylvie*" (196) he pointed out that the roundelay of the young girls in *Sylvie* was reminiscent of a scene in *Thérèse Aubert*. His *Nerval, expérience et création* (263) contains numerous examples to show that "l'influence de Charles Nodier devait s'exercer de façon diffuse sur de larges secteurs de l'œuvre nervalienne" (p. 95). One other critic, Hubert Juin in *Chroniques sentimentales* (249), made penetrating observations on the parallels to be found in Nodier and Nerval.

Hugo's debt to Nodier was a great one and had, of course, been examined before. But during the present period new aspects of their literary relationship were considered by Charles Dédéyan and N. Wilson. Dédéyan's *Victor Hugo et l'Allemagne* (266) included a detailed study of the Germanic influence transmitted through Nodier to Hugo. In "Charles Nodier, Victor Hugo and *Les Feuilles d'automne*" (289) Wilson presented the idea that many of the contradictions to be seen in the *Feuilles d'automne* resulted from Hugo's desire to mend the rift with Nodier.

It was also during the period since 1950 that Nodier began to be cited in connection with Balzac. The first mention came in 1956 with Moïse Le Yaouanc's "Autour de *Louis Lambert*" (202), in which it was suggested that Nodier may have imitated Balzac's Louis Lambert in creating his character Jean-François les Bas-Bleus. Pierre-Georges Castex's valuable study of 1962, "Balzac et Charles Nodier" (244), treated both the personal relations and the reciprocal literary borrowings of Nodier and Balzac during a time in the early 1830's when their thought was similar, and found that in spite of their evolution in opposite directions Balzac appreciated in Nodier

> des qualités d'esprit qui ne lui sont pas toujours reconnues: une vigueur d'analyse, une lucidité de jugement qui font de lui, dans quelques-uns de ses ouvrages, un témoin implacable des erreurs de l'âge moderne. (p. 211)

Pierre Citron's "Aux Sources d'*Une Fille d'Ève*" (277) disagreed with scholars who have seen Nodier as the essential model behind Balzac's composite portrait of the character Nathan. "Balzac et Stendhal, romanciers de l'évasion" (280) by Bernard Guyon linked Nodier with the two great novelists by suggesting that escapes effected in Balzac's *La Muse du département* and Stendhal's *La Chartreuse de Parme* may have been taken from hearing Nodier's relation of a similar incident.

Four foreign critics have broadened even further since 1950 the knowledge of Nodier's influence on other authors. Maria Bianca Luporini in "Un Paesaggio italiano dell' *Evgenij Onegin*" (250) proposed Nodier's *Jean Sbogar* as a source for certain passages in Pushkin's poem. "Postille francesi di Allesandro Manzoni a Charles Nodier" (260) by Francesco Isola published Manzoni's marginal comments in French on a copy of Nodier's *Examen critique des dictionnaires de la langue françoise* and considered what influence Nodier's work might have had on Manzoni's linguistic studies. J. Mitchell Morse's "Charles Nodier's Dreams and *Finnegans Wake*" (303) pointed out the similarity in the theories of dream as seen in the literature of Nodier and Joyce. And Louise S. Blanco in "Origin and History of the Plot of *Marianela*" (276-A) saw Nodier's *Les Aveugles de Chamouny* as an influence on Pérez Galdós' *Marianela*.

Nodier's relationship to the Surrealists was investigated in some detail in Mme Melahat Menemencioglu's "Un Aspect surréaliste de Charles Nodier" (270-A). Christian Dédéyan's article, "Charles Nodier annonciateur du rêve" (246), suggested, in a general manner, Nodier's literary influence by noting that all French art since Nerval, Baudelaire, and the Symbolists is indebted to him. "S'il est un titre que Nodier réclamera, un 'vice' dont il fera sa vertu la moins vaine, c'est le titre de rêveur, la pente à la rêverie. Tous ses livres en témoignent" (p. 28). Thus, he is an important precursor of the Surrealists, for whom, as for him, sleep is the most active state of the soul.

Since 1950 there has been a large current of interest in individual works of Nodier. During this period *La Fée aux Miettes* definitely emerges as the single work commanding the widest attention. In 1950 Albert Béguin in "Charles Nodier ou l'enfance restaurée" (156) examined the psychological reasons for the writing of *La Fée aux Miettes* and *Trilby* and considered them the two masterpieces by which Nodier deserves a place as one of the great creators of French Romanticism. However, the largest share of attention to *La Fée aux Miettes* has been directed toward its interpretation. Béguin, in the main, accepted Vodoz' explanation of 1925 (17). But others proposed widely differing solutions to this difficult work. André Lebois in *Un Bréviaire du compagnonnage: "La Fée aux Miettes" de Charles Nodier* (241) offered a detailed analysis of the story as a Masonic allegory. Antoine Fongaro demonstrated in passing, in "A-t-on lu la *Fée aux Miettes?*" (248), that the story lends itself to the possibility of a gnostic or even Cathar explanation. In his dissertation on "The Fictional Confession of Adolescent Love" (299) Gerald H. Storzer found in Michel a hero who represents the efforts of all men to rise above their condition. "L'Analisi del sogno in *La Fée aux Miettes*" (253) by Piero Battista, proposing that the symbols do not necessarily have specific explanations but allude generally to man's situation, seems to be an effort to put the story back into perspective after the various psychological and esoteric explanations that have been proposed since Vodoz. Albert George, although dealing with the body of Nodier's fiction rather than specifically with *La Fée aux Miettes* in *Short Fiction in France 1800-1850* (269), did offer a simple and interesting solution to the story — that it really is a fairy tale, though a didactic one, in which in traditional manner the hero is placed in jeopardy three times.

But aspects of *La Fée aux Miettes* other than its interpretation also received the attention of scholars. Pierre-Georges Castex in "Une Source de *La Fée aux Miettes*" (157) and Marcel Schneider, who analyzed this *conte* at some length in his overall consideration of Nodier's fiction in *La Littérature fantastique en France* (275), proposed new sources for various elements of the story. Jean Richer's "Le Manuscrit et les premières éditions de *La Fée aux Miettes* de Charles Nodier" (192) examined the original manuscript to find what inferences could be drawn from Nodier's own corrections. And Antoine Fongaro in "A-t-on lu la *Fée aux Miettes?*" (248) pointed out many of the errors that have been repeated in succeeding editions, which, when corrected, remove some of the difficulties of the story. Yet, in spite of all that has been written on *La Fée aux Miettes,* everything has not been said; and it seems likely that attention will continue to be devoted to it.

The other work of Nodier which received a considerable, but far less, amount of study and which also seems assured of attracting further commentary is *L'Histoire du roi de Bohême et de ses sept châteaux*. Yanette Delétang-Tardif's article of 1950, "Je visite les soleils ..." (160) suggested that *Le Roi de Bohême* not only looked back from Sterne to Apuleius, but also forward to Laforgue, Gourmont, Jarry, and the *Calligrammes* of Apollinaire. In the same year a reprint of the 1830 edition of *Le Roi de Bohême* by the Club Français du Livre appeared, with an important postface by Jean Richer entitled "*Le Roi de Bohême* ou les tentations du langage" (166), which pointed out the many authors Nodier is indebted to and indicated some of the parodies and satires. Two years later Richer published *La Plus Petite des pantoufles* (176), which was the preliminary sketch for *L'Histoire du Roi de Bohême*. Both of these publications were incorporated, with the addition of pertinent documents, into Richer's *Autour de "L'Histoire du roi de Bohême," Charles Nodier "dériseur sensé"* of 1962 (252).

A few other works of Nodier were singled out for attention for various reasons. Marius Dargaud reported, in "L'Édition originale du *Génie Bonhomme* de Charles Nodier" (158), the discovery of an 1836 edition of the story that replaces the one of 1837 as the earliest known. In "Variations sur un succube; *Histoire de Thibaud de la Jacquière*" (257) Jean Decottignies traced the source of Nodier's *Aventures de Thibaud de la Jacquière* to a seventeenth-century tale by François de Rosset. A nice comparative study of the differences in treatment of the story of Hélène Gillet by Nodier *(Histoire d'Hélène Gillet)* and Anatole France *(Les Opinions de Jérôme Coignard)* was done by J. Perret in "L'Utilisation littéraire d'un drame judiciaire bressan. Hélène Gillet" (164). And Pierre Mornand commented on Nodier's delightful essay, *L'Amateur de livres,* in "Des Physiologies en général, de celles des bouquinistes et bouquineurs en particulier" (225).

The period since 1950 has seen an increased rate of publication of previously unpublished material by Nodier. Letters continue to turn up, in large numbers. (See 162, 163, 171, 209, 213, 217-A, 224, 288, and 295.) But perhaps more important are the rare, or hitherto unpublished texts, both poetry and prose. Jean Richer has made four important contributions (in addition to his unpublished edition of *Le Voleur* to be considered along with other editions produced during the present period). In no. 304 of the *Cahiers du Sud*, which is in part devoted to Nodier, Richer published the last chapter of *Le Voleur* (163). In 1952, following his "Charles Nodier, dériseur sensé" (176) he published chapter IV of *Le Voleur*, and *La Plus Petite des pantoufles*. His "Notes bibliographiques sur Charles Nodier" (171) contains excerpts of three documents: the project for an *Histoire des califats*, a contract with Renduel, and a letter. And "Textes rares au inédits" (288) contains Nodier's self-portrait, as well as twelve letters cited above.

Other scholars have made less numerous, but equally interesting contributions. Pierre-Georges Castex in "Un Inédit de Charles Nodier: *Ferry Barbis*" (198) proposed that *Ferry Barbis* is the first chapter to a historical novel contemplated by Nodier, which was to have been situated in seventeenth-century Franche-Comté. A. Richard Oliver's "An Unpublished Analysis of Some Fine Editions by the Young Bibliophile Charles Nodier" (234) presented in translation the "Essai sur l'imprimerie et ses progrès" written by Nodier in 1798 and followed by a list of the rare editions in his collection at that time. Finally, Albert Kies in "Deux Inédits de Charles Nodier" (221) and Albert J. George in "Nodier: *Le Vieux Marinier*" (228) published examples of Nodier's *inédits*, the former presenting youthful efforts, and the latter more mature work.

Interest in Nodier's journalistic and critical career, which was active in the period 1923 through 1939 but almost totally lacking during the war years, gained new momentum, which it is to be hoped will continue, in the present period. Three studies concerned Nodier's part in forwarding the Romantic movement. A recent dissertation, "Charting French Romanticism: The Criticism of Charles Nodier" (301) by Edmund J. Bender, investigated Nodier's literary criticism as it relates to the movement. Michel Vivier suggested a sizeable extension of Nodier's journalistic production when in "Victor Hugo et Charles Nodier collaborateurs de *L'Oriflamme*" (217) he proposed Nodier as the most likely author of a series of aggressively Romantic articles in the *Oriflamme* called "Les Sabbats" and signed "Le Vieux Sorcier." C. Jensen showed that "The 'Romanticism' of the *Annales de la Littérature et des Arts*" (281) was confined almost exclusively to articles by Nodier, manifesting here a somewhat subdued form of Romanticism.

Several other studies are indicative of the relatively important role that Nodier seems to have played in literary criticism of the time. Marguerite Iknayan's *The Idea of the Novel in France: the Critical Reaction, 1815-1848* (240) considered Nodier the primary novelist and *conteur* who was also worthy of being cited for his critical articles. "Nodier's Criticism of the *Dictionnaire de l'Académie Française*" (212) by A. Richard Oliver demonstrated that Nodier's critical attacks on the *Dictionnaire* were made largely to attract attention to his own qualifications for election to the Académie. The important question of Nodier's contribution to Shakespeare criticism of the time was examined by two scholars who came to opposite conclusions. In 1961 O. G. Brockett in "Charles Nodier's Estimate of Shakespeare" (237) found that Nodier's appreciation was essentially the same as that of others of his time. But the next year A. Richard Oliver's "Charles Nodier's Cult of Shakespeare as a Facet of French Romanticism" (251) more convincingly showed him to be ahead of his contemporaries in his understanding and appreciation of Shakespeare's genius. One other article was devoted to Nodier's role as a critic. Stephen J. Gendzier in "Diderot's Impact on the Generation of 1830" (259) discussed Diderot's rehabilitation through the writings of Nodier and others.

Nodier's learned work, which received a certain amount of attention in the period from 1923 through 1939, has been almost ignored since. A single study, but one of interest, concerned a side of Nodier that has fascinated one segment of his admirers from time to time over the years. "Nodier as Bibliographer and Bibliophile" (203) by A. Richard Oliver sought to restore Nodier to the important rank he held in the nineteenth century in bibliography and bibliophilism.

It is noteworthy that during this period proportionately far less attention was directed toward Nodier the man than in the years from 1923 through 1949, and far more toward his work and literary influence. Very few biographical studies can be cited here, though one very good book must be mentioned. A. Richard Oliver's *Charles Nodier, Pilot of Romanticism* (271), which was published in 1964, was the first biography since Marguerite Henry-Rosier's fictionalized *Vie de Charles Nodier* (62) in 1931. Up-to-date and factual, Oliver's book helped to fill the need for a well-documented, modern treatment of Nodier's life. Two other smaller contributions might also be mentioned. Maurice Billey's "Un Magistrat révolutionnaire: le père de Charles Nodier" (194) is informative on Nodier's lineage, his early years, and his relations with his father. And Pierre Moreau in "Les Faux Jours de Charles Nodier" (191) presented Nodier as primarily a man of the eighteenth century and of the province of Franche-Comté.

Of perhaps equal significance with the decline in biographical studies is the almost total lack of concern with the salon at the Arsenal. In 1960 Jean Vagne, in his preface to *La Fée aux Miettes* [et autres contes] (55a), wrote of Nodier:

> La légende de l'Arsenal s'est, dirait-on, retournée contre lui. Le plaisant diseur de fariboles, l'aimable faiseur de saugrenu a éclipsé l'écrivain. Dans les histoires de la littérature, il ne sera plus que le maître effacé du grand salon romantique. De temps à autre une voix proteste qu'il est infiniment mieux que cela, et puis le silence retombe. Disons-le à notre tour: il est mieux que cela. (p. 17)

Vagne was partly right: Nodier *is* better than that. But he was wrong in believing that Nodier is still a victim of the fame of his salon, as I believe this study has already demonstrated.

A further proof of Nodier's current rehabilitation is the great amount of interest shown since 1950 in almost any previously uninvestigated aspect of his work, thought, or life. A wide diversity of good studies has turned up numerous new or little explored subjects of interest. Many of these works are concerned with various aspects of Nodier's literary production. Laurence Minot Porter's dissertation of 1965, "Le Style et l'art narratif de Charles Nodier dans les Contes" (287-B), was the first detailed investigation of Nodier's style. Another doctoral dissertation, Henriette Horchler's "Dream and Reality in the Works of Charles Nodier" (302) demonstrated the fusion of the real and the dream worlds in his settings, his characters, and his treatment of historical and social problems. Two papers during the present period, Marius Dargaud's "Nodier mémoraliste: *Suites d'un mandat d'arrêt* (fragment inédit)" (170) and Francesco Orlando's "Charles Nodier memoralista: una infanzia sotto la Rivoluzione" (287) sought to vindicate Nodier in an area in which he has been much criticized, as a writer of memoirs. Orlando also devoted a chapter of his *Infanzia, memoria e storia da Rousseau ai romantici* (291-A) to a further look at this aspect of Nodier's work. In another article by Dargaud, "Charles Nodier poète et l'épopée napoléonienne" (169), Nodier was upheld as a poet of some merit, and a rare poem of his, "Le Conscrit," was republished. In a book of unusual interest, *Piranèse et les romantiques français, le mythe des escaliers en spirale* (290) by Luzius Keller, Nodier was shown to be, through his *Piranèse*, the precursor of better-known nineteenth-century authors who were concerned with the same theme. A secondary study of the same subject, "Piranèse et les poètes romantiques français" (292 and 293) by Georges Poulet, is also of some interest. Alfred G. Engstrom in "The Voices of Plants and Flowers and the Changing Cry of the Mandrake" (279) found *La Fée aux Miettes* to be perhaps the first literary work where the mandrake sings. And Pierre Moreau's *La Tradition française du poème en prose avant Baudelaire* (223) situated Nodier among the many French writers using that form.

A few critics were concerned with different facets of Nodier's thought. The most ambitious undertaking in this area was Robert Maples' somewhat unsuccessful attempt, in his dissertation on "Technique and Vision in the Fiction of Charles Nodier" (285), to see a unified vision of life evinced in Nodier's work. On the other hand, Laurence Minot Porter's dissertation, "Le Style et l'art narratif de Charles Nodier dans les Contes" (287-B), mentioned above, succeeded in demonstrating the way in which Nodier's style related to his cosmology and in proving the essential coherence of his thought. Jean Mennessier-Nodier's "Charles Nodier et l'éducation du peuple" (187) is highly informative on a small segment of his ancestor's intellectual activity.

Two final articles are concerned with other aspects of Nodier's life or career. A. Richard Oliver's "Charles Nodier and the

Marquis de Sade" (233) shows the impossibility of a meeting of the two in spite of Nodier's claim to the contrary. And André Mongland in "Éditeurs romantiques: Nicolas Delangle et Charles Nodier" (190) is concerned with a joint publishing project of these two men.

A backward glance at the pages dealing with the period since 1950 shows not only a preoccupation with a wide variety of aspects of Nodier, but also the greatly increased attention of foreign scholars. At least a part of the change in direction of Nodier studies can be ascribed to the new ideas contributed and areas of inquiry opened up by scholars from other countries.

It is highly significant that literary histories, manuals, and encyclopedias, which usually mirror "standard" thought, and which prior to 1950 had not begun to reflect the awakening interest of scholars in Nodier's work and literary influence, since 1950 have caught up with the current trend. Pierre Moreau in the 1957 edition of *Le Romantisme* (211) gave an excellent three-page summary of Nodier's life and importance as a *conteur* of dream and madness, and as a precursor of Lautréamont and the Surrealists, in contrast to his dismissal of Nodier in the 1932 edition (74) as a "flâneur" (p. 160). Albert J. George in his important *Short Fiction in France 1800-1850* (269) found that Nodier's work is of value not only historically but also intrinsically. As early as 1950 Pierre-Georges Castex and Paul Surer in their *Manuel des études littéraires françaises. XIXᵉ siècle* (Paris: Hachette) came close to giving Nodier his just due as an important precursor when they recognized that:

> ... il peut être considéré comme l'initiateur en France d'une littérature qui a été illustrée au XIXᵉ siècle par des chefs-d'œuvre comme l'*Aurélia* de Nerval et qui trouve son expression la plus audacieuse au XXᵉ siècle dans le mouvement surréaliste. (p. 52)

But it is especially revealing to compare the appreciation of Larousse forty years ago and that of today. The *Larousse du XXᵉ siècle* (Paris: Librairie Larousse, 1928-1933) summed Nodier up as "un amateur en toutes choses." Today the *Grand Larousse encyclopédique* (Paris: Librairie Larousse, 1960-1964) says:

L'influence de Nodier a certainement contribué à élargir l'horizon littéraire du romantisme; il a surtout exploré le domaine du fantastique et des chimères, et préparé ainsi la voie à Nerval et au surréalisme.

A look at the publication record since 1950 is also meaningful to an interpretation of those years. The most important event was the reprinting (1a) in 1967 of Nodier's *Œuvres complètes,* which were originally published from 1832 to 1837 and had not been reprinted since. This would seem to be indicative of the greatly increased present interest in Nodier. In addition, there were twenty-one editions of selected works published in France, Belgium, Italy, and Spain. One of these was of major importance. The Garnier edition of Nodier's *Contes* (57a), with introduction, notices, and notes by Pierre-Georges Castex, is the best edition of the *contes* available, and the only one that can be called scholarly. One other edition, the *Contes fantastiques* (50a), with introductory, biographical, and bibliographical material by Michel Laclos, is worthy of mention for its effort to arouse favorable interest in an exceptional *conteur.*

Only approximately a dozen editions of Nodier's individual works have been published since 1950. But at least three of the dozen were notable. The 1951 edition of Nodier's essay *The Book Collector* (113a) was beautifully printed and illustrated with reproductions of Daumier lithographs. Of the three editions of *La Fée aux Miettes,* the work which was published the most times individually during the period, that of Auguste Viatte (76a) is the best. Viatte disclaims any pretensions to a critical edition but has tried to rid Nodier's text of the "innombrables coquilles qui le déparent dans les éditions courantes." One of the most important publications of the period was the 1950 Club Français du Livre reprinting of the rare *L'Histoire du roi de Bohême* (95a), with an informative postface by Jean Richer. This republication, along with the evident pre-eminence of interest in *La Fée aux Miettes,* is an indication of the attention being given Nodier as a precursor of later nineteenth-century and twentieth-century literature. One other edition might be mentioned, although it exists at the present only in typewritten form as a "thèse secondaire." Jean Richer's critical edition of the unpublished *roman,*

Le Voleur (112a), should point the way for similar work by others in the future.

While the editions of Nodier appearing since 1950 represent a definite decrease in rate of publication from that of the two preceding periods, they would seem, at the same time, to indicate an increase in quality and scholarly interest.

All the evidence, then, for the period since 1950 points toward a current tendency to re-evaluate the literary work and influence of Nodier. A few voices, like that of Roger Duhamel in "De Nouveaux Noms, des œuvres nouvelles" (267), continue to express a dissenting attitude. However, others actively call for a reassessment. In 1954-1955 Richard Switzer in "Charles Nodier: A Re-examination" (193) made a plea for recognition of Nodier as an important precursor in his own right. A few years later Fred Bérence in his treatment of Nodier in *Grandeur spirituelle du XIXe siècle français* (214) expressed surprise that the élite of the twentieth century continue to ignore Nodier and fail to realize that he speaks of essential problems. It is my contention that, beginning with Jean Larat's *La Tradition et l'exotisme dans l'œuvre de Charles Nodier* (4) in 1923, a new interest in the literary work and influence was manifested and that this interest has gradually but steadily evolved until at the present time a re-evaluation is, in fact, in the process of being made, and that wider and wider recognition of Nodier's position as an important precursor is being accorded.

Yet, in spite of the progress that has been made in Nodier scholarship since 1923, there is still much to be done. In 1965 Jean Richer (288) pointed out what he considered to be the three most urgent tasks: to rework Larat's *Bibliographie* (3), completing, correcting, and bringing it up-to-date; to produce a scholarly edition of Nodier's articles of criticism; and to publish an edition of at least selected correspondence. It is hoped that the present study will fill the need to complement Larat, while Edmund J. Bender's bibliography,[3] recently published, up-dates and corrects many aspects of it. The need for an edition of Nodier's articles of criticism, which have never been brought together in

---

[3] See footnote 2 of the Preface.

one place, became particularly evident in the course of this research; and I am at the present undertaking the project. M. Marius Dargaud, Adjoint d'Archives at Alençon, writes me that he is working on the correspondence. Three additional opportunities for study should be pointed out. Much has been said of Nodier's style; but except for Laurence Minot Porter's unpublished dissertation on "Le Style et l'art narratif de Charles Nodier dans les Contes" (287-B) no analysis of it has yet been made.[4] And although a beginning of interest in critical editions can be discerned since 1950, very few have been produced to the present. More should appear in the future. The discovery of a number of autographical manuscripts since Larat's *Bibliographie* (3) in 1923 indicated that none was known to exist ought to facilitate publication of such editions. And, finally, a detailed analysis of *L'Histoire du roi de Bohême* would cast light on Nodier as both an imitator and a precursor.

Thus, it may be seen that, while a great deal has been accomplished in Nodier research since 1923, some of the most important studies are yet to be undertaken or completed.

---

[4] The section dealing directly with style has been published as "Charles Nodier's Prose Rhythms: a Study of Manuscript Variants in the *Contes*," *The French Review*, XLII (1968-69), 533-539.

BIBLIOGRAPHY

PART I

A CRITICAL BIBLIOGRAPHY OF NODIER STUDIES, 1923-1967

1923

1. Callet, Albert. "Une Audience de Charles Nodier à l'Arsenal," *Rev. Franche-Comté et Monts Jura*, avril 1923, p. 156.
Not seen.

2. Killen, Alice M. *Le Roman terrifiant ou roman noir de Walpole à Anne Radcliffe et son influence sur la littérature française jusqu'en 1840.* Bibliothèque de la Revue de Littérature Comparée, Vol. IV. Paris: Édouard Champion, 1923. xvi, 255 pp.

> Considers Nodier "le pivot du nouveau movement et un des premiers romantique à donner des gages à l'école 'noire.' " The influence of the *noir* can be seen in his poetry *(Essai d'un jeune barde)*, *contes* and novels (primarily *Mademoiselle de Marsan* and *Inès de las Sierras)*, and drama *(Le Vampire* and *Bertram, ou le château de Saint-Aldobrand).* But his novels, especially, are written with a style and art not usually present in this kind of work. See pp. 135, 144-146, 184-187, 190-191. See also Hartland (40).

3. Larat, Jean. *Bibliographie critique des œuvres de Charles Nodier, suivie de documents inédits.* Bibliothèque de la Revue de Littérature Comparée, Vol. X. Paris: Édouard Champion, 1923. 144 pp.

The most comprehensive bibliography available covering the period to 1923.[1] The title notwithstanding, the treatment is largely noncritical. Research continues to uncover material unknown to, or not cited by Larat; but his bibliography is an indispensable research tool for Nodier scholarship. Includes bibliographies, both general and specifically on Nodier; catalogues of his book sales; manuscripts; correspondence; works planned by him and works which appeared under other names but are attributed to him; works, prefaces, and articles by Nodier; works and articles on Nodier; and iconography. Appendices contain previously unpublished documents from several periods of Nodier's life.

 a.   F. Baldensperger. *Revue Critique d'Histoire et de Littérature*, 1924, 30-31.

    Not seen.

 b.   J. Marsan. *Revue de Littérature Comparée*, IV (1924), 355-362.

4. Larat, Jean. *La Tradition et l'exotisme dans l'œuvre de Charles Nodier (1780-1844): étude sur les origines du romantisme français.* Bibliothèque de la Revue de Littérature Comparée, Vol. IX. Paris: Édouard Champion, 1923. vi, 450 pp.

Aware of a number of recent studies of Nodier, Larat confesses "que notre crainte fut ... d'arriver trop tard dans un champ moissonné." On the contrary, his book opened a new area of Nodier research: the works rather than the man. Abandoning the traditional picture of Nodier as primarily the "Patron du Romantisme," he makes a thorough exploration of the successive influences and the themes in the many facets of Nodier's prose work, disentangles the part played by tradition and that played by exoticism, and shows that foreign influences led Nodier to a renewed interest in national traditions. He concludes that "à défaut de son charme, son œuvre aurait donc le mérite de nous éviter une conception trop sommaire du romantisme." This is the first such study of Nodier's work, and is still the most extensive one. Although later scholars have dug deeper in specific areas, this book remains the basic work of its kind.

---

[1] The recent publication of Edmund J. Bender's *Bibliographie: Charles Nodier* has already been noted in footnote 2 of the Preface.

Unfortunately, there is no index; but a detailed table of contents partially remedies the lack.

    a. J. Marsan. *Revue de Littérature Comparée,* IV (1924), 355-362.

5. Pilon, Edmond. "Charles Nodier," in Charles Nodier, *Thérèse Aubert,* avec une préface d'Edmond Pilon. Bibliothèque Plon, no. 41. Paris: Plon-Nourrit, s. d. [1923?]. Pp. 7-24.

Not a biography. Concerns the part that the tales (told by an old servant, Denise, and by an old man of the environs of Besançon) heard by Nodier in his childhood played in the development of his special kind of storytelling. With the exception of differences in the first two pages, the same material is found in Pilon's "Un Précurseur. Charles Nodier et le roman fantaisiste," *Revue Universelle,* 1er janv. 1921.

6. Trahard, Pierre. *Prosper Mérimée et l'art de la nouvelle.* Paris: Les Presses Universitaires de France, 1923. 28 pp.

Page 8 shows Mérimée's comparison of the *nouvelle* with the *conte* and the *roman.* He thought that with *Mateo Falcone* he had created, or refound, the art of the *nouvelle,* because he judged that Nodier had lost it in his *contes de fées.* Same material may be found in the third edition, 1952 (177), p. 18.

1924

7. Aynard, Joseph. "Les Idées et les livres: Charles Nodier," *Journal des Débats,* Édition Hebdomadaire, 26 janv. 1924, pp. 185-187.

The point of departure for this article was the recent publication of Larat's *La Tradition et l'exotisme dans l'œuvre de Charles Nodier* (4). While Aynard admits the utility of Larat's work because of its insights into many literary modes, he takes him to task, for "c'est son [Nodier's] caractère et sa vie surtout qui pourraient nous amuser, et c'est de son œuvre que nous parle M. Larat." Denying any basic conflict in Nodier between the traditionalist and the Romantic, Aynard sees him as purely a product of the eighteenth century. Of interest largely because of the extreme statement of the view that Nodier's contribution to literature lies in the ideas he advanced and the friendships he fostered rather than in the works he wrote.

8. Gauthier-Ferrières. "Charles Nodier (1780-1844)," in Charles Nodier, *Contes fantastiques*. Notice et annotations par Gauthier-Ferrières. Bibliothèque Larousse. Paris: Larousse, 1924. Pp. 5-20.

>A good account of Nodier's life and literary salon and appreciation of his qualities as a writer. Includes three of Nodier's poems and a short evaluation of him as a poet.

9. Gazier, Georges. "Nodier à l'Arsenal, d'après les carnets de voyage de son ami Ch. Weiss," *Revue d'Histoire Littéraire de la France*, XXXI (1924), 419-433.

>A charming article giving some intimate glimpses into the character of Nodier and those around him, 1822-1834. Based on the recently discovered "carnets de route" of Charles Weiss, one of Nodier's dearest friends.

10. Larat, Jean. "Une première esquisse inédite des *Proscrits* de Nodier," *Revue de Littérature Comparée*, IV (1924), 111-120.

>Presents a hitherto unpublished work of Nodier written ca. 1798 in the form of six letters that constitute a first sketch of the youthful work, *Les Proscrits* (1802), and points out the principal differences in the two versions.

11. Maixner, Rudolf. "Charles Nodier en Illyrie," *Revue des Études Slaves*, IV (1924), [252]-263.

>Fragments of Maixner's thesis in Croatian: *Charles Nodier i Illirija* (304), written in 1922. Represents Maixner's earliest work on Nodier and Illyria. For his definitive statement of the results of thirty-eight years' study and research see *Charles Nodier et l'Illyrie* (231).

12. M[iquel y] P[lanas], R. "Una Vida de bibliófilo Nodier," in Charles Nodier, *Franciscus Columna, novela bibliográfica de Carlos Nodier, precedida de El Bibliómano del mismo autor*. Traducción de Rafael V. Silvari. Pequeña Colección del Bibliófilo, dirigida por R. Miquel y Planas, Vol. III. Madrid: Librería de los Bibliófilos Españoles, 1924. Pp. ix-clxxxiv.

> Intended to introduce Nodier to the Spanish reader, who may not know him, and to present a background for the reading of *Franciscus Columna*. Fills its purpose well, indeed. Places emphasis on Nodier as a bibliophile personally and as a writer about bibliophiles. Discusses the *Songe de Poliphile* as the source for Nodier's *conte*. One serious drawback, however, is the small format of the book and the exceedingly fine print resulting.

13. Monnot, Abel. "La Slovénie et Charles Nodier," *Bulletin Trimestriel de l'Académie des Sciences, Belles-Lettres et Arts de Besançon*, 1924, pp. 195-211.

> A pleasant and personal little evocation of Nodier's stay in Illyria, soundly based on research. But for a more factual, fuller, and more recent treatment see Maixner's *Charles Nodier et l'Illyrie* (231). Reprinted in Monnot's *Études comtoises* (141).

14. Partridge, Eric. *The French Romantics' Knowledge of English Literature (1820-1848) according to Contemporary Memoirs, Letters and Periodicals*. Bibliothèque de la Revue de Littérature Comparée, Vol. 14. Paris: Édouard Champion, 1924. xv, 370 pp.

> This extensively documented study packs much into two good pages on Nodier's knowledge of English literature and its influence on him, as witnessed by contemporary critics. See pp. 51-52.

15. Rudwin, Maximilian J. "Nodier's Fantasticism," *Open Court*, XXXVIII (1924), 8-15.

> Rudwin, who has written widely on diabolism and the supernatural in literature, here considers these elements in Nodier. Is of especial interest because of the conclusion of rare and little-known works in addition to those which are better-known. See also Rudwin (34, 53-A, and 99), Cailliet (72), Grillet (90), and Milner (232).

1925

16. Henriot, Émile. *Courrier littéraire, XIX⁰ siècle.* Paris: Plon, Nourrit, 1925.

Not seen. See also no. 59 and no. 148.

17. Vodoz, Jules. *"La Fée aux Miettes." Essai sur le rôle du subconscient dans l'œuvre de Charles Nodier.* Paris: Honoré Champion, 1925. xvi, 321 pp.

> A controversial study of Nodier's often-analysed story. Vodoz calls his work "une simple étude du symbolisme de *La Fée aux Miettes,*" but in reality it is a detailed psychoanalytical investigation of Nodier's life based on this one story. The most debatable features of the book are the arbitrary nature of a large part of the symbolism, and seeing symbolism where perhaps none exists. Although admittedly much of Nodier can be discerned in the character of Michel, Vodoz carries his parallels too far. He sees in La Fée aux Miettes Nodier's wife Désirée and in Belkiss Marie. Thus the whole narrative becomes a sort of expiation for a guilty love for his daughter. This is an interesting and original study, with some valuable insights into the character of Nodier and the interpretation of his story. But the rapprochements between man and fiction are often forced.
>
> a. P. Kohler. *Gazette de Lausanne,* 6 déc. 1925. Not seen.
>
> b. J. L. *Revue de Littérature Comparée,* VI (1926), 539-542.
>
> c. L. P. Shanks. *Modern Language Notes,* XLI (1926), 346-347.
>
> d. J. Giraud. *Revue d'Histoire Littéraire de la France,* XXXIV (1927), 271-273.
>
> e. V. Klemperer. *Die Neueren Sprachen,* XXXV (1927), 231-232.

1926

18. Ancelot, Mme. "Le Salon de Charles Nodier; souvenirs," *Les Annales Politiques et Littéraires,* LXXXVII (1926), 597-598.

This unflattering "souvenir" of Nodier's salon in the "Numéro romantique" of the *Annales Politiques et Littéraires* is obviously a reprint from a nineteenth-century account. (See Larat [3], p. 77.) However, at the present moment materials are unavailable for specific identification.

19. Kos, Milko. "*Télégraphe Officiel* in njegove izdaje. (Le *Télégraphe Officiel* et ses éditions.)," *Muzejsko društvo za Slovenijo, Ljubljana. Glasnik. Bulletin de l'Association du Musée de Slovénie*, VII-VIII, Cahier 1-4 (1926-27), 5-12.

A résumé in French gives a very brief statement of Nodier's part as editor of the *Télégraphe Officiel* in 1813. A reference of only limited interest for most purposes.

20. Marsan, Jules. *Notes sur Charles Nodier (documents inédits)*. Toulouse: Privat, 1926.

Not seen. Apparently a reprint of the paper in the *Mémoires de l'Académie des Sciences, Inscriptions et Belles-Lettres de Toulouse*, 1912, which is again reprinted in no. 98.

21. Palfrey, Thomas R. "Charles Nodier et l'*Europe Littéraire*," *Revue de Littérature Comparée*, VI (1926), 130-131.

Intended to supplement Larat's work (4) on Nodier's journalistic activities. Concerns Nodier's contributions to the short-lived but luxuriously produced *L'Europe Littéraire*.

22. Pourrat, Henri. *La Fontaine au bois dormant*. Les Cahiers de Paris, 2. sér., 1926, Cahier IV. Paris: Les Cahiers de Paris, 1926. 127 pp.

On pp. 9-46 the author gives an agreeable but undocumented account of Nodier's life, the literary influences he underwent, and his regionalism as a facet of exoticism. Apparently based largely on Larat and intended for the general reader.

23. Schutz, A. H. "The Nature and Influence of Charles Nodier's Philological Activity," *Studies in Philology*, XXIII (1926), 464-472.

Puts into perspective what the author considers an incomplete picture by Larat (4) and Michel Salomon (*Charles*

Nodier et le groupe romantique d'après des documents inédits [Paris: Perrin, 1908]) of Nodier's linguistic work. Here, a scholar "whose interest lies primarily in the history of the French language" reviews Nodier's philological activity with two things in mind: the times in which Nodier's linguistic ideas were formed, and his influence in linguistic matters on his contemporaries. Schutz does not hesitate to say that the imposing list of philological works draws only a shrug from a modern philologist. He concludes that Nodier's program in many respects paralleled rather than molded the reforms of other Romanticists but that in the question of influence he was in a position to contribute much to this group.

1927

24. Baldensperger, F[ernand]. "Les Années 1827-1828 en France et au dehors: I. [Introduction]," *Revue des Cours et Conférences*, XXIX, sér. 1, (1927-28), [405]-420; "II. Les Nouveaux Contacts de société," XXIX, sér. 1, (1927-28), [494]-511; "V. L'Appel au romantisme des provinces," XXIX, sér. 2, (1928), [227]-240; "VII. Les 'Moyennes' romantiques de 1827-1828," XXX, sér. 1, (1928-29), [177]-192; "IX. Les Représentations anglaises à Paris en 1827-28," XXX, sér. 1, (1928-29), [629]-645.

> Contains a number of scattered but good references to Nodier, including an excellent statement of the real import of Nodier and his salon for the younger Romantics in II, 502-504.

25. Blaser, Edouard. "Um Charles Nodier," *Neue Schweizer Rundschau*, XX (1927), 599-605.

> A major portion of this article is simply a retelling of the literary influences felt by Nodier and the works he wrote manifesting those influences. In the last third, which is of more interest, Blaser asks whether Nodier in writing *La Fée aux Miettes* was working from instinct or from remembrances of actual dreams. Was he aware of the influence of his own dreams on his writings? Blaser reproaches Vodoz (17) for not asking these questions and for making up his mind in advance what conclusion he would reach.

26. Calot, Frantz. " 'Le Salon de Charles Nodier et les romantiques,' exposition à la Bibliothèque de l'Arsenal (16 mai-16 juin 1927)," *Bulletin du Bibliophile et du Bibliothécaire*, n. s., VI (1927), [266]-272.

> Points out the rare pictures, portraits, sculpture, autographs, albums, books, and manuscripts in the collection that was assembled for the exposition at the Arsenal to celebrate the one hundredth anniversary of Romanticism. See also no. 33.

27. Charlier, Gustave. "Sœur Béatrice et Béatrijs," in *Mélanges publiés en l'honneur de M. le professeur Vaclav Tille à l'occasion de son 60ème anniversaire, 1867-1927*. Prague: Éditions Orbis, 1927. Pp. 26-30.

> In his consideration of Maeterlinck's *Sœur Béatrice,* Charlier mentions Nodier's story on the subject. Nodier, himself, said that he took it from Bzovius, continuator of the *Annales ecclésiastiques* of Baronius. But his source might also have been Césaire de Heisterbach, whose *Dialogus miraculorum* contains the same instructive example.

28. Deslandres, Paul. "La Bibliothèque de l'Arsenal, berceau du romantisme et sanctuaire du théâtre," *Le Correspondant*, CCCVII (1927), 737-743.

> In this short history of the administration of the Arsenal from Nodier's time, when its fame began, to 1927 Nodier is shown, as far as possible, in his little-known role as librarian of this famous library. A sympathetic picture of his salon adds nothing new to this aspect of his life.

29. Eggli, Edmond. *Schiller et le romantisme français.* 2 vols. Paris: J. Gamber, 1927.

> For the reader who can wade through the numerous page references to Nodier in the index there are interesting bits of information not to be found elsewhere relating to the influence of Schiller on Nodier and to Nodier's literary criticism of Schiller. But there is no systematic discussion of this aspect of Nodier's work.

30. Henriot, Émile. "Le Salon de Charles Nodier; la jeunesse des romantiques; pastels français du XVIIe et du XVIIIe siècles," *Revue Universelle*, XXIX (1927), 743-748.

Comments on the expositions featuring Nodier at the Arsenal and Hugo at the Place des Vosges in honor of the centenary of Romanticism. Describes well the atmosphere of the *dimanches* at the Arsenal—a little bourgeois, a little provincial, but extremely hospitable, gracious, and worldly—in contrast to the atmosphere of the field of battle at Victor Hugo's salon.

31. Jaloux, Edmond. "Charles Nodier," in Charles Nodier, *Contes et nouvelles;* publiés avec une introduction d'Edmond Jaloux. Paris: Payot, 1927. Pp. vii-xxi.

A perfunctory description of Nodier's salon and résumé of his life, with a few actual errors, are redeemed by Jaloux's good personal observations on Nodier's character and work. It is difficult to know Nodier exactly, "non parce qu'il est obscur, mais parce qu'il reste mystérieux. On a pu faire sur lui les appréciations les plus diverses et les plus contradictoires; tout semble vrai." But "il arrive cependant aujourd'hui que les deux romantiques en qui nous trouvions le plus de romantisme réel, je veux dire le romantisme psychologique, aient été Nodier et Nerval...."

32. "Une lettre inédite de Charles Nodier," *Le Figaro*, 28 mai 1927, *Supplément Littéraire*, p. 2.

A hitherto unpublished letter of Nodier, from the collection of. M. Hugues Delorme, shows Nodier, at the height of his success, in his customary need of money. The letter, dated Paris, 18 avril 1833, is addressed to his publisher, Renduel, and asks an advance on two of his literary projects.

33. Paris. Bibliothèque de l'Arsenal. *Le Salon de Charles Nodier et les romantiques, exposition à la Bibliothèque de l'Arsenal, rue de Sully, mai-juin 1927*. Paris: Albert Morancé [1927?]. 22 pp.

A highly valuable catalogue of the exposition at the Arsenal celebrating the centennial of Romanticism. Includes items associated not only with Nodier but with family and friends who surrounded him. The list includes: objects in the Arsenal of former days, paintings, water colors, drawings, sculpture, engravings, lithographs, vignettes, original manuscripts, autographs, albums, printed matter, and bindings. The owner or location of each is indicated. The catalogue is preceded by an introduction by Louis Batiffol, the administrator of the library of the Arsenal, describing the salon as it appeared in Nodier's day; by a poem of Alfred de Musset, "À M. Charles Nodier," describing the soirées at the Arsenal; and by Alexandre Dumas père's description of the soirées taken from his *Mémoires*.

34. Rudwin, Maximilian. "Romantisme et Satanisme," *La Grande Revue*, CXXIII (1927), 549-573.

Cites Nodier among the principal authors writing in the fantastic genre. Calls the reunions at the Arsenal "de vraies débauches de fantastique." See also Rudwin (15, 53-A, and 99), Cailliet (72), Grillet (90), and Milner (232).

35. Simon, Gustave. "Charles Nodier; lettres inédites à Victor Hugo," *La Revue Mondiale*, CLXXVII (1927), 329-339; and CLXXVIII (1927), 11-17.

The author publishes ten letters of Nodier and of his daughter, Marie, to Victor Hugo, and a letter and poem of Hugo to Nodier, and comments on each or situates it in the historical background of the moment. This technique confirms Simon's assertion that the letters throw new light on Nodier the man. They range in date from 1825 until after Nodier's death.

    a. In volume CLXXVII:

        (1) Letter from Nodier looking forward to trip to Reims with Hugo. Personal affairs.

        (2) Letter from Nodier concerning his rivalry with Alexandre Guiraud for a seat in the Académie Française.

        (3) Letter of thanks by Nodier for a letter Hugo wrote in the above matter.

        (4) Letter from Nodier asking Hugo to write in favor of a proposed Académie Provinciale.

        (5) Letter from Hugo introducing to Nodier a young M. Planche who wanted to borrow books from the Arsenal.

        (6) Poem "Billet à Charles Nodier," from Hugo. About Nodier's *Histoire du roi de Bohême* that had just been published.

b. In volume CLXXVIII, preceded by Simon's comment on the break between Nodier and Hugo after Nodier's article on *Les Orientales:*

(1) Letter from Nodier praising *Les Chants du crépuscule.*

(2) Letter of Marie concerning Nodier's illness in 1844.

(3) Letter of Marie asking Hugo to write a *post-scriptum* to Nodier's unfinished *Expédition des portes de fer. Post-scriptum* reproduced.

(4) Letter of Marie asking Hugo to be godfather of her first child.

(5) Letter of Marie to Hugo on birth of his grandson, Georges.

(6) Letter of Marie assuring Hugo that her child whom he mistakenly thought to be dead, is well.

36. Souriau, Maurice. *Histoire du romantisme en France.* 2 vols. in 3. Paris: "Éditions Spes," 1927.

Though written forty years ago, this book is still one of the best for the Romantic period in France. But it is somewhat outdated for Nodier, to whom Souriau devotes a long chapter in Tome I, pt. 2, pp. 115-136. He admits that "la grande influence littéraire et royaliste est alors celle de Nodier", but "moins par son œuvre, qui est de second ordre, que par sa personnalité qui est de premier plan." Nodier's biography is "la plus romanesque de ses œuvres, et nous ne nous y attarderons guère." Souriau dedicates approximately one half of the chapter to Nodier's youth, with emphasis on its disorders, and to a generally valid critique of his literary works. Significantly, almost half of the study concerns the soirées at the Arsenal, where Souriau obviously thinks that Nodier's greatest sphere of influence and historical importance lie. The soirées have been described only too often, but never more charmingly than by Souriau, whose apparent antipathy for Nodier, the man and the author, is not evident here.

37. Vodoz, J. "Zu Charles Nodier's *Moi-même*," *Jahrbuch für Philologie,* II (1927), 35-[61].

Scholars have generally refused to take Nodier's youthful autobiographical novel, *Moi-même*, seriously; but Vodoz, continuing the vein of investigation begun with *La Fée aux Miettes* (17), again examines the work to find the man. He sees the key to Nodier's character under the mocking exterior of the story, and finds that little by little such an individual as the one revealed here loses contact with reality. "Das war Nodiers Los."

38. Vuillame, Camille. "Nodier journaliste," *Journal des Débats,* Édition Hebdomadaire, mai 22 1927, pp. 853-854.

Gives interesting information on the unfortunately somewhat neglected career of Nodier as both literary and political journalist.

1928

39. Gazier, Georges. "Une Œuvre de jeunesse inédite de Charles Nodier," *Procès-Verbaux et Mémoires de l'Académie des Sciences, Belles-Lettres et Arts de Besançon,* 1928, pp. [95]-102.

Concerns a recently discovered discourse of Nodier written in 1807 for the "concours d'éloquence" of the Académie des Sciences, Belles-Lettres et Arts de Besançon on the subject of the influence great men, especially Napoleon, have exerted on the century in which they lived. The Académie judged that none of the contenders for the gold medal had fully understood the subject and did not make an award. Nodier himself seems to have forgotten this pompous and mediocre discourse, but Gazier's account of it provides information on Nodier's early literary activities.

40. Hartland, Reginald W. *Walter Scott et le roman frénétique, contribution à l'étude de leur fortune en France.* Bibliothèque de la Revue de Littérature Comparée, Vol. LII. Paris: Honoré Champion, 1928. 266 pp.

Hartland's expressed intention is to examine all the important works of the English school that is today called "frénétique." But the works of Nodier are "un si bel exemple du cosmopolitisme littéraire que j'ai cru passer en revue ses romans, nouvelles et contes." Thus, Chapter VI, "Charles Nodier," pp. 91-134, examines a large part of Nodier's fiction. Parts of the chapter are a restatement of old material, but the information on English and other influences is worth reading. See also Killen (2).

41. Miquel y Planas, R. [Article on the personal relations of Nodier with the great bibliophile and book seller of Valencia, V. Salvá], *Correo Catalán,* 19 avril 1928.

Not seen.

42. Munksgaard, Ejnar. "Charles Nodier et son cercle," in Charles Nodier, *Le Bibliomane,* publié avec préface et annotations par Ejnar Munksgaard. 24 Illus. par Maurice Leloir. Paris: H. Champion, 1928. Pp. 13-28.

> An interesting preface that describes Nodier's ample opportunities as a youth to come into contact with rare books, tells of his adult passion for books and his activities as a bibliophile, and relates stories concerning his bibliophile friends in an effort to show that Nodier's picture of the bibliomaniac in the story published here is by no means exaggerated.

43. Souday, Paul, ed. *Les Romantiques à l'Académie, suivi des discours de réception de MM. de Lamartine, Charles Nodier, Victor Hugo, Sainte-Beuve, Alfred de Vigny, Alfred de Musset, et des réponses de MM. le baron Cuvier, de Jouy, de Salvandy, Victor Hugo, le comte Molé, Nisard.* Paris: Ernest Flammarion, 1928. xiii, 284 pp.

> Nodier's discourse, pp. 76-90. It is, according to Souday, a little timid: "le brave homme voudrait contenter tout le monde" (p. xxxvi). See also C., G. (83).

44. Viatte, Auguste. *Les Sources occultes du romantisme: illuminisme—théosophie, 1770-1820.* Bibliothèque de la Revue de Littérature Comparée, Vols. XLVI-XLVII. 2 vols. Paris: Honoré Champion, 1928.

> In pages 145-167 of volume II Viatte examines Nodier's relations with the illuminati and points out their influence in his work, seeing in *Trilby* Nodier's best utilization of this type of material. The author wisely finds, however, that Nodier did not formulate any system. "On voit qu'en dépit de son illumination passagère, Nodier amprunte [sic] surtout aux mystiques leurs attitudes les plus connues et les

plus *voyantes*. Il trouve chez eux une mine inépuisable de récits fantastiques: sa curiosité se plaît à l'impossible; il ne va guère au delà." See also Amadou (155) and Richer (197).

1929

45. Koch, Theodore W., ed. and tr. *Tales for Bibliophiles; Translated from the French*. Chicago: The Caxton Club, 1929. 212 pp.

> Contains *The Bibliomaniac* by Nodier and *The French Pastry Cook* by Dumas père, the chapter from his *Mémoires* telling how he met Nodier and was first introduced to bibliophily. Preface and notes have material on Nodier's attitude toward bibliophily and on his activities as a book collector.

46. Stadelmann, Josef. *Charles Nodier im Urteil seiner Zeitgenossen*. Inaugural-Dissertation, zur Erlangung der Doktorwürde der philosophischen Fakultät (I. Sektion) der Ludwig-Maximilians-Universität zu München. [Tag der mündlichen Prüfung: 19 Dezember 1929] 1929.

> A doctoral dissertation on Nodier as seen by his contemporaries. Shows Nodier in the judgment of the great Romantics who frequented his salon, the literary critics of the time, and the Stendhal-Mérimée opposition. Helpful, but leaves much to be said on the subject.

1930

47. Gazier, Georges. "Un Centenaire romantique: le mariage de Marie Nodier," *Mémoires de la Société d'Émulation du Doubs*, 1930, pp. [11]-30.

> Informative on the close relationship between Nodier and his daughter, Marie, the friendship between Nodier and Charles Weiss, and the difficulty in persuading Nodier to arrange a marriage for Marie. Also published separately under same title at Besançon: Imprimerie de l'Est, s. d.

48. Henry-Rosier, Mme Marguerite. "Autour du Romantisme. Deux Épisodes de la vie de Charles Nodier. I. Marie," *Le Figaro*, 18 oct. 1930, p. 6; and "II. Illyria," 25 oct. 1930, p. 6.

These pages appear almost integrally—there are minor changes, mostly of wording—in Mme Henry-Rosier's *La Vie de Charles Nodier* (62).

49. Henry-Rosier, Mme Marguerite. "Autour du Romantisme. La Jeunesse de Charles Nodier," *La Revue de France*, 10ᵉ année, III (1930), [304]-333.

Appears, with only minor changes in wording, and not always on consecutive pages, in Mme Henry-Rosier's *La Vie de Charles Nodier* (62).

50. Larat, Jean. "Charles Nodier en Alsace," *L'Alsace Française, Revue Hebdomadaire d'Action Nationale*, 10ᵉ année, XX (1930), 417-422.

Adds to the rather sparse knowledge of Nodier's early years. Describes his sojourn, at the age of thirteen, in Strasbourg to commence Hellenist studies under Euloge Schneider and indicates his works in which the impact of that violent and tumultuous atmosphere can be seen.

51. Lods, Armand, C. M. R., and R. B. "Charles Nodier," *L'Intermédiaire des Chercheurs et Curieux*, XCIII (1930), 776-777.

Of no help to the informed Nodier scholar.

52. Patin, Jacques. "Sur un exemplaire de Charles Nodier," *Le Figaro*, 13 déc. 1930, pp. 5-6.

An interesting article concerning a copy of *Trilby* inscribed with a dedicatory poem and given by Nodier to Hugo, who presented it later to Juliette Drouet as a memento of the beginning of their liaison. Contains a superfluous account of Nodier's well-known literary activities around 1822.

53. Prinet, Gaston. "Charles Nodier," *L'Intermédiaire des Chercheurs et Curieux*, XCIII (1930), 738-739.

Supplies the names of Nodier's descendants living in 1930.

53-A. Rudwin, Maximilian. "The Devil-Compact in Legend and Literature," *The Open Court*, XLIV (1930), [321]-341, [419]-437.

Includes a brief consideration, largely summaries, of Nodier's *L'Amour et le grimoire* and *La Combe de l'homme mort*, pp. 424-425. Says that Nodier imitated Matthew Gregory Lewis in *Inès de las Sierras*, p. 428. See also Rudwin (15, 34, and 99), Cailliet (72), Grillet (90), and Milner (232) for related studies on diabolism in Nodier.

54. Soudain, J., and Georges Goyau. "Charles Nodier," *L'Intermédiaire des Chercheurs et Curieux*, XCIII (1930), 932.

Of no importance to the informed Nodier scholar.

1931

55. Bain, Margaret I. *Les Voyageurs français en Écosse, 1770-1830, et leurs curiosités intellectuelles*. Bibliothèque de la Revue de Littérature Comparée, Vol. 79. Paris: Honoré Champion, 1931. 226 pp.

Nodier and his companions (Taylor, Cailleux, and Isabey) were, after the prisoner Lezeverne, the first French Romantic voyagers to Scotland. Pages 137-142 relate this 1821 trip as told by Nodier in his correspondence and in the *Promenade de Dieppe aux montagnes d'Écosse*, which was "le signal et le prototype du voyage romantique." Pages 174-175 concern the influence of Scott and Scotland in the salon at the Arsenal. Various articles and fragments inspired by the visit to Scotland are listed on pages 181 and 183, and pp. 195-202 concern the contributions of this trip to Nodier's larger works. Miss Bain concludes on pp. 208-209 that it was such voyages, primarily, rather than the novels of Scott, that led to French literary regionalism in authors like Nodier. Other scattered references. A thorough treatment. See also Gordon (105).

56. Dollot, René. "Les Romans illyriens de Charles Nodier," *Revue de Littérature Comparée*, XI (1931), 285-314.

A very well-documented study of the Illyrian influences in *Jean Sbogar* and *Mademoiselle de Marsan*. The author places them in their historical framework, seeks what they contain that is Illyrian, and judges that there are more Illyrian elements than had been thought before. See also Larat (4), Warnier (87), and Maixner (231).

57. Hartmann, Georges. "Charles Nodier et la Garde Nationale à l'Arsenal pendant les journées de juillet 1830," *La Cité*, janv. 1931, pp. [253]-262.

> With the aid of previously unpublished correspondence, reveals some little-known aspects of Nodier's role as librarian at the Arsenal. Although not the administrator of the library, he actually fulfilled the duties of that office. In the uprising of 1830 Nodier, fearing pillage, as a friend of the regime, demanded and received guards for the Arsenal. With the change in regime he began maneuvers to keep his position. After several months, having friends in all camps, he was maintained as librarian. Certainly, with the aid of the National Guard, he had kept the Arsenal from being pillaged in July, 1830.

58. Hawkins, Richmond-Laurin. "Lettres inédites de romantiques français [Nodier]," *Le Figaro*, 16 mai 1931, p. 6; and 22 août 1931, p. 5.

> In *Le Figaro* of 1931 Hawkins publishes a series of the Romantics' letters in American libraries. In the issue of May 16 he publishes a letter of Nodier to Sir Herbert Croft dated Quintigny, près Lons-le-Saunier (Jura), 30 octobre 1813, relating the disasters of his flight from Illyria and his financial and physical troubles and offering his services once again to Croft. The August 22 issue prints Nodier's letter from Paris, 2 juillet 1831, thanking Auguste-Marseille Barthélemy, founder of the satirical pamphlet *Némésis,* for some verses he had written (reproduced here) in praise of Nodier.

59. Henriot, Émile. "Courrier littéraire: Charles Nodier ou le mythomane," *Le Temps*, 21 juil. 1931, p. 3.

> An essay on the character of Nodier and what remains of him for today's reader. For Henriot, the outstanding characteristic is the unreliability of what Nodier says. Nor should his reputation as a "bonhomme" be examined too closely. Nodier can still be found in his *contes*, "toujours un peu mous et souvent étirés." Henriot is one of the few writers who like Nodier neither as a man nor as a writer. Reprinted in *Courrier littéraire. XIXe siècle* (148).

60. Henry-Rosier, Mme Marguerite. "Un Chapitre inédit de la vie de Charles Nodier," *Franche-Comté, Monts-Jura et Haute Alsace,* avril 1931.

Not seen.

61. Henry-Rosier, Mme Marguerite. "Un Pamphlet de Charles Nodier," *Le Figaro,* 5 sept. 1931, p. 5.

> Describes the contents of Nodier's satirical pamphlet, *Le Parnasse du jour,* written in 1801, recounting a literary voyage to Parnassus and ridiculing the authors of the day, including Chateaubriand. Quotes from letters of Nodier showing that he published it because he needed money and that he later regretted having done so. Reprinted, with only slight amplification, as "Une Satire de Charles Nodier, ou la surprise de M. Geoffroy" (91).

62. Henry-Rosier, Mme Marguerite. *La Vie de Charles Nodier.* Vies des Hommes Illustres, no. 73. Paris: Gallimard, 1931. 258 pp.

> This biographical work has all the lively interest of a well-written novel, which is not surprising, as the author is a novelist and poet as well as a Nodier scholar. The book obviously has a solid base in fact. The author herself tells us that she drew from recently discovered material and unpublished sources. However, the treatment is fictionalized, with décors and conversations supplied. As no bibliography or references are given, it is often impossible to determine where fact ends and fiction begins. The work's main merit, then, of reading like a good novel also becomes its main drawback for the scholarly reader. But Mme Rosier does make Nodier live for us.

63. Lenôtre, G., pseud. of Louis Léon Théodore Gosselin. *La Compagnie de Jéhu; épisodes de la réaction lyonnaise, 1794-1800.* Paris: Perrin, 1931. 296 pp.

> Pages 249-259 deal with the manner in which Nodier depicts the Compagnie de Jéhu in a chapter of his *Souvenirs.* Lenôtre tries to determine "la part de la vérité et celle de l'enjolivement" by examining an episode involving the Compagnie as related by Nodier and as records show it to be. He finds that Nodier groups in a single episode components

gathered from various incidents and greatly idealizes the participants. It was Nodier's account of the Compagnie rather than documents that influenced Dumas père's *Compagnons de Jéhu.*

64. Mönch, Walter. *Charles Nodier und die deutsche und englische Literatur, eine Studie zur romantischen Denkform in Frankreich.* Romanische Studien, Vol. XXIV. Berlin: Emil Ebering, 1931. 128 pp.

This book examines Nodier's political, social, philosophical, and mystical thought, as revealed in his work, in relation to Rousseau and other immediate French predecessors and to German and English literature. The Romantic side of Nodier was at home in these northern literatures, and the analyses of specific influences and rapprochements are good. But on the whole this is an over-philosophized treatment. Also published in part as an inaugural dissertation (65). Reprinted in 1967 (296).

65. Mönch, Walter. *Charles Nodier. Zusammenhang von Erlebnisübertragung und Denkform in der Wesensbestimmung des literarischen Einflusses.* (Teildruck). Inaugural-Dissertation zur Erlangung der Doktorwürde genehmigt von der Philosophischen Fakultät der Friedrich-Wilhelms-Universität zu Berlin. Tag der münlichen Prüfung: 16.1.1930. Tag der Promotion: 24:2.1931. Berlin: Ebering, 1931. 50 pp.

Published also in expanded form under different title. See no. 64.

66. Pitollet, Camille. "Charles Nodier," *L'Intermédiaire des Chercheurs et Curieux,* XCIV (1931), 112-115.

Useful for its incidental references to out-of-the-way materials relating to Nodier.

67. Pourrat, Henri. "Une imagination de province: Charles Nodier," *Nouvelles Littéraires, Artistiques et Scientifiques; Hebdomadaire d'Information, de Critique et de Bibliographie,* 25 juil. 1931, p. [1].

Overemphasizes the regional background of Nodier, seeing in his adult life and in his writings only an attempt to recapture his Romantic youth in Franche-Comté.

68. Sauvage, R. N. "Nodier et les Vaudevires," *Normannia, Revue Bibliographique et Critique d'Histoire de Normandie*, déc. 1931, pp. [166]-169.

Shows that Nodier planned a new edition of the Vaudevires based on the 1811 edition by Asselin and asks: "Mais faut-il sérieusement regretter de ne pas être redevable à sa fantaisie érudite d'une édition des Vaudevires?"

69. Thiébaut, Marcel. "À Propos de Charles Nodier," *La Revue de Paris*, 38e année, V (1931), [209]-229.

Takes as an excuse for writing about Nodier the recent publication of Mme Henry-Rosier's *La Vie de Charles Nodier* (62), and also the fact that one hundred years ago Nodier was writing for the *Revue de Paris*. Is largely a retelling of Nodier's life, which is of little interest, and a review of his *contes*, which is remarkable for the singularity of some of the literary judgments. If Nodier's works are "tout près de sombrer dans un définitif oubli," at least he will be remembered for his salon at the Arsenal.

70. Vial, Francisque, and Louis Denise. *Idées et doctrines littéraires du XIXe siècle (extraits des préfaces, traités et autres écrits théoriques)*. Paris: Delagrave, 1931. iv, 344 pp.

Excerpts from Nodier's review of Byron's *Vampire* translated by Faber, from his *Du Fantastique en littérature*, and from his review of *La Gaule poétique* of Marchangy. (See pp. 100-102 and 226-227.) A small addition to the sparse amount of Nodier's literary criticism available in twentieth century editions.

1932

71. Bray, René. *Chronologie du Romantisme (1804-1830)*. Bibliothèque de la Revue des Cours et Conférences. Paris: Boivin, 1932. vii, 238 pp.

Nodier figures frequently in this book. But as the purpose is to show the year by year development of Romanticism, and as there is no index, it is necessary to read the entire contents to find the numerous good references to him.

72. Cailliet, Émile. *The Themes of Magic in Nineteenth Century French Fiction.* English Translation by Lorraine Havens. Paris: Les Presses Universitaires de France, 1932. xii, 228 pp.

> Accords Nodier an unreservedly high place in the literature of the marvellous. "The wonder literature of the nineteenth century is inseparable from the name of Charles Nodier." Discusses the various aspects of the marvellous in Nodier, dwelling at length on *Trilby*, "still the purest jewel of this genre." Curiously, the author almost ignores *La Fée aux Miettes*. An entirely undocumented but seemingly well-informed, though overly eulogistic, study. See pp. 12-14, 28-39, 88-89, 214, 220. See also Rudwin (15, 34, 53-A, and 99), Grillet (90), and Milner (232).

73. Charles, Paul-A. "Charles Nodier et Victor Hugo," *Revue d'Histoire Littéraire de la France*, XXXIX (1932), 568-586.

> Presents two recently-discovered and entirely favorable articles in *Le Temps* of 1831 by Nodier on Hugo's *Marion Delorme* and traces the relations between the two authors to that time. See also Bauer (89), Dédéyan (266), and Wilson (289).

74. Moreau, Pierre. *Le Romantisme.* Histoire de la Littérature Française, pub. sous la direction de J. Calvet, Vol. VIII. Paris: J. de Gigord, 1932. 546 pp.

> An important book on French Romanticism deals, on pp. 159-161, with Nodier with a definite 1930's accent. Moreau admits that Nodier had a real part in the advent of Romanticism in his use of fantasy and the fantastic, popular legends, and an exotic folklore. But he does not seem to feel that one work is more important than another. He seems, rather, to dismiss Nodier and his writings with the words "flâneur," and "charmant bavardage." Compare with the change in tone of the treatment in the 1957 edition (211), where emphasis is placed on Nodier as a *conteur* of dream and madness, as well as fantasy, and the link is made with Lautréamont and the Surrealists.

75. Tisseau, Paul. "Deux lettres de Charles Nodier," *Revue d'Histoire Littéraire de la France,* XXXIX (1932), 260-262.

> Publishes two letters of Nodier. One, written from Lons-le-Saunier on 28 novembre 1813, to M. Tamisier, concerns Nodier's material situation on his return from Illyria. The other, dated 21 avril 1834, shows his effort to sell to M. Crapelet in advance his *Notions élémentaires de linguistique.*

1933

76. Broyer, Ch. "Charles Nodier, cryptogamiste," *Bulletin de la Société Botanique de France,* LXXX (1933), 30-31.

> Calls attention to several pages in Nodier's *Promenade de Dieppe aux montagnes d'Écosse* "célébrant le charme, la variété des Mousses, des Lichens et des Fougères." Working from the two finely engraved and colored plates accompanying the text, Broyer lists the plants and gives their current scientific names. Suggests Nodier's friend Bory de Saint-Vincent as the source of his interest in this humble vegetation.

77. Eggli, Edmond, and Pierre Martino. *Le Débat romantique en France, 1813-1830. Pamphlets. Manifestes. Polémiques de presse.* Publications de la Faculté des Lettres d'Alger, IIe sér., Vol. VI. Paris: Société d'Édition "Les Belles Lettres," 1933—. 498 pp.

> Volume I covers the years 1813-1816. Apparently no further volumes were published. This undertaking contains only the texts that are hard to get, presented in a chronological arrangement. The following articles of Nodier are included and commented on:
>
> > *a.* Article of criticism that appeared in the *Journal de l'Empire,* 4 mars 1814, on Schlegel's *Cours de littérature dramatique.* Pp. 111-115.
> >
> > *b.* Article in the *Journal de l'Empire,* 20 mars 1814, on *La Rançon de Duguesclin,* and an article in the *Journal des Débats,* 14 mai 1814, on the *Hamlet of Ducis.* Pp. 131-137.
> >
> > *c.* Articles in the *Journal des Débats,* 19 juin 1814, on *Ossian, ou les bardes,* an opera; 29 août 1814,

on Beaumarchais' *Eugénie;* 6 septembre 1814, on *Andromaque;* and 13 septembre 1814, on *Athalie.* Pp. 193-199.

d. Article in the *Journal de l'Empire,* 4 avril 1815, on *Antigone* by Ballanche. Pp. 294-295.

There is a need for the publication of Nodier's critical articles, and those selected here are good as a revelation of his critical thought, 1813-1816. But the period covered is far too short, and the lack of an index seriously hampers the availability of what there is.

78. Evans, Serge. "La Jeunesse d'un conteur comtois," *Le Pays Comtois,* 20 août 1933, pp. 573-576.

Not seen.

79. *Guyot, Charly. Voyageurs romantiques en pays neuchâtelois.* Neuchâtel, Paris: Delachaux et Niestlé, 1933. 181 pp.

Pages 41-43 are about Nodier's stay of a few weeks in Switzerland at the end of 1805 or the beginning of 1806 when he fled from the police for political activities. A charming description of the environs of Yverdon is quoted from the Romantic story of *Amélie* in the *Souvenirs de jeunesse.*

80. Moraud, Marcel. *Le Romantisme français en Angleterre de 1814 à 1848; contributions à l'étude des relations littéraires entre la France et l'Angleterre dans la première moitié du XIXe siècle.* Bibliothèque de la Revue de Littérature Comparée, Vol. 90. Paris: Honoré Champion, 1933. 479 pp.

A few isolated references (the only ones I have found on the subject) show that Nodier was well-received in England.

81. Souza, Robert de. "À Propos du phonographe.—Il faut remonter à Charles Nodier et pour l'idée et pour le mot," *Mercure de France,* CCXLVI (1933), 462-466.

Shows that in the introduction to his *Vocabulaire de la langue française* Nodier several times used the terms *phonographe* and *phonographique* in the sense of "des vocables précis les plus naturels pour bien rendre ce qui se rapporte à *l'écriture* des sons." He also wondered why a means could not be devised to reproduce the sound of the voice. Then

Nodier invented both the idea for the phonograph and the word. Souza proposes that Bloch amend his article on *phonographe* in his *Dictionnaire étymologique de la langue française* (1932) to show the origin of the word with Nodier and the inversion in meaning through which it has gone.

1934

82. Brandicourt, Virgile. "Charles Nodier naturaliste." *La Nature,* LXII, pt. 1 (1934), 369-371.

Gives a quick sketch, useful for the literary scholar, of the natural history works of Nodier, both published and unpublished, and his contacts with natural scientists. Drawn largely from Antoine Magnin, *Charles Nodier naturaliste* (Paris: Hermann, 1911).

83. C., G. "Le Centenaire de la réception de Nodier à l'Académie," *Journal des Débats* [Édition Hebdomadaire?], 5 janv. 1934, p. 36.

The *Journal des Débats,* for which Nodier once wrote, marks the centenary of his reception into the Académie Française with a column recalling some of the main points of his discourse and the reply by M. de Jouy. See also Souday (43).

84. Cummings, Edith Katharine. *The Literary Development of the Romantic Fairy Tale in France.* Bryn Mawr, Pa., 1934. 100 pp.

A published Ph. D. dissertation from Bryn Mawr College. The author devotes the first chapter to what she considers Nodier's *contes de fées* for adults, *Trilby* and *La Fée aux Miettes;* and to his two *contes de fées* for children, *Le Génie Bonhomme* and *Trésor des Fèves et Fleur des Pois.* She analyses these stories to see how they differ from the traditional fairy tale and in what ways they are Romantic, finding that the greatest difference between the seventeenth-century *conte de fées* and Nodier's is that the setting for Nodier's is a "vague borderland between reality and illusion," while Perrault's is situated in a real world. The other main novelty of Nodier's two tales for adults is the emphasis on the love theme. Miss Cummings sees in his heroes and heroines the romantic young people of Nodier's time. The tales for children differ especially from seventeenth-century fairy stories in use of a richer vocabulary and irony. Although some of the observations are valid, seen from Miss Cummings' point of view, the two *contes* for adults, in particular *La Fée aux Miettes,* are unbelievably oversimplified.

85. Gaiffe, Félix. "Quand Nodier pense à la petite patrie," *Le Pays Comtois,* 20 juil. 1934, pp. 453-455.

Not seen.

86. P., J. G. "Bibliographie de Charles Nodier et de Noël et Chapsal," *Mercure de France,* CCLIV (1934), 666-667.

Examines the number of editions of Nodier listed in the just-published vol. 125 of the *Catalogue général des livres imprimés de la Bibliothèque nationale* and finds that Nodier is somewhat forgotten, or at least neglected, in our day.

87. Warnier, R. "Contribution à la biographie intellectuelle de Ch. Nodier," *Revue de Littérature Comparée,* XIV (1934), 191-208.

"On ... trouvera dans Larat [4] le bilan" of the copious literature on Illyrian influences in Nodier; but the *Statistique illyrienne* (19a), published in 1933, fills an important gap by making available the articles written by Nodier for that paper. This collection of articles provides more than just an inventory of Nodier's Illyrian interests. It also shows some of the general aspects of his literary formation and helps place the interlude in Illyria in the general framework of his thought. Warnier finds that some of Nodier's observations in his works showing Illyrian influence are truer than have been admitted and are often in accord with reality. See also Larat (4), Dollot (56), and Maixner (231).

88. Wood, Kathryn L. *Criticism of French Romantic Literature in the "Gazette de France," 1830-1848.* Philadelphia, 1934. ix, 139 pp.

Published Ph. D. thesis from Bryn Mawr College, 1934. Pages 7-9 show Turquéty's favorable review in the *Gazette de France,* supplément, 19 août 1840, of a new edition of Nodier's tales.

1935

89. Bauer, Henri François. *Les "Ballades" de Victor Hugo.* Paris: Les Presses Modernes, 1935. xlv, 199 pp.

> Says the two French predecessors of Hugo were Millevoye and, especially, Nodier, whose passion for national antiquities and the Middle Ages, and whose interest in the fantastic and frenetic were important influences. Traces the friendship of Nodier and Hugo as shown in letters, poems, Hugo's use of epigraphs from Nodier, and articles of literary criticism by Nodier accompanying the publications of Hugo. A valuable table shows Hugo's debt in specific poems to specific works of Nodier and others. See pp. 33-34, 41-51, and 71-122. See also Charles (73), Dédéyan (266), and Wilson (289).

90. Grillet, Claudius. *Le Diable dans la littérature au XIXe siècle.* Paris: Desclée de Brouwer, 1935. 226 pp.

> "Au Satan de Chateaubriand et de Lamennais, qui est celui du catéchisme, succéda le diable de Nodier qui est celui des légendes médiévales, proche parent des lutins, des gnomes et des sylphes." Considers the influence of Nodier in the realm of the fantastic on the four great Romantics, the influence being in proportion to their frequentation of the Arsenal. But behind the influence of Nodier is that of Scott, Goethe, and Hoffmann. However, these authors had taken their types and legends from the French Middle Ages. So the Arsenal, rather than being a center of Germanic propaganda, was "un office de restitutions." Author goes farther, seeing influence of Nodier on Gautier and Balzac. See pages 35-45, 62-63, 78, 87-88. See also Rudwin (15, 34, 53-A, and 99); Cailliet (72); and Milner (232).

91. Henry-Rosier, Mme Marguerite. "Une Satire de Charles Nodier, ou la surprise de M. Geoffroy," *Procès-Verbaux et Mémoires de l'Académie des Sciences, Belles-Lettres et Arts de Besançon,* 1935, pp. [120]-129.

> A slight amplification of her "Un Pamphlet de Charles Nodier" (61).

92. Steib, Charles. *Les Secrets d'un conte populaire (Le Chien de Brisquet, de Charles Nosier* [sic]). Thann, 1935. 16 pp.

Not seen.

    a. P. S. *Revue de Folklore Français et de Folklore Colonial,* VI (1935), 67.

1936

93. Broyer, Ch. "La Jeunesse agitée de Charles Nodier en Franche-Comté," *Bulletin de la Société des Naturalistes et Archéologues de l'Ain,* no. 50 (1936), pp. 271-285.

A picturesque and impressionistic relation of several of the episodes of Nodier's youth connected with his anti-Napoleon activities. Undocumented, but apparently relies on Nodier's own versions of the events. Also published separately at Bourg: Impr. Berthod, 1936.

94. Moreau, Pierre. "Les Origines du réalisme franc-comtois," *Procès-Verbaux et Mémoires de l'Académie des Sciences, Belles-Lettres et Arts de Besançon,* 1936, pp. [22]-43.

This *discours de réception* for the Académie of Besançon has some interesting references to Nodier. Moreau uses him as an example in reply to those who might limit the Franc-Comtois genius to realism. But though Nodier's genius is somewhat foreign to his native province, he does have realistic elements. "Dans son œuvre d'immortel mythomane, les traits les plus fermes, ceux où la vie est cernée d'un contour net, lui viennent de la province abandonnée mais non pas oubliée." And again: "Dans cette œuvre touffue de légendes et de fantômes, les clairières d'humaine et simple vérité étaient des clairières comtoises."

1937

95. Aymonnier, Camille. "Charles Nodier linguiste," *Le Pays Comtois,* CVII (août 1937), 227-233.

Not seen.

96. Béguin, Albert. *L'Âme romantique et le rêve; essai sur le romantisme allemand et la poésie française.* 2 vols. Marseille: Éditions des Cahiers du Sud, 1937.

Excellent pages on dream and nightmare in Nodier, and in particular on *La Fée aux Miettes,* whether or not one believes in "l'étrange cristallisation amoureuse qui, secrètement accomplie dans une région très obscure, mais très efficace, de lui-même, avait fixé sur sa fille Marie tous les pouvoirs affectifs de Nodier." See vol. II, pp. 333-346.

97. Henry-Rosier, Mme Marguerite. "Quand M. de Lamennais s'inspire de Charles Nodier," *Procès-Verbaux et Mémoires de l'Académie des Sciences, Belles-Lettres et Arts de Besançon,* 1937, pp. [16]-23.

Compares a forgotten work of Nodier, *L'Apocalypse du solitaire,* published in 1821, with Lamennais's somewhat revolutionary *Paroles d'un croyant* (1834). Shows, with examples, that while there was no question of plagiarism, "M. de Lamennais n'avait pas toujours inventé ses musiques et ... tel mot de *L'Apocalypse du solitaire* chantait ouvertement dans un verset du *Croyant.*" At least Nodier had a sort of glory as a precursor.

98. Marsan, Jules. "Notes sur Charles Nodier (documents inédits)," in his *Autour du romantisme.* Toulouse: Aux Éditions de l'Archer, 1937. Pp. 33-55.

Reprinted from the *Mémoires de l'Académie des Sciences, Inscriptions et Belles-Lettres de Toulouse,* 1912. See also no. 20. A pleasant but sketchy biography of Nodier, the function of which is to hold together the numerous letters that are reproduced. Provenance of the letters not indicated.

99. Rudwin, Maximilian J. *Les Écrivains diaboliques de France.* Paris: Éditions E. Figuière, 1937. 186 pp.

This fascinating little book, which for the most part deals only briefly with each author, treats Nodier on p. 49 as the inaugurator of the fantastic and of the diabolic in French literature. Nodier himself, according to Hugo, was possessed of a devil, "le diable Elzévir"! See also Rudwin (15, 34, and 53-A), Cailliet (72), Grillet (90), and Milner (232).

100. Smith, Francis Prescott. "Peter Irving, Translator of *Jean Sbogar,*" *Franco-American Review,* I (1937), 341-346.

Identifies the 1820 translation of *Giovanni Sbogarro, A Venetian Tale* by Peter Irving (brother of Washington) as being a translation of Nodier's *Jean Sbogar*, which had been published anonymously in 1818. There is no indication that either brother knew of Nodier's existence, though later in the century George Sumner compared Washington Irving's prose to that of Nodier. *Giovanni Sbogarro* is a literal translation, with a "few interpolations of incident or description."

1938

101. Lévy, Paul. "Les Romantiques français et la langue allemande," *Revue Germanique: Allemagne. — Autriche. — Pays-Bas. — Scandinavie,* XXIX (1938), [225]-252.

An inquiry into what the Romantics knew and thought of the German language. Nodier's knowledge of German is considered on p. 232. The fact that the three sales catalogues of his personal library (1827, 1829, and 1844) did not contain a single book in the German language seems to confirm Sainte-Beuve's statement that Nodier did not know German. However, Nodier's imitations of German literature, his trip to Austria, and his youthful studies at Strasbourg would tend to show that he must have had at least a vague idea of the language.

1939

102. Béguin, Albert. *L'Âme romantique et le rêve; essai sur le romantisme allemand et la poésie française.* Nouv. éd. Paris: José Corti, 1939. xvii, 413 pp.

Contains the same material on Nodier as the 1937 edition (96). See pp. 336-345.

1940

103. Benassis, Docteur. "Essais de clinique romantique: Charles Nodier ou l'onirique," *Revue Thérapeutique des Alcaloïdes; Recueil d'Études Physiologiques et Cliniques sur les Alcaloïdes et Autres Principes Actifs Retirés du Règne Végétal,* 4e sér., 48e année (1940), pp. 70-76, 94-101, 118-126; 5e sér., 49e année (1941), pp. 8-15, 30-38, 54-65.

A curious mélange of biography, literary criticism, and detailed medical and psychological analyses of Nodier which does not follow in any particular order. But it is highly interesting for the questions it raises as to the reasons for certain aspects of Nodier's character and works.

104. C[alot], Fr[antz]. "En 1844 Charles Nodier mourait," *Bulletin du Bibliophile et du Bibliothécaire*, 1940-45, pp. [157]-168.

Commemorates the centenary of Nodier's death by recalling his last moments, friends at the cemetery, and the discourses pronounced at his burial. Traces the changes in the vogue of Nodier since that time. Calls him an amiable *conteur;* a prophet in linguistics, foreshadowing Esperanto; and a truly immortal bibliophile. A note appended to the article expresses regret that circumstances did not permit a commemoration at Paris, but indicates that a medal bearing Nodier's profile was being cast.

105. Gordon, R. K. "Le Voyage d'Abbotsford," *Proceedings and Transactions of the Royal Society of Canada*, 3d. sér., XXXIV, Sec. II (1940), 71-85.

Many foreign visitors were attracted to Scotland by the fame of Sir Walter Scott. Among them was Charles Nodier, who made a two-weeks' trip in 1821. Pages 73-75 are an amusing sketch of this journey and a consideration of its influence on Nodier based on his correspondence, his articles for various journals, and other contemporary sources. See also Bain (55).

1941

106. Engstrom, Alfred G. "The French Artistic Short Story before Maupassant." Unpub. Diss., Univ. of North Carolina, 1941. v, 331 pp.

Examines the shorter narratives of Nodier in the framework of a definition of the *Conte* as the artistic short story and finds only one, *Inès de las Sierras,* first part, that can be called a *Conte.* See pp. 239-246.

107. Morrow, Christine. *Le Roman irréaliste dans les littératures contemporaines de langues française et anglaise.* Paris: Didier, 1941. 332 pp.

>Scattered but good references to Nodier as an important precursor of such French authors as Alain-Fournier, Jean Giraudoux, and Julien Green; and of British and American authors like Virginia Woolf, James Stephens, and James Branch Cabell. See pp. 9, 43-46.

108. Raimbault, R.-N. "Charles Nodier et son temps," in Charles Nodier, *Contes choisis.* Introduction, choix et notes de R.-N. Raimbault. Collection Les Lettres et la Vie Française, 1re Sér., 6. Angers: Jacques Petit, 1941. Pp. vii-lxvi.

>A long and fairly complete biography of Nodier, but more evocative than factual. The last 16 pages describe the soirées at the Arsenal, showing that most descriptions have been inexact because they were static, whereas in reality the salon evolved over a period of years.

109. Trahard, Pierre. *Prosper Mérimée et l'art de la nouvelle.* 2e éd. Paris: Jean-Renard, 1941.

>Not seen. Presumably has same material on Nodier as the 1st edition (6), and the 3rd edition (177).

1942

110. Maixner, Rudolf. "L'Élément illyrien dans *Jean Sbogar* de Charles Nodier," *Annales de l'Institut Français de Zagreb,* no. 20-23 (1942-43), pp. 101-123.

>A well-documented and detailed inquiry into the Illyrian elements in *Jean Sbogar.* Summarizes the story, presents accusations of plagiarism and Nodier's defense, and shows in what measure Nodier's stay in Illyria influenced the composition of the book. The same material comprises Chapter V of Maixner's *Charles Nodier et l'Illyrie* (231).

1944

111. Aubert, R. "Le Centenaire de la mort de Charles Nodier a été commémoré à Lons-le-Saunier," *Le Nouvelliste* (de Lyon), 8 févr. 1944.

>Unverified. Seen only as a clipping in 127.

112. Aubert, R. "Le Centenaire de la mort de Charles Nodier; conférence et théâtre; la journée de dimanche," *Le Nouvelliste* (de Lyon), 10 févr. 1944.

Unverified. Seen only as a clipping in 127.

113. Aubert, R. "Le Centenaire de la mort de Charles Nodier. Une voix du terroir," *Le Nouvelliste* (de Lyon), 9 févr. 1944.

Unverified. Seen only as a clipping in 127.

114. Béguin, Albert. "Nodier et Nerval," *Labyrinthe*, no. 1 (1944).

> *La Fée aux Miettes* and *Aurélia* are the masterpieces of French "romantisme intérieur." The former is a desperate attempt to assuage the anguish of the knowledge of a heavy but imprecise guilt. This is true also of *Aurélia*, with the difference that with Nerval the sense of guilt does not remain imprecise and subjective, but is "l'objet d'une conscience très réellement religieuse." *Aurélia* is the stronger work. But *La Fée aux Miettes* deserves to be as well-gnown, for French literature does not have another "roman féerique" of this quality.

115. Bernard, Jean-Jacques. *Le Camp de la mort lente (Compiègne, 1941-42)*. Paris: Éditions Albin Michel, 1944. 246 pp.

> Has a single, but touching, reference on page 141 to the soirées at the Arsenal, which the author evoked for his fellow inmates of the concentration camp at Compiègne.

116. Dargaud, Marius. "Les Amis jurassiens de Charles Nodier vont célébrer le centenaire de sa mort," *Journal des Débats*, 29-30 janv. 1944.

> Summarizes Nodier's ties with the Jura mountains area.

117. Dargaud, Marius. "Autour de Charles Nodier. Antoine de Mailly de Châteaurenaud, curieuse figure de la Révolution, et la famille Charve," *Le Nouvelliste* (de Lyon), 12 janv. 1944.

> Seen only as a clipping in 127. Bibliographical data supplied by the author.

118. Dargaud, Marius. "Autour d'un Centenaire. Charles Nodier au *Journal des Débats*," *Journal des Débats*, 24 janv. 1944.

>A general summary of Nodier's journalistic activity for the *Journal des Débats*.

119. Dargaud, Marius. "Autour d'un Centenaire. Charles Nodier, jurassien," *Le Nouvelliste* (de Lyon), 7 janv. 1944.

>Seen only as a clipping in 127. Bibliographical data supplied by the author.

120. Dargaud, Marius. "Le Centenaire de la mort de Charles Nodier," *Chroniques* (Vichy), no. 38, 1944.

>Not seen. Bibliographical data supplied by the author. According to M. Dargaud, the text is "identique à celui du *Journal des Débats*."

120-A. Dargaud, Marius. "Le Centenaire de la mort de Charles Nodier," *Lyon Républicain*, 25 janv. 1944.

>Not seen. Bibliographical data supplied by the author. According to M. Dargaud, the text is "identique à celui du *Journal des Débats*."

121. Dargaud, Marius. "Le Centenaire de la mort de Charles Nodier," *Le Mois à Lyon*, no. 4, 25 avril 1944.

>Not seen. Bibliographical data supplied by the author. According to him, this is the "texte du discours prononcé par M. DARGAUD à Quintigny, le 5 février 1944."

122. Dargaud, Marius. "Le Centenaire de la mort de Charles Nodier," *La Page* (Lyon), 4 févr. 1944.

>Not seen. Bibliographical data supplied by the author. According to M. Dargaud, the text is "identique à celui du *Journal des Débats*."

123. Dargaud, Marius. *Centenaire de la mort de Charles Nodier (1780-1844), Lons-le-Saunier, 5 et 6 février, 1944. Théâtre Municipal. Représentations littéraires et artistiques avec le con-*

cours du Cercle Artistique Lédonien. Programme. Lons-le-Saunier: M. Declume, 1944. 4 pp.

> The program includes a lecture by Dargaud, a reading of the famous sonnet of Félix Arvers written for Marie Nodier, and two little plays (analyses on p. 4): *Le Secret d'Arvers* by Jean-Jacques Bernard, and the third act of the unpublished *Conteur féerique* by Dargaud.

123-A. Dargaud, Marius. "Charles Nodier dans ses horizons," *Journal des Débats,* 6 juil. 1944.

> A brief consideration of the place that the village of Quintigny had in the life and work of Nodier.

124. Dargaud, Marius. "Charles Nodier, jurassien," *Le Mois à Lyon,* no. 2, 25 févr. 1944; et no. 3, 25 mars 1944.

> Not seen. Bibliographical date supplied by the author.

125. Dargaud, Marius. *Exposition organisée à la Chambre de Commerce de Lons-le-Saunier par le Comité des Amis Jurassiens de Charles Nodier à l'occasion du centenaire de sa mort, 5-6 février, 1944. Autour de Charles Nodier.* Catalogue établi par M. Marius Dargaud. Lons-le-Saunier: M. Declume, 1944. 39 pp.

> Because of the evacuation of manuscript collections of Besançon and Paris libraries during the war, an exposition devoted exclusively to Nodier was not possible. Therefore a collection was assembled of materials concerning not only Nodier and his family, but also his wife's family and his Jurassien friends. The catalogue gives a valuable list of family documents, correspondence, manuscripts, editions, portraits, and other items displayed and indicates their location.

125-A. Dargaud, Marius. "Une Lettre inédite de Charles Nodier," *Journal des Débats,* 17 juil. 1944.

> Sees Nodier as the probable author of an undated, unsigned letter to Lucile Franque written in 1803, not long before her death.

126. Maixner, Rudolf. "Voyageurs français en Dalmatie, réels et imaginaires: Xavier Marmier, Albert Dumont et Francis

Levasseur," *Annales de l'Institut Français de Zagreb,* 8ᵉ année, nos. 24-25 (1944), pp. 84-119.

> Marmier's translation of the popular Dalmatian elegy of the *Femme d'Hassan-Aga* goes back to the Italian translation of Fortis. He evidently did not know Nodier's translation. In contrast, Levasseur in his *La Dalmatie ancienne et moderne* constantly purloins form both Fortis and Nodier. His "Triste Ballade de la noble épouse d'Asan-Aga" is reproduced alongside Nodier's "Femme d'Asan" to show the borrowings.

127. *[Recueil de documents concernant la célébration du centenaire de la mort de Charles Nodier—Lons-le-Saunier et Quintigny, 5-6 février 1944.]* (Dossier comprenent 1 br. in 8° et 27 ff. in 4°.)

> Collection of materials assembled in the Bibliothèque de l'Arsenal. Contains documents concerning a subscription for a monument to Nodier and a catalogue (125) and photographs of the exposition at the Chamber of Commerce of Lons-le-Saunier. There are also five newspaper articles, which together give a complete picture of the event. They are labelled as being from *Le Nouvelliste* (de Lyon). I was unable to verify the three by Aubert, but M. Dargaud personally verified his.
>
> > *a.* Dargaud, Marius. "Autour d'un centenaire, Charles Nodier, jurassien," 7 janv. 1944.
> >
> > *b.* Dargaud, Marius. "Autour de Charles Nodier. Antoine de Mailly de Châteaurenaud, curieuse figure de la Révolution; et la famille Charve," 12 janv. 1944.
> >
> > *c.* Aubert, R. "Le Centenaire de la mort de Charles Nodier a été commémoré à Lons-le-Saunier," 8 févr. 1944.
> >
> > *d.* Aubert, R. "Le Centenaire de la mort de Charles Nodier. Une Voix du terroir," 9 févr. 1944.
> >
> > *e.* Aubert, R. "Le Centenaire de la mort de Charles Nodier; conférence et théâtre la journée de dimanche," 10 févr. 1944.

128. Rosenfeld, Paul. "Nodier After a Century," *The Nation,* CLIX (1944), 18-19.

Looking back over the century since Nodier's death, Rosenfeld sees him as an innovator. In *Jean Sbogar* Nodier introduced to his readers the social revolutionary. The *Novena of Candlemas* revealed other new material for fiction, the lyrical expression of provincial themes. And the *Castles of the King of Bohemia* anticipates Mallarmé, Apollinaire, and E. E. Cummings. This critic holds that if Nodier excelled at nothing, at least in these inventions the mark of genius can be seen.

129. Thérive, André. "La Cité des plumes—Nodier précurseur," *Aujourd'hui (Paris)*, N° des 1er-2 juil. 1944, p. 2.

A newspaper article of one paragraph regretting that the centenary of Nodier's death passed almost unnoticed in Paris. Calls Nodier a European and cosmopolitan writer, and a precursor of Nerval and Heredia. Dargaud (136) defends Nodier against the title of European, which he considers pejorative.

130. Visan, Tancrède de. "Ce Bon Nodier," *Le Nouvelliste* [de Lyon], 5 janv. 1944, p. 1.

A newspaper article saluting the forthcoming celebration for Nodier at Besançon and Lons-le-Saunier, sketching Nodier's life, and citing his judicious selection of books for the Arsenal and his work for the *Bulletin du Bibliophile*.

1945

131. Baldensperger, Fernand. *La Critique et l'histoire littéraires en France au dix-neuvième et au début du vingtième siècles*, en collaboration avec H. S. Craig, Jr. Bibliothèque Brentano's, Études d'Histoire et de Critique Littéraires. New York: Brentano's, 1945. 244 pp.

Pages 49-52 present, with comment, a portion of Nodier's "Recherches sur l'éloquence révolutionnaire." If the importance of the selection to represent Nodier as a literary critic may be questioned, even a minor addition to his few readily available articles of criticism is welcome.

131-A. Dargaud, Marius. "Charles Nodier et le marquis de Moustier," *La République de Franche-Comté et du Territoire de Belfort* (Besançon), 12 sept. 1945.

>Not seen. Bibliographical data supplied by the author.

131-B. Dargaud, Marius. "L'Étrange Nuit de Ghismondo," *La Liberté* (Lyon), 24 déc. 1945.

>Not seen. Bibliographical data supplied by the author.

132. Engstrom, Alfred G. "The Formal Short Story in France and Its Development before 1850," *Studies in Philology*, XLII (1945), 627-639.

>Having equated the term *Conte* with the formal short story, the author concludes that "aside from the tales of Mérimée, Balzac, and Gautier, the only first-rate *Conte* I have been able to find in France before 1850 is Nodier's *Inès de las Sierras* (part one, 1837), and Nodier seems not to have employed the form again." Page 638.

133. Guischard, John A. *Le Conte fantastique au XIX⁰ siècle*. Les Publications de l'Université Laval. Montréal: Fides, [1945?]. 181 pp.

>A somewhat naïve treatment of Nodier, with generally acceptable conclusions but some details which are open to question, is found on pp. 74-78.

134. Marc, Fernand. "Une lettre inédite de Charles Nodier," *Les Lettres; Poésie, Philosophie, Littérature, Critique*, I (1945-46), 213-216.

>Presents a letter written by Nodier at the age of seventeen to his friend Pertusier in Paris concerning the admission of a new member to the Philadelphes and telling of projects for the future.

135. Martino, Pierre. *L'Époque romantique en France, 1815-1830*. Le Livre de l'Étudiant, coll. dirigée par Paul Hazard, 16. Paris: Boivin, 1945. 186 pp.

>A brief manual for the years 1815-1830. Nodier's works are covered in routine fashion on pp. 40-42. A more important

reference occurs on pp. 106-107: In Nodier's article, "De Quelques Logomachies classiques," that appeared in *La Muse Française* of April 1824, one can recognize the ideas that Sainte-Beuve will advance later in his *Pensées de Joseph Delorme:* "C'est la première apparition d'une théorie du romantisme fantaisiste et pittoresque, du romantisme artiste, du culte de la forme; au bout il y a les *Orientales.*"

1946

136. Dargaud, Marius. "Charles Nodier (1780-1844). La Commémoration du centenaire de sa mort sous l'oppression," *Bulletin du Bibliophile et du Bibliothécaire,* n. s. 1946, pp. [216]-223.

Relates the difficulties the Comité des Amis Jurassiens de Charles Nodier had during the Occupation in staging the centenary commemoration of Nodier's death. Also printed separately (Paris: L. Giraud-Badin, 1947).

137. Dargaud, Marius. "Une Lettre retrouvée de Charles Nodier," *Bulletin du Bibliophile et du Bibliothécaire,* n. s., 1946, pp. [102]-110.

Reestablishes in its complete text a letter that was partially mutilated in its previous publication. The letter, to Désiré Monnier in 1808, thanks him for dedicating some verses to Nodier. Shows Nodier as a philologist and critic of epic poetry in his early years. Also printed separately (Paris: L. Giraud-Badin, 1947).

138. Delétang-Tardif, Yanette. "Souvenir de Nodier; cheval pâle," *Paris, les Arts et les Lettres,* 2ᵉ année, no. 6 (9 janv. 1946), 1.

The author has just made the discovery of Nodier's *L'Histoire du roi de Bohême et de ses sept châteaux,* "cet objet délicieux, ce divertissement éblouissant, ce texte de haute désinvolture," and suggests an edition of it with Romantic illustrations.

139. Duhamel, Georges, ed. *Anthologie de la poésie lyrique en France de la fin du XVᵉ siècle à la fin du XIXᵉ siècle.* Paris: Flammarion, 1946. xxxix, 532 pp.

It is of some interest that Nodier should be included in a current anthology of French poetry. Although the editor says in his Preface, "Nodier est une figure sympathique entre toutes celles de ce temps; mais c'est dans la prose qu'il se fait justement apprécier" (p. xxxvi), his "Elle était bien jolie" is worthy of inclusion. See p. 377.

140. Maixner, R[udolf]. "Le Projet de l'édition illyrienne du *Télégraphe*," *Annales de l'Institut Français de Zagreb*, no. 28-29 (1946-47), pp. [232]-242.

Contains *Avis* no. 47, of June 13, 1813, by Nodier, as Director of the *Télégraphe Officiel,* to subscribers, concerning renewal of subscriptions. This *Avis* does not appear in the *Statistique illyrienne* (19a). See pp. 239-240 of the above article.

141. Monnot, Abel. "La Slovénie et Charles Nodier," in his *Études comtoises*. Besançon: Imprimerie de l'Est, 1946. Pp. 51-69.

Reprinted from the *Bulletin Trimestriel de l'Académie des Sciences, Belles-Lettres et Arts de Besançon*, 1924, pp. 195-211 (13).

> *a.* P. Moreau. *Revue d'Histoire Littéraire de la France*, XLVII (1947), 373-374.

142. T., L. S. "Charles Nodier and the Don Vicente Legend," *American Notes and Queries, a Journal for the Curious,* VI (1946-47), 134-135.

The author corrects a "grievous but unintentional calumny of the Roman clergy which I committed in my 'Notes on Bibliokleptomania' in the September, 1944, issue of the *New York Public Library Bulletin*." He has found that the alleged murder by Don Vicente of a book dealer who outbid him was not true. According to Miquel y Planas in *La Llegenda del llibreter assasí de Barcelona* (305) the whole affair was a fabrication of Nodier.

1947

143. Adhémar, Jean. "Le Livre romantique," *Le Portique,* no. 5 (1947), [93]-110.

Very little on Nodier. Reproduces, p. 98, a frontispiece by Tony Johannot for the 1844 edition of Nodier's *Contes* published by Hetzel. In connection with the very popular

Romantic album mentions (p. 107) Nodier, Taylor, and Cailleux's *Voyages pittoresques et romantiques dans l'ancienne France*, which was begun in the form of illustrated texts, but ended as albums of pictures preceded by an introduction.

144. Castex, Pierre-Georges. *Anthologie du conte fantastique français*. Paris: José Corti, 1947. 326 pp.

Two good pages, pp. 61-62, introduce an excerpt from *Smarra*. In a century when science was rapidly extending its sway, "ses [Nodier's] œuvres d'imagination peuvent ... apparaître comme la protestation d'un génie mystique laissé insatisfait par les vérités d'expérience et les évidences rationnelles, d'un poète soucieux de ne pas laisser immoler la Poésie sur les autels de la Science." Nodier would have approved of Freudian researches and subscribed to the formula of André Breton denying the opposition of "folie" and reason. The same material appears in the 1963 edition of the *Anthologie* (254).

144-A. Dargaud, Marius. "Autour d'une Exposition littéraire. Le Douzième Fauteuil académique, de Charles Nodier à Marcel Pagnol (1833-1947)," *L'Espoir* (Saint-Étienne), 7 et 8 avril 1947.

Not seen. Bibliographical data supplied by the author.

1948

145. Brunot, Ferdinand. *Histoire de la langue française des origines à nos jours*, Vol. XII: *L'Époque romantique*, by Charles Bruneau. Paris: Armand Colin, 1948. xix, 593 pp.

Pages 212-215 quote and summarize Nodier's ideas on language, the two dominant ideas being that of the divine origin of language, and that similar to Rousseau's of a linguistic perfection possessed in the past but progressively lost.

146. Charlier, Gustave. *Le Mouvement romantique en Belgique (1815-1850)*. 2 vols. Bruxelles: Palais des Académies, 1948-59.

An addition to the literature on Nodier's reception in foreign countries. In Vol. I, pp. 116-121 recount the fortune of Nodier in the Belgian press from 1818 to the early 1820's. Reaction was largely, but not always, favorable. Other scattered references give reactions as late as 1828. In Vol. II, pp. 92-94 show praise of Nodier in the 1830's, and the notice taken by the press of his trip to Belgium in 1835. Pages 406-408 concern the high favor in which he stood in Belgium at his death, and his continuing reputation today.

147. Dargaud, Marius. "Deux Lettres de jeunesse de Marie Nodier (1827)," *Bulletin du Bibliophile et du Bibliothécaire,* n. s., 1948, pp. [560]-569.

A brief letter written by Marie for her father, who is sick, to M. Péricaud, a librarian of Lyons, shows the existence of relations of Nodier with bibliophiles and scholars of that city.

148. Henriot, Émile. "Charles Nodier ou le mythomane," in his *Courrier littéraire. XIXe siècle.* Vol. I: *Autour de Chateaubriand.* Paris: Marcel Dauban, 1948. Pp. [311]-318.

Reprinted from *Le Temps,* 21 juillet 1931 (59).

149. Stambak, Dinko. "La Complainte de la noble femme d'Asan-Aga ou l'invitation romantique au voyage illyrien," *Revue de Littérature Comparée,* 22e année (1948), 296-303.

Among all the popular Slavic ballads the famous *Hasanaghinitsa* occupies an exceptional place. It had fifteen translations into French, and the two by Nodier are considered along with the others. Nodier was the most important of those to introduce Illyrian themes into France. Not many had travelled in Illyria, and his experience there permitted him to pose as an authority. The Illyria that was created by the imaginary travelers received its start at the Arsenal.

1949

150. Dargaud, Marius. "Une Correspondance familiale inédite de Marie Nodier (1833-1868)," *Bulletin du Bibliophile et du Bibliothécaire,* n. s., 1949, pp. [371]-399.

Correspondence of Marie Nodier after her marriage. Listed in Drevet and RHL under Charles Nodier, but does not concern him.

151. Deharme, Lise. "Charles Nodier," in Francis Dumont, ed., *Les Petits Romantiques français*. Liguge: Les Cahiers du Sud, 1949. Pp. 189-205.

> Lise Deharme introduces ten pages of miscellaneous fragments from Nodier with a little essay that makes no attempt to add anything in the way of scholarship but shows a fine feeling for the atmosphere of his works.

> *a.* L. Gros. *Cahiers du Sud*, no. 303 (1950).
> Not seen.

152. Fontana, Luigi. "L'Arte di Charles Nodier," *Annali della Scuola Friulana*, 1949-50, pp. 21-64.

> This is a very good attempt at an analysis of the art of Nodier to see what his especial charm is. Fontana proceeds by examining in some detail examples of Nodier's Wertherian works and then those of fantastic inspiration, discussing the weaknesses, strong points, and special characteristics of both modes. It was with the latter that Nodier finally created something completely his own. He saw poetry as a basis of his art. "Il miracolo stupisce lo stesso Nodier per la semplicità della formula, ma c'eran voluti cinquant'anni di tentativi faticosi e sterili, di prove, di dubbi, di scoraggiamenti, prima di trovare la strada maestra, il filone lucente di poesia."

153. Held, Mariette. *Charles Nodier et le romantisme*. Thèse présentée à la Faculté des Lettres de l'Université de Berne pour obtenir le grade de docteur. Bienne: Éditions du Chandelier, 1949. 100 pp.

> The well-realized aim of this book is to look at Nodier, the man and the work, in order to determine the expressions of his Romantic side, without neglecting his realism. The first section of this three-part essay defines the historical role of Nodier in the Romantic movement, treating less well-known documents. Nodier's influence as a critic was not preponderant, but often he was the first to express new ideas that were in the air. Part Two shows the romantic elements in the fantastic reveries of Nodier: a feeling for nature, exoticism, love of the Middle Ages, influence of English and German literatures, fantasy, and a predilection for archaisms and the language of the people. But realistic

touches are seen throughout his *contes*. Part Three is an excellent psychological analysis of Nodier's character that avoids the pitfalls of applying psychoanalytical techniques to literary criticism. Miss Held sees lack of maternal love and deficiency of maternal intelligence as the seat of many of Nodier's disorders. All his life, like Gérard de Nerval, he sought the ideal woman, at once mother, lover, and goddess. *La Fée aux Miettes* is the most complete expression of that nostalgia, but his reveries do not admit integral reconstruction of his psychological portrait. Nodier is a figure apart, resisting classification in any particular category. His Romanticism, being innate, never became a program.

> *a.* P. Moreau. *Revue d'Histoire Littéraire de la France*, L (1950), 328-329.

154. [Weigert, Roger-Armand, and Ferdinand Boyer. *Le Testament de Charles Le Brun* [et] *Inventaire des tapisseries de Charles-Maurice Le Tellier,* par Roger-Armand Weigert. *Catalogue raisonné de l'œuvre de Charles Natoire,* par Ferdinand Boyer. Paris: A. Colin, 1949. 109 pp.

> This reference, which is listed in *Zeitschrift für Romanische Philologie* under Charles *Nodier* is, rather, for Charles *Natoire.*]

1950

155. Amadou, Robert, and Robert Kanters, eds. *Anthologie littéraire de l'occultisme.* Paris: R. Juliard, 1950. 365 pp.

> Fragments of Nodier's *De la Palingénésie humaine* are preceded by a good one-page appreciation of Nodier's occultism (pp. 212-217). See also Viatte (44) and Richer (197).

156. Béguin, Albert. "Charles Nodier ou l'enfance restaurée," *Cahiers du Sud,* no. 304 (1950), pp. [353]-357.

> Some very good insights into the psychological reasons for the writing of *Trilby* and *La Fée aux Miettes* and why they are great works. In these two stories Nodier was seeking a return to childhood. "Deux fois il a recréé le paradis d'enfance, mais un paradis dont la félicité poétique inclut, transfigure, illumine jusqu'aux plus cruelles souffrances, jusqu'aux terreurs du cauchemar. Et ce sont les deux chefs-d'œuvre grâce auxquels il mérite vraiment de survivre,

non pas parmi les poètes mineurs, les écrivains de transition, les précurseurs, mais parmi les très grands créateurs du romantisme français." Accepts Vodoz' study of *La Fée aux Miettes* (17) as "une des seules études psychanalytiques valables que l'on ait écrites sur une œuvre de poésie." Reprinted in *Poésie de la présence* (206). For a fuller study of the idea of paradise in Nodier see Engler (247). See also Orlando (291-A).

157. Castex, Pierre-Georges. "Une Source de *La Fée aux Miettes*," *Revue des Sciences Humaines*, n. s., 1950, pp. [205]-208.

Vodoz and Béguin have revealed the personal elements in *La Fée aux Miettes*. But the interior life of Nodier does not explain certain details. For example, why did Nodier locate the "maison de santé" at Glasgow? Castex proposes as the source of the idea an article in the *Revue de Paris* of May, 1829, entitled "Lettre à M. le docteur A... sur l'hospice des fous de Glascow [sic] par M. le duc de Lévis," praising the methods of that insane asylum.

158. Dargaud, Marius. "L'Édition originale du *Génie Bonhomme* de Charles Nodier (1836)," *Bulletin du Bibliophile et du Bibliothécaire*, n. s., 1950, pp. [42]-50.

Heretofore the original edition of *Le Génie Bonhomme* has been considered that of 1837. Dargaud has found an 1836 edition. Except for a few minor variations the texts are the same.

159. Dargaud, Marius. "Une Pseudo-Édition du *Livre de beauté* (1846)," *Bulletin du Bibliophile et du Bibliothécaire*, n. s., 1950, pp. [298]-302.

Gives the date of 1846 to an undated reprinting of the 1834 edition of *Le Livre de beauté*, a *keepsake* with a preface by Nodier.

160. Delétang-Tardif, Yanette. "Je visite les soleils ...," *Cahiers du Sud*, no. 304 (1950), pp. [358]-363.

Nodier was amusing himself in *L'Histoire du roi de Bohême et de ses sept châteaux*, and amusing things are divine. Though Nodier said that in this work he was plagiarizing Sterne, who plagiarized Swift, and on back to Apuleius,

Yanette Delétang-Tardif says that he went forward as well, anticipating Laforgue, Gourmont, Jarry, and the *Calligrammes* of Apollinaire. "L'œuf surréaliste est dans ces pages, sous les verts gazons de la résurrection." Written with obvious delight in this "livre exquis."

161. Henry-Rosier, Mme Marguerite. "Charles Nodier à Dole," *Le Pays Jurassien*, 5ᵉ année, no. 40 (oct. à déc. 1950), pp. 99-103.

Published from a talk given by the author before the Société d'Émulation at Dole in 1950. Recounts, with the addition of little that is unknown, Nodier's sojourn in Dole following his anti-Napoleon activities.

162. "Lettre [inédite] de Charles Nodier [1ᵉʳ juillet 1828]," *Le Vieux Papier. Bulletin de la Société Archéologique, Historique et Artistique*, XX (1950-53), 354.

A letter of Nodier, ostensibly to his publisher, with a request for two hundred francs in advance on a proposed new edition of his *Dictionnaire des onomatopées*. From the collection of M. Ferrand.

163. Nodier, Charles. "Textes de Charles Nodier: 'Jugement dernier' [présenté par J. Richer]; 'Lettre sur les origines de l'alphabet' [présentée] par Marius Dargaud; 'Piranèse. Contes psychologiques à propos de la monomanie réflexive,'" *Cahiers du Sud*, no. 304 (1950), pp. [372]-386.

Richer's text is the last chapter of a novel, *Le Voleur*, of the period 1803-1807, which he hopes to publish. See 112a. Dargaud, in presenting Nodier's letter, discusses further work along the same lines being done at the same time by Nodier and others.

164. Perret, J. "L'Utilisation littéraire d'un drame judiciaire bressan. Hélène Gillet," *Annales de la Société d'Émulation de l'Agriculture, Sciences, Lettres et Arts de l'Ain*, 1950, pp. [83]-94.

A nice comparative study of the use of the same historical event in two different manners. Perret first reviews the facts in the case of Hélène Gillet and then examines Nodier's treatment in *L'Histoire d'Hélène Gillet* and Anatole France's treatment in *Les Opinions de Jérôme Coignard.* Nodier's story is characterized by: suppression of some of the details and modification of others to appeal to the audience of his time; insistence on the Christian marvellous; a lyrical, dramatic, emphatic account of the trial and attempted execution of Hélène; and a plea against the death penalty. It is a Romantic treatment. Anatole France's is more sober, with elimination of any melodrama, emphasis, or the marvellous, Christian or otherwise. It is a rationalistic relation for an audience that would have rejected Romantic techniques.

165. Richer, Jean. "Nodier et Nerval," *Cahiers du Sud,* no. 304 (1950), pp. [364]-371.

> An unusually good paper. On the direct borrowings of Nerval from Nodier and common themes in the two authors. It was only after Nodier's death that Nerval permitted himself to borrow directly from his friend. *L'Histoire du roi de Bohême et de ses sept châteaux* had a profound influence on both "Angélique" and *Les Petits Châteaux de Bohême.* Part of the scenario of *Les Monténégrins* was inspired by *Jean Sbogar* and *Inès de les Sierras.* And *Aurélia* owes much to the preface of *Smarra.* But along with these borrowings there are many similarities in themes: the Queen or Sheba, "amours enfantines," illuminism and secret societies, and prison. Such resemblances may be explained by common sources of inspiration and similarities in lived experience. But "l'ombre portée par ce petit homme [Nerval] empêche parfois de distinguer le tuteur qui se tient derrière lui." For other material on similarities in Nodier and Nerval, see Richer (263) and Juin (249).

166. Richer, Jean. "*Le Roi de Bohême* ou les tentations du langage," in Charles Nodier, *Histoire du roi de Bohême et de ses sept châteaux.* Paris: Delangle Frères, 1830. [Réimpression... 1950.]

> Richer's postface is an informative "introduction" to the reading of Nodier's fantasy. Discusses the many authors Nodier is indebted to: Sterne, Montaigne, Charron, Cervantes, Cyrano, Swift, Amyot, Marot, Bonaventure Despériers, and especially Rabelais. Searches into the origins of the names of the characters and the themes, and points out some of the parodies and satires. Has also been incorporated

into Richer's *Autour de "L'Histoire du roi de Bohême," Charles Nodier "dériseur sensé"* of 1962 (252).

1951

167. Castex, Pierre-Georges. "Nodier et ses rêves," in *Le Conte fantastique en France de Nodier à Maupassant.* Paris: José Conti, 1951. Pp. [121]-167.

This important book devotes a long chapter, of major interest, to Nodier as one of the masters of the fantastic *conte,* giving him an eminent place in the history of a genre which had a successful vogue in France throughout the nineteenth century. Analyses penetratingly and in detail, with excellent summaries, all the principal works of Nodier in the fantastic vein and characterizes the fantastic elements in each. Is especially good in analyses of *Smarra, Trilby,* and *Inès de las Sierras.* But we must learn to know Nodier himself if we are to understand his work. "Sa vie intérieure transparaît dans ses fictions, son univers fantastique exprime un romantisme profond." Good bibliographies at end of book. Reprinted exactly in the new edition, 1962 (245). Also appears, without footnotes and bibliography, as a postface to Nodier's *Contes du pays des rêves* (207).

    a. Annales de l'Université de Paris, XXI (1951), 265-267.

    b. S. de Sacy. Mercure de France, CCCXII (1951), 339-343.

    c. H. Godin. French Studies, VI (1952), 262-263.

    d. J. Pommier. Revue d'Histoire Littéraire de la France, LII (1952), 241-245.

    e. J. Voisine. Revue de Littérature Comparée, XXVI (1952), 153-155.

    f. E. Noulet. Diogènes, no. 1 (1953), pp. 98-107.

168. *Cuentos de bibliófilo:* originales de C. Nodier [*et al.*], precedidos de un prólogo de R. Miguel y Planas. Ilus. de Triadó [*et al.*] con ornamentaciones de J. Figuerola. Barcelona: Instituto Catalán de las Artes del Libro, 1951. 101, 349 pp.

Pages 31-38 of a long prologue are devoted to Nodier but consist largely of résumés of his two works included in the anthology: *El Bibliómano* and *Franciscus Columna.* Some information on the origin of sach.

169. Dargaud, Marius. "Charles Nodier poète et l'épopée napoléonienne (1833)," *Bulletin du Bibliophile et du Bibliothécaire,* n. s., 1951, pp. [211]-217.

Republishes and comments on a poem of Nodier to be found only in the *Revue de Sainte-Étienne* of 1833. "Le Conscrit," about a soldier's departure from home, the battle of Waterloo, and his father's futile wait for his return, is a strange poem coming from the author of the *Napoléone.* But it was written after the fall of the Restoration, when Napoleon's legend was growing. Also published separately at Chartres, 1951.

170. Dargaud, Marius. "Nodier mémoraliste: *Suites d'un mandat d'arrêt* (fragment inédit)," *Revue des Sciences Humaines,* n. s., 1951, pp. [273]-281.

Dargaud presents here a fragment of the *Suites d'un mandat d'arrêt* that Nodier did not include in his published version, and goes to great pains to document the whole affair of Nodier's return to Besançon after his arrest in Paris. Dargaud points out that of all Nodier's work his *Souvenirs* remain the most criticized parts; yet he has just demonstrated that they are not all to be questioned. A critical edition should be done, seeking Nodier's source for each episode and putting each in its historical light. See also Orlando (287 and 291-A).

171. Richer, Jean. "Notes bibliographiques sur Charles Nodier," *Revue des Sciences Humaines,* n. s., 1951, pp. [282]-284.

For the benefit of whoever may undertake to prepare a more complete bibliography of Nodier than Larat's (3), Richer describes and gives excerpts from three unpublished documents: I. Projet d'une *Histoire des califats* (1825); II. Un Contrat inconnu avec Renduel (1840); III. Lettre de Charles Nodier au libraire Dumont (1842).

172. Vivier, Michel. "Charles Nodier, romantique et royaliste," *Aspects de la France,* V, no. 158 (1951), 3.

Follows Richer (165) in his observations on Nodier's influence on Nerval. Adds nothing to knowledge of Nodier "royaliste."

1952

173. Duban, Edmund. "Charles Weiss, un ami de Charles Nodier." Thèse compl. Lettres, Paris, 1952.

Not seen.

174. Duban, Edmund. "La Jeunesse de Charles Nodier." Thèse. Lettres, Paris, 1952.

Not seen.

175. Oliver, A. Richard. "Nodier at the Newberry," *The Newberry Library Bulletin*, n. s., III (1952-55), 237-241.

Praises the Newberry Library in Chicago as a place for research in French literature. In particular, finds that it is well equipped to serve not only the Nodier scholar, but researchers in other areas of Romanticism.

176. Richer, Jean. "Charles Nodier, dériseur sensé, [suivi de] 'Ce pacte inouï' (*Le Voleur,* chapitre IV) [et] *La Plus Petite des pantoufles,* par Charles Nodier," *Mercure de France,* CCCXV (1952), [92]-119.

At every opportunity Nodier attacked the idea of progress and perfectibility. As a young man he even went further, believing that society was bad in its essence. An unpublished novel, *Le Voleur,* written around 1805, is very revealing in this respect. Nodier also had a precocious satiric streak that may be seen in a text that remained long unpublished: *La Plus Petite des pantoufles,* also written around 1805. It is really the sketch for the *Histoire du roi de Bohême, though* it lacks Nodier's principal idea in the latter of putting himself on the scene as three different personages. However, very few lines, textually, of *La Plus Petite des pantoufles* are found in *Le roi de Bohême*. This very informative material is, except for "Ce Pacte inouï," incorporated into Richer's *Autour de l'Histoire du roi de Bohême* (252).

177. Trahard, Pierre. *Prosper Mérimée et l'art de la nouvelle. Troisième édition avec un fac-simile.* Paris: Nizet, 1952. 53 pp.

Has same material as first edition (6). See p. 18.

1953

178. Maixner, Rudolf. "Un Article 'illyrisant' posthume de Charles Nodier," *Annales de l'Institut Français de Zagreb,* 2ᵉ sér., nos. 2 et 3 (1953-54), pp. 163-171.

Maixner comments on an "illyrisant" fragment which he had recently discovered. Shows that Nodier's observations on Illyrian literature in this article have inexactitudes and errors and that at the time they were written, probably between 1826 and 1840, Nodier had not made any new studies, but was drawing on his articles for the *Télégraphe* of 1813. This material is included in Chapter XIII of *Charles Nodier et l'Illyrie* (231).

179. Monchoux, André. *L'Allemagne devant les lettres françaises de 1814 à 1835.* Paris: Armand Colin, [1953?]. 526 pp.

A few scattered references to Nodier, mostly in regard to his statements on the importance of German literature to French literature. Exactly the same material on Nodier contained in the second edition, 1965 (286).

    a. J.-M. Carré. *Revue de Littérature Comparée,* XXVII (1953), 475-478.

180. Prévost, Jean-Laurent. *Le Prêtre, ce héros de roman d'Atala aux Thibault.* Collection Présence du Catholicisme. Paris: P. Téqui, 1953.

In this study on the evolution du personage of the priest as the novel form evolves, the role of the priest in two of Nodier's stories is considered. *Franciscus Columna* shows a Romantic treatment. That in *Thérèse Aubert* is more realistic. See pp. 24 and 52.

1954

181. Banachévitch, N. "Les Romantiques français et la Serbie," *La Revue des Lettres Modernes,* no. 10 (nov. 1954), pp. 9-15.

Two short paragraphs (p. 13) on Nodier are of no interest to the informed Nodier scholar.

182. Clouard, Henri. "Nodier et sa multiple figure," in Charles Nodier, *La Fée Aux Miettes ... L'Homme et la fourmi.* Bibliothèque Mondiale, no. 8, 7 mai 1953. Paris: Éditions de la Bibliothèque Mondiale, 1954. Pp. 185-192.

An introduction for the general reader to Nodier's character and the literary influences he underwent. Also appears in 183.

183. Clouard, Henri. "Nodier et sa multiple figure," in Charles Nodier, *La Fée aux Miettes ... suivi de L'Homme et la fourmi, apologue primitif.* Paris: Le Livre Mondiale, s. d. [Entre 1936-1959.]

Contains the same material as the 1954 edition (182).

184. Descaves, Pierre. "Charles Nodier," in Charles Nodier, *La Fée aux Miettes ... L'Homme et la fourmi.* Bibliothèque Mondiale, no. 8, 7 mai 1953. Paris: Éditions de la Bibliothèque Mondiale, 1954. Pp. 1-5.

A good account of Nodier's life and salon at the Arsenal for the general reader. Also appears in 185 and 200.

185. Descaves, Pierre. "Charles Nodier," in Charles Nodier, *La Fée aux Miettes ... suivi de L'Homme et la fourmi, apologue primitif.* Paris: Le Livre Mondiale, s. d. [Entre 1936-1959.]

Contains the same material as the 1954 edition (184) and the 1956 edition (200).

186. Jaloux, Edmond. *Visages français. Avant-propos par Henri Mondor.* Paris: Albin Michel, 1954. 254 pp.

Jaloux shows a marked predilection for Nodier, but the pages devoted to him (pp. 165-180) are largely a recounting of the well-known facts of his life and the soirées at the Arsenal.

    a. M. Thiébaut. "Edmond Jaloux ou l'anti-Hugo," *La Revue de Paris,* 61ᵉ année (juin 1954), 151-152.

    b. P. M. Jones. *French Studies,* IX (1955), 180-181.

187. Mennessier-Nodier, Jean. "Charles Nodier et l'éducation du peuple, pages inédites," *Revue des Sciences Humaines,* n. s., no. 76 (1954), [393]-401.

Nodier was against proposals for collective education among the proletariat, which were to him contradictory to the monarchic order. However, he did not always oppose advancement. Toward the end of his life he drew up a plan for a treatise on the education of the people, the hitherto unpublished outline of which is published here. It shows that he feared instruction given to the people without discrimination, but felt that one who raised himself above his estate by ability should advance. It also shows his interest in technical education, moral education, and a number of reforms, including that of the death penalty. Followed by a list of other references by Nodier to the same subject. Enlightening on a little-studied aspect of Nodier's thought.

188. Miomandre, Francis de. "*La Fée aux Miettes,*" in Charles Nodier, *La Fée aux Miettes ... L'Homme et la fourmi.* Bibliothèque Mondiale, no. 8, 7 mai 1953. Paris: Éditions de la Bibliothèque Mondiale, 1954. Pp. 7-12.

A good analysis of *La Fée aux Miettes* for the general reader. Also appears in 189.

189. Miomandre, Francis de. "*La Fée aux Miettes,*" in Charles Nodier, *La Fée aux Miettes ... suivi de L'Homme et la fourmi, apologue primitif.* Paris: Le Livre Mondiale, s. d. [Entre 1936-1959.]

Contains the same material as the 1954 edition (188).

190. Mongland, André. "Éditeurs romantiques: Nicolas Delangle et Charles Nodier," in *Mélanges d'histoire littéraire et de bibliographie offerts à Jean Bonnerot,* conservateur en chef honoraire de la Bibliothèque de la Sorbonne, par ses amis et ses collègues. Paris: Nizet, 1954. Pp. [317]-326.

This paper concerns Nicolas Delangle, one of the little-known Romantic publishers who helped carry the art of the book to a high level in the Romantic period, and his relation, in both friendship and finance, with his favorite author, Charles Nodier, who played the role of a sort of protector to him. Both Nodier and Delangle were lovers of fine books. One of their joint projects was the publishing of the *Collection des petits classiques français* with emphasis on fine physical production. Delangle published a number of Nodier's works. In 1830 he tried to surpass himself with a generously illustrated edition of *L'Histoire du roi de Bohême et de ses sept châteaux*. The enormous expense ruined him, and he had to close his publishing house and was soon lost from sight. An interesting addition to knowledge of Nodier's relations to the publishing world.

191. Moreau, Pierre. "Les Faux Jours de Charles Nodier," *Droit et Liberté; Revue Bimestrielle de l'Union Chrétienne des Professeurs de l'Enseignement Officiel de Belgique*, VI (1954-55), 112-124.

For Moreau, Nodier is primarily a man of the eighteenth century and of the province of Franche-Comté. He finds justification for these views in Nodier's *contes*. "Nodier, homme du XVIIIe siècle dans le XIXe, franc-comtois dans la bataille parisienne des lettres, conteur de beaux mensonges en un temps qui fait de l'histoire une science et de la science une religion: tel est le triple paradoxe de cette âme légère." A well-documented article.

192. Richer, Jean. "Le Manuscrit et les premières éditions de *La Fée aux Miettes* de Charles Nodier (matériaux pour une édition critique)," in *Mélanges d'histoire littéraire et de bibliographie offerts à Jean Bonnerot*, conservateur en chef honoraire de la Bibliothèque de la Sorbonne, par ses amis et ses collègues. Paris: Nizet, 1954. Pp. [365]-371.

Compares the original manuscript of *La Fée aux Miettes* with a copy of the second edition of Renduel (1835) and points out the principal variants and corrections, the most revealing being those that confirm Nodier's identification of himself with Michel and the relation of this work to the formative period of his life.

193. Switzer, Richard. "Charles Nodier: A Re-examination," *The French Review*, XXVIII (1954-55), 224-232.

Literary history has always misunderstood Nodier, classing him as a second-rate Romantic instead of according him his rightful place as an important precursor of Symbolism and as a significant author in his own right. Nodier's importance as a precursor is apparent in both the form and the content of his work, as can be seen especially in *L'Histoire du roi de Bohême et de ses sept châteaux* and *Smarra*. He should be recognized as an important influence foreshadowing post-Romantic literature.

1955

194. Billey, Maurice. "Un Magistrat révolutionnaire: le père de Charles Nodier," *Bulletin de la Fédération des Sociétés Savantes de Franche-Comté*, no. 2 (1955), pp. 116-164.

Though this article primarily concerns Nodier's father, it traces the Nodier family from the middle of the seventeenth century and devotes approximately four pages to Nodier's illegitimate birth, later regularized; his father's tender care of him; and Nodier's love for his father.

195. Picon, Gaëtan. "Le Roman et la prose lyrique au XIXe siècle," in Raymond Queneau, *Histoire des littératures*. Encyclopédie de la Pléiade. 3 vols. Paris: Gallimard, 1955-58. III, [999]-1107.

Pages 1034-36 are a short but good essay on the place of Nodier in the literature of dream and madness, with special attention to *Trilby* and *La Fée aux Miettes*.

196. Richer, Jean. "Gérard de Nerval et *Sylvie*," *La Revue de Paris*, 62e année (oct. 1955), pp. [116]-126.

A single, but interesting, reference to Nodier on p. 119; "Mais on n'a pas signalé, à notre connaissance, que la célèbre scène de la ronde des jeunes filles, au chapitre II de *Sylvie*, reprend un épisode semblable de *Thérèse Aubert* de Charles Nodier."

197. Richer, Jean. "Romantiques français devant les sciences occultes," in *Proceedings of the Sixth Triennial Congress of the International Federation for Modern Languages and Literatures. Literature and Science. Oxford, 1954.* Oxford: Basil Blackwell, 1955. Pp. 242-250.

Considers occultism in Nodier, Hugo, Balzac, and Nerval. In this area, as in many others, Nodier was a precursor. He uses occultism for literary purposes, showing especial fondness for the phenomena "de visions à distance, de sympathies obscurs entre les âmes, de correspondances mystérieuses entre les divers degrés de la création." Dream, for Nodier, opened the gates of the spiritual universe, and occultism for him is the equivalent of a sort of waking dream. It probably was not by accident that the authors treated here frequented and admired each other. Though all very different, they lived in a "décor mental commun" brought about partly by occultism. A good juxtaposition of four authors sharing a common interest. See also Viatte (44) and Amadou (155).

1956

198. Castex, Pierre-Georges. "Un Inédit de Charles Nodier: 'Ferry Barbis,'" *Annales Publiées par la Faculté des Lettres de Toulouse. Littératures,* IV, fasc. 1-2 (1956), 7-19.

Castex adds informative comments to "Ferry Barbis" published here. Between 1820 and 1830 Nodier had harbored the idea of writing a historical novel on the theme of seventeenth-century Franche-Comté. Marie Mennessier-Nodier said that her father actually wrote the first chapter in 1823. Castex proposes that "Ferry Barbis" is that chapter. It is of good literary quality, has its settings near Besançon, and apparently takes place in the reign of Louis XIII.

199. Cluzel, Étienne. "Une Édition fantôme des *Petits Châteaux de Bohême,*" *Bulletin du Bibliophile et du Bibliothécaire,* n. s., 1956, pp. [80]-86.

French VI lists this under Nodier instead of Nerval. Deals with Nerval's *Petits Châteaux de Bohême,* but "il est permis de supposer que c'est à dessein et en souvenir de son ami Nodier que ce titre fut choisi."

200. Descaves, Pierre. "Charles Nodier," in Charles Nodier, *La Fée aux Miettes,* présentée par Pierre Descaves. Paris: Éditions de la Bibliothèque Mondiale, 1956.

Identical with the presentation, "Charles Nodier," in the 1954 edition (184) and the undated edition (185).

201. Freymann, Hella-Henriette. "Aspects littéraires des tendances platoniciennes dans la France du XIXe siècle (Literary Aspects of Platonic Tendencies in XIXth Century France)." Ann Arbor, Mich: University Microfilms, 1956. 321 pp.

>Doctoral dissertation at Columbia University, 1956. Concerned with Nodier, Nerval, Baudelaire, Rimbaud, and Villiers de l'Isle-Adam, as representatives of the idealistic literature stemming from Romanticism and evolving into Symbolism. Chapter III, pp. 70-119, passes in review a large part of Nodier's fictional output, showing his idealistic tendencies.

202. Le Yaouanc, Moïse. "Autour de *Louis Lambert*," *Revue d'Histoire Littéraire de la France*, LVI (1956), [516]-534.

>Pages 532-534 call attention to similarities in Nodier's character, Jean-François les Bas-Bleus, and Balzac's Louis Lambert in the *Comédie Humaine*. The likenesses are so striking that one of the writers must have imitated the other. As *Louis Lambert* was published first, Nodier would have to be the imitator. Furthermore, Balzac called Nodier's attention to Louis Lambert in a letter published in the *Revue de Paris* in October, 1832. It does not seem, however, that Balzac ever complained of this borrowing. For other material on similarities in Nodier and Balzac see Castex (244).

203. Oliver, A. Richard. "Nodier as Bibliographer and Bibliophile," *The Library Quarterly*, XXVI (1956), 23-30.

>Nodier was an avid collector of rare books and fine bindings. He conceived the first bibliographical journal of any importance, the *Bulletin du Bibliophile*, and published in it fine lead articles on bibliographic, literary, and linguistic subjects. By 1830 his many activities in this field had gained him the reputation as an international authority on books. At the end of the nineteenth century he was still ranked as one of the great bibliophiles of all time, but since then has been more or less forgotten. This article presents a good case for restoring him to his former rank in the fields of bibliography and bibliophilism.

204. Ruff, Marcel A. "Maturin et les romantiques français," in C. R. Maturin, *Bertram, ou le château de Saint-Aldobrand*.

Traduit Librement de l'Anglais par Taylor et Ch. Nodier. Éd. commentée et précédée d'une introduction sur Maturin et les romantiques français par Marcel A. Ruff. Paris: José Corti, 1956. Pp. [7]-66.

> A few pages are devoted to Nodier's literary criticism of Maturin, which was mostly favorable, and to his collaboration in the translation of *Bertram* into French. Ruff speculates that Nodier may also have been a collaborator in the writing of the melodrama, *Bertram, ou le pirate*, on the same subject, which was a great stage success in 1822. See pp. 28-31, 37.

1957

205. Archer, E. A. "The Prose Poem in French Literature from 1800 up to and Including the Publication of Baudelaire's 'Petits Poèmes en prose,' in 1869, with Special Reference to Ch. Nodier, Aloysius Bertrand, Maurice de Guérin and Gérard de Nerval." Diss., London, Westfield College, 1957-58.

> Not seen.

206. Béguin, Albert. "Charles Nodier ou l'enfance restaurée," in his *Poésie de la présence. De Chrétien de Troyes à Pierre Emmanuel.* Les Cahiers du Rhône, 95. Sér. Blanche, 29. Neuchâtel: La Baconnière; Paris: Éditions du Seuil, 1957. Pp. [169]-175.

> A reprinting of his article by the same title in the *Cahiers du Sud*, 1950 (156).

207. Castex, Pierre-Georges. "Nodier et ses rêves," in Charles Nodier, *Contes du pays des rêves.* Saverne: Club des Libraires de France, 1957. Pp. [391]-443.

> Reprinted, without footnotes and bibliography, from Castex's *Le Conte fantastique en France de Nodier à Maupassant* (167). The same material appears also in the new edition of the *Conte fantastique* (245).

208. Kies, Albert. "À propos d'un exemplaire de *Trilby* ayant appartenu à Victor Hugo," *Bulletin du Bibliophile et du Bibliothécaire*, n. s., 1957, pp. [91]-93.

Jacques Patin (52) has preceded Kies in describing the copy of *Trilby* given by Nodier to Hugo (who presented it, in turn, to Juliette Drouet) and in publishing Nodier's accompanying poem to Hugo. Patin's article has an added interest in that he sees the book as a gift for the two-month anniversary of the commencement of Hugo's and Juliette Drouet's liaison.

209. Kies, Albert. "Charles Nodier et Sir Herbert Croft d'après des documents inédits," *Bulletin du Bibliophile et du Bibliothécaire*, n. s., 1957, pp. [53]-56.

Presents a letter from Nodier to Sir Herbert Croft accepting a position at Amiens as his secretary. Kies is struck by Nodier's enthusiasm and effusion for a man whom he hardly knew, and explains them by saying that Nodier, disillusioned with life, had taken refuge in a dream world. Sir Herbert, with the advantages he offered, now became a part of his dreams and was to appear later as a character in *Amélie*, where the real world and dream world are mingled.

210. Marquardt, Hans. *Französische Liebesgeschichten von Nodier bis Maupassant*. Ubertr. v. Helmut Bartuschek. Ill. v. Max Schwimmer. Leipzig: Reclam, 1957. 637 pp.

A second edition appeared in 1957, a third in 1959, a fourth in 1961, and a fifth in 1962. None seen.

211. Moreau, Pierre. *Le Romantisme*. In Jean Calvet, ed., Histoire de la Littérature Française, Vol. VIII. Paris: Del Duca, 1957. 470 pp.

An excellent three-page résumé (pp. 129-131) of Nodier's work and influence. Since the first edition in 1932 (74) the section on Nodier has been completely recast in order to bring it in line with current appraisals of his significance as a *conteur* of dream and madness, and as a forerunner of Lautréamont and the Surrealists.

212. Oliver, A. Richard. "Nodier's Criticism of the *Dictionnaire de l'Académie Française*," *The Modern Language Journal*, XLI (1957), 20-25.

The Académie Française did not welcome the Romanticists wholeheartedly. Nodier knew that if he were elected it would be because of his dictionaries and other erudite works rather than because of his fiction. His attacks on the *Dictionnaire de l'Académie Française,* which appeared mainly in *Le Temps,* increased just before his election in 1833 and turned to tolerance and even defense afterwards, although his acceptance of the dictionary was with reservations. The conclusion drawn is that Nodier's criticism was mainly to attract attention to his own qualifications.

213. Oliver, A. Richard. "An Unpublished Letter of Charles Nodier," *Modern Language Notes,* LXXII (1957), 578-579.

Publishes a previously unpublished letter, dated 10 avril 1817, of Nodier to M. le Comte de Pradel, ministre de la Maison du Roi, in which Nodier, because of his health and the press of work, resigns from the "jury littéraire de l'Académie Royale de Musique." Oliver comments that it is a surprising letter, as there is no other evidence of an interest in music on Nodier's part.

1958

214. Bérence, Fred. "Charles Nodier ou les sources de la poésie (1780-1844)," in his *Grandeur spirituelle du XIXe siècle français.* I. *Les Aînés.* Paris: La Colombe, 1958. Pp. [153]-176.

In a book whose overall purpose is a reconsideration of the nineteenth century as a great artistic century, Nodier receives competent treatment as a precursor of post-Romantic literature. However, the principal contribution of Bérence is his fine perception of Nodier as a man "d'une intélligence raffinée, subtile, intuitive." He says that it is understandable that the second half of the nineteenth century, in reaction against the excesses of Romanticism, should consider Nodier "fade." It is not understandable that the élite of this century fail to realize that he speaks of essential problems.

215. Chouan's, Geneviève. "Ceux du Cénacle, vus par les frères Pavie, d'Angers," *La Revue Moderne des Arts et de la Vie,* 1er juil. 1958, pp. 28-29; 1er août 1958, pp. 28-29.

A fragmented account of Nodier's salon that manages to drop the names of most of those who frequented it, but

with an obscure comment or a quotation from Victor or
Théodore Pavie, or less frequently from David d'Angers.
Seems to be largely an excuse to draw into print the memory
of the author's ancestors.

216. Gaulmier, Jean. "Nodier manqua d'être Nerval! En Tout
Cas l'auteur d'*Aurélia* et des *Filles du feu* reconnaît en celui de
La Fée aux Miettes son 'tuteur littéraire,'" *Le Figaro Littéraire*,
13ᵉ année (4 janv. 1958), 3.

Points with surprise to the fact that Nodier is not cited
more frequently as a source of Nerval, who, in *Angélique*,
calls Nodier his "tuteur littéraire." If Nodier did not have
a masterpiece like *Aurélia*, at least he announced some of
the themes "dont le génie Nervalien saura tirer une in-
comparable intensité poétique." For work on this subject
see Richer (165 and 263) and Juin (249).

217. Vivier, Michel. "Victor Hugo et Charles Nodier collaborateurs de *L'Oriflamme* (1823-1824)," *Revue d'Histoire Littéraire
de la France*, LVIII (1958), [297]-323.

The short-lived Romantic and royalist paper, *L'Oriflamme*,
has escaped the attention of most historians. Its most original
aspect is the amount of space devoted to cultural matters.
The young intellectuals associated with it wanted to restore
art and letters as well as the throne. There is one article
obviously by Nodier, and several others can be almost
certainly attributed to him. Starting on February 7, 1824, a
series of articles called "Les Sabbats" and signed "Le Vieux
Sorcier" manifested an aggressive Romanticism. "... Cette
fantaisie railleuse et drolatique, digne de l'école qui va
bientôt faire l'apologie du burlesque, relève assurément d'un
journalisme de grande classe et conserve après cent trente
ans une saveur très vive." Vivier considers as possible
authors of "Les Sabbats" Émile Deschamps, Adolphe de
Saint-Valry, Gaspard de Pons, and Victor Hugo, but makes
a well-reasoned choice of Nodier, thus extending considerably his journalistic career.

   a. *Studi Francesi*, II (1958), 512.

1959

217-A. Clarac, Pierre. "Onze Lettres adressées à Chateaubriand (1819-1825)," *Société Chateaubriand Bulletin*, n. s., no. 3 (1959), pp. 19-30.

> Includes a previously unpublished letter, dated September, 1825, of Nodier to Chateaubriand recommending Alexandre Barginet.
>
> *a. Studi Francesi*, IV (1960), 565.

218. Dollot, René. "Trieste et la France. Histoire d'un consulat. La Révolution et l'Empire (Suite et fin)," *Revue d'Histoire Diplomatique*. LXXIII (1959), [137]-164.

> Pages 154-161 recount the well-known episode of Nodier's Illyrian stay and briefly discuss its influence on his literary works. The chief contribution, as far as Nodier is concerned, is to situate him in the complete picture of the French consulate in Illyria. Dollot has done a much more detailed study of the Illyrian influences on Nodier (56). Reprinted in no. 238.

219. Durry, Marie-Jeanne, *see* Morlanwelz, Belgium. Musée de Mariemont.

220. *Festgabe für Eduard Berend zum 75. Geburtstag am 5. Dezember 1958.* Weimar: Hermann Böhlaus Nachfolger, 1959. xi, 479 pp.

> Although *French VI* lists this book as having material on Nodier, there is only one reference to him, on page 113 in the article "Jean Paul in Frankreich," by Robert Minder. He is simply mentioned among a number of French Romantic writers who underwent a certain influence from the German poet.

221. Kies, Albert. "Deux Inédits de Charles Nodier ['Description d'une nuit orageuse dans le style des anciens bardes'; 'Le Mariage d'un faune']," *Bulletin de l'Académie Royale de Langue et de Littérature Françaises*, XXXVII (1959), 146-154.

The two youthful works published here for the first time are intrinsically unimportant, but the comments which accompany them, pointing out the tendencies manifested, are excellent.

222. Maingot, Éliane. "Le Baron Taylor (1789-1879)," *Le Bouquiniste Français*, 39ᵉ année, n. s., no. 14 (Noël 1959), 17-24.

Although listed by *French VI* as having material on Nodier, this article mentions him only twice, briefly: first, as the collaborator with Taylor upon the only one of Taylor's long list of dramas that had any success, *Bertram ou le château de Saint-Aldobrand;* and second, as the frequent host of Taylor in his salon at the Arsenal.

223. Moreau, Pierre. *La Tradition française du poème en prose avant Baudelaire.* Archives des Lettres Modernes, 1959 (III), no. 19-20. Paris: Lettres Modernes, 1959. 52 pp.

Scattered references place Nodier in the long line of French writers using the form of the *poème en prose*. In 1821 he published his Morlaque songs, written in that form. An especially interesting reference shows the kinship of Aloysius Bertrand's *Gaspard de la nuit* to Nodier. See pp. 18, 25, 32, and 33.

224. Morlanwelz, Belgium. Musée de Mariemont. *Autographes de Mariemont.* By Marie-Jeanne Durry. Deuxième partie, Vol. II: *De Marchangy à Victor Hugo.* Paris: Nizet, 1959.

Four letters of Nodier which are believed to be unpublished are presented here, with comments. See pages 647-662.

    a. A letter of 30 Nov., 1823, to Joseph Michaud summarizing Nodier's financial difficulties and asking for an advance on his journalistic work, or a personal loan.

    b. A letter to the Comte de Pradel pointing out that Nodier is dedicating his new edition of the *Fables* of La Fontaine to him, and that he has not yet received a decoration.

    c. A letter of 27 Dec., 1833, to the Marquis de Custine thanking him for his felicitations on Nodier's discourse to the Académie Française.

  d. A letter written at the end of 1835 or the beginning of 1836 recommending a M. André Delrieu to someone, possibly Fr. de Reiffenberg, in Brussels.

  (1) *Studi Francesi,* V (1961), 363-364.

225. Mornand, Pierre. "Des Physiologies en général, de celles des bouquinistes et bouquineurs en particulier," *Le Bouquiniste Français,* n. s., no. 5 (févr. 1959), pp. 11-14.

  Rightly calls Nodier's essay, *L'Amateur de livres,* "une véritable étude, aussi spirituelle que pertinente," and quotes from his description of the bibliophile, the bibliomaniac, and the *bouquiniste.*

1960

226. Coindre, Gaston. *Mon Vieux Besançon; histoire pittoresque et intime d'une ville.* Éd. abrégée avec la collaboration de *Guy Chassagnard et Jean Ledoux.* Besançon: Imprimerie Jacques & Demontrond, 1960. 525 pp.

  A short paragraph on pp. 105-106 describes the house in which Nodier grew up: "Celle-ci (numéro 11), de coquetterie bourgeoise, comme une aïeule parée d'un bijou, à son balcon, de ferronnerie élégante, où s'entrelacent les initiales du propriétaire et les chiffres d'une date, 1768."

227. Dargaud, Marius. "Une Filleule de Madame Nodier à l'Arsenal (d'après des documents inédits)," in *Mélanges d'histoire du livre et des bibliothèques offerts à Monsieur Frantz Calot,* conservateur en chef honoraire de la Bibliothèque de l'Arsenal. Paris: Librairie d'Argences, 1960. Pp. [337]-368.

  Concerned chiefly with the niece and godchild of Mme Nodier, Louise-Désirée-Victoire Charve. However, there are a few glimpses of Nodier and his wife and of their kindness and indulgence for the girl during the years she lived with them at the Arsenal. The author feels that perhaps the Nodiers, in bringing her from the provinces and raising her in the midst of bourgeois Paris society without teaching her a means of support, made a "déclassée" of her.

228. George, Albert J. "Nodier: 'Le Vieux Marinier,'" *Modern Language Notes,* LXXV (1960), 139-143.

Publishes a fragment of Nodier's work, apparently from his later period. The larger part of the fragment is a poem written in the person of an old mariner who kills himself because of the death of his wife and daughter. George says of the fragment: "The philologist in him [Nodier] played happily with unusual sea terms; the eighteenth-century writer recalled the graveyard poetry once in vogue; and the romantic in him built his verse around the emotional content of poetry written by a man who committed suicide because he had lost his wife and daughter, and hence his reason for living."

229. Kies, Albert. "Imitation et pastiche dans l'œuvre de Charles Nodier," *Cahiers de l'Association Internationale des Études Françaises*, no. 12 (juin 1960), pp. [67]-77.

Summarizes, with examples, Nodier's imitative tendencies. He imitated classical antiquity; writers of the Middle Ages; German writers; and, more specifically, Chateaubriand, Bernardin de Saint-Pierre, Ballanche, Sénancour, Constant, Sylvain Maréchal, La Fontaine, La Bruyère, Sterne, and Villon. Says that this aptitude for imitation is one of the most troubling aspects of a personality about which all has not yet been found out.

230. Maingot, Éliane. "Les Voyages pittoresques du baron Taylor," *Le Bouquiniste Français*, n. s., no. 15 (janv. 1960), pp. 7-17.

Speaks briefly of Nodier's collaboration with his friend Taylor on the first volumes of the monumental *Voyages pittoresques à travers l'ancienne France*, "le plus bel ouvrage romantique français," and reproduces a letter written by Nodier in strong defense of Taylor when in 1843 he was accused in the press of having signed pages not written and sketches not drawn by himself.

231. Maixner, R[udolf]. *Charles Nodier et l'Illyrie*. Études de Littérature Étrangère et Comparée, 37. Paris: Didier, 1960. 132 pp.

This book is a scholarly, and by far the most complete, study of Nodier's rapports with Illyria, its literature, its folklore, and its culture. It represents a lifetime of interest in the subject. Maixner shows exactly what Nodier owed not only to Illyria, but also to the Illyrian work of Fortis.

He also points out his numerous mistakes. Inclined by temperament to be interested in little-known countries and peoples, Nodier found in Illyria material to color his literary activity for twenty-five years and to satisfy his need for the imaginary and fantastic. Maixner sees three stages in Nodier's interest in Illyria: between 1818-21, with *Jean Sbogar, Smarra*, and translations of Illyrian material; in 1832, with *Mademoiselle de Marsan;* and finally in 1836, with his revision of the article on "La Langue et la littérature illyriennes" in the *Dictionnaire de la conversation*. However, there were many instances where Nodier could have exploited Illyrian themes but did not; and he completely abandoned this vein toward the end of his life. Footnotes and bibliographies are excellent. See also Larat (4), Dollot (56), and Warnier (87).

    a. A. Kies. *Revue d'Histoire Littéraire de la France*, LXIII (1963), 480-481.

    b. A. Kies. *Les Lettres Romanes*, XVII (1963), 293-295.

These two reviews are almost identical.

232. Milner, Max. *Le Diable dans la littérature française de Cazotte à Baudelaire, 1772-1861.* 2 vols. Paris: J. Corti, 1960.

This massively documented work has some very good pages on Nodier's part in introducing frenetic and Satanic literature into France, his criticism of it, and his principal works in this style. See especially: Vol. I, 269-281, 479-480, 494-495; Vol. II, 182-183, 201-202. See also Rudwin (15, 34, 53-A, and 99); Cailliet (72); and Grillet (90).

233. Oliver, A. Richard. "Charles Nodier and the Marquis de Sade," *Modern Language Notes*, LXXV (1960), 497-502.

Nodier claims to have met the Marquis de Sade in Sainte-Pélagie prison and even describes him in his *Souvenirs*. Various biographers have tried to prove the claim and determine the date. But Oliver examines it in the light of Nodier's whereabouts on the dates cited and shows the impossibility of a meeting.

    a. A. P. *Studi Francesi*, V (1961), 564.

234. Oliver, A Richard. "An Unpublished Analysis of Some Fine Editions by the Young Bibliophile Charles Nodier," *The Library Quarterly*, XXX (1960), 140-143.

Presents in translation, with explanatory footnotes, Nodier's "Essai sur l'imprimerie et ses progrès," written in the form of a letter to Pierre Joseph Briot, probably to seek his influence in obtaining a position as assistant librarian in the Besançon École Centrale in the summer of 1798. The manuscript shows errors and oversights but reveals the unusual interest of a young boy in books. Followed by Nodier's list of the fine editions in his personal library at the time.

235. Whyte, Lancelot Law. *The Unconscious before Freud.* New York: Basic Books, 1960. xi, 219 pp.

Has a brief reference to Nodier as one of the eighteenth- and nineteenth-century discoverers of the unconscious mind. See pp. 145-146.

1961

236. Bazziconi, Michèle. "Le Rêve dans l'œuvre de Charles Nodier. Diplôme d'études supérieures." [s. d. 1961?]

A survey of the role of dream and imagination in the fiction, theory, and memoirs of Nodier. Cited in the catalogue of the Bibliothèque de l'Arsenal.

237. Brockett, O. G. "Charles Nodier's Estimate of Shakespeare", *Shakespeare Quarterly*, XII (1961), 345-348.

Since the late nineteenth century it has been said from time to time that Nodier's appreciation of Shakespeare considerably surpassed that of his countrymen prior to the Romantic movement. Brockett re-examines the evidence and comes to the conclusion that Nodier's appreciation was not essentially different from that of others of his time. Like late eighteenth-century critics and his own contemporaries Nodier recognized Shakespeare's natural genius but saw also his supposed faults. He associated Shakespeare with the new Romanticism but classified his plays as melodramas and compared him to Pixérécourt. "Thus Nodier reduced Shakespeare, melodrama, and the new Romantic drama to the common denominator of melodrama and applauded only those aspects of Shakespearian and Romantic tragedy which he found also in popular melodrama." For a completely different view, see Oliver (251).

238. Dollot, René. *Trieste et la France (1702-1958); histoire d'un consulat.* Paris: A. Pedone, 1961. 259 pp.

> Reprinted from the *Revue d'Histoire Diplomatique,* 1958-1960 (218). For Nodier, see pp. 98-105.

239. Hoffmann, Léon-François. *Romantique Espagne; l'image de l'Espagne en France entre 1800 et 1850.* Publications du Département de Langues Romanes de l'Université de Princeton. [Princeton], N. J.: Université de Princeton, Dépt. de Langues Romanes; Paris: Presses Universitaires de France, 1961. 202 pp.

> Has a few references to Nodier that are of some interest. Says that when a fantastic tale is situated in Spain, in general it is in Catalonia, the least typically Spanish province. This is true of *Inès de las Sierras.* Also, in this *conte* French characters make the story less strictly Spanish. See p. 38. Page 51 mentions Nodier's visit to Spain in 1827. Page 54 lists four Spanish words used in *Inès de las Sierras: arriero, mozo, vino, rancio.*

240. Iknayan, Marguerite. *The Idea of the Novel in France: the Critical Reaction, 1815-1848.* Genève: E. Droz; Paris: Minard, 1961. 199 pp.

> This study is an "effort to find out to what degree the critics were concerned with the novel as a genre" (p. 11). It is interested more in the writings of the critics than the novelists themselves. Nodier is the main novelist and *conteur* drawn from for his critical articles. However, there is no systematic treatment of his ideas. The thirty-six references to him, ranging from a sentence to a paragraph, have to be located through the index.

241. Lebois, André. *Un Bréviaire du compagnonnage: "La Fée aux Miettes" de Charles Nodier.* Archives des Lettres Modernes, 1961 (III), no. 40. Paris: Lettres Modernes, 1961. 40 pp.

> It is Lebois's contention that *La Fée aux Miettes* is a breviary for Freemasonry and *compagnonnage,* the secret code of the perfect worker based on Masonic principles. It

was written to spread among rebellious working youth of the early 1830's the basic elements of Masonic teaching. For Lebois, La Fée aux Miettes is the "Mère des Compagnons," Michel is the "compagnon parfait," and the action is a series of "épreuves initiatiques." This is an original idea, thought out in detail, but nonetheless unconvincing.

241.-A. Masson, André, and Paule Salvan. *Les Bibliothèques.* Que Sais-je?, No. 944. Paris: Presses Universitaires de France, 1961. 128 pp.

Calls Nodier "la figure la plus représentative du bibliothécaire homme de lettres et bibliophile." See p. 47. The same statement appears in the second edition (260-A).

242. Teichmann, Elizabeth. *La Fortune d'Hoffmann en France.* Genève: E. Droz; Paris: Minard, 1961. 288 pp.

Many writers have spoken vaguely of Hoffmann's influence or lack of it on Nodier. Here the juxtaposition of these two authors, though in only a few references, is more specific. Pages 60-61 and 130 show Nodier's defense of Hoffmann and the fantastic, and his role in Hoffmann's diffusion in France. Page 92 points out Nodier's new preface to *Smarra* in 1832 written to show that he was not an imitator of Hoffmann. And on p. 183 the author says that Sainte-Beuve "constate que la venue et la naturalisation d'Hoffmann en France 'durent imprimer à l'imagination de Nodier un nouvel ébranlement, une toute récente émulation de fantaisie.' C'est un jugement que Nodier avait confirmé d'avance."

    a. E. Caramaschi. *Studi Francesi,* VIII (1964), 364-365.

1962

243. Caillois, Roger. "Puissances du rêve," *Tel Quel,* no. 8 (hiver 1962), pp. [14]-25.

Of Nodier this article says only: "Pour Charles Nodier, *Smarra* demeure un exercise érudit, à mon sens exécrable, d'une ridicule emphase et dont l'académisme, s'agissant de donner l'impression de cauchemar, représente un contresens presque grotesque" (p. 23). An overly harsh judgment, whether or not one likes *Smarra.*

244. Castex, Pierre-Georges. "Balzac et Charles Nodier," in *L'Année balzacienne, 1962.* Paris: Éditions Garnier Frères, 1962. Pp. [197]-212.

Valuable information on both the personal relations and the reciprocal literary borrowings and influence of Nodier and Balzac during a three year period in the early 1830's. Their thought was quite close at that time. But "Balzac et Nodier, après avoir manifesté des tendances et des curiosités communes au temps du *Roi de Bohême* et des premiers *Contes philosophiques*, vont évoluer dans des directions opposées." See also Le Yaouanc (202).

  a. *Studi Francesi*, VII (1963), 568-569.

245. Castex, Pierre-Georges. "Nodier et ses rêves," in *Le Conte fantastique en France de Nodier à Maupassant.* Nouvelle ed. Paris: José Corti, 1962. Pp. [121]-167.

Reprinted exactly from the first edition, 1951 (167). Also appears, without footnotes and bibliography, as a postface to Nodier's *Contes du pays des rêves* (207).

246. Dédéyan, Christian. "Charles Nodier annociateur du rêve," *Points et Contrepoints,* no. 62-63 (déc. 1962), pp. 28-32.

A well-written article that offers nothing new in the way of scholarship but shows a good appreciation of Nodier's importance as an initiator into the world of dream. All French art from Nerval, Baudelaire, and the Symbolists is indebted to him. His penetrations into the world of dream were made discreetly, keeping the mask of real life. But by the "éclairage indirect" of his words objects assumed a meaning different from their usual significance. For Nodier, as for the Surrealists, sleep is the most active state of the soul. Thus he is an important precursor. Seen in this light the fantastic reveals a profound meaning.

247. Engler, Winfried. "Der Mythos vom verlorenen Paradies bei Charles Nodier," *Antaios,* IV (1962-63), 521-535.

Examines the idea of paradise in Nodier and finds that there are two kinds: the *locus amoenus,* which rises and falls again with the downfall of society; and the paradise of childhood which is lost with maturity. Nodier seems to feel that living things below the level of human beings, and therefore unaware of death, have more of a concept of paradise than human beings. In contrast to the impersonal, many-sided idyll of the eighteenth century and to the later rustic novels of George Sand, Nodier's works are a mixture of the personal and mythical that was influential in the development of the idea of paradise up through Alain-Fournier and Truman Capote. An interesting inquiry into an aspect of Nodier that has heretofore been studied only obliquely. Ses also Béguin (156) and Orlando (291-A).

248. Fongaro, Antoine. "A-t-on lu la *Fée aux Miettes?*" *Revue des Sciences Humaines*, n. s., no. 107 (1962), pp. [439]-452.

Fongaro demonstrates briefly that *La Fée aux Miettes* might be given a gnostic or even Cathar explanation, in contrast to the psychoanalytical interpretation of Vodoz (17) or the Masonic exegesis of Lebois (241) and Viatte (76a). But his primary concern here is a careful study of the language and style of this *conte*. He points out numerous errors in spelling that have been repeated in succeeding editions, examples of negligence in style, and inexactnesses in choice of words, which, when corrected, remove some of the ambiguities and difficulties of the story. Though Viatte's edition is more correct than others, much study of this text remains to be done.

    a. *Studi Francesi*, VII (1963), 173.

249. Juin, Hubert. *Chroniques sentimentales.* Paris: Mercure de France, 1962. 232 pp.

Shows that the character, Maxime Odin, who is the hero in the five *récits* composing the *Souvenirs de jeunesse*, in *Mademoiselle de Marsan*, and in *La Neuvaine de la chandeleur*, is Nodier, himself. Contains penetrating pages on the similarities and differences in Nodier and Nerval and in the themes found in their work. See pp. 107-138. For other material on similarities in Nodier and Nerval, see Richer (165 and 263).

250. Luporini, Maria Bianca. "Un Paesaggio italiano dell' *Evgenij Onegin*, Charles Nodier e 'La superba lira d'Albione,'" in *Studi in onori di Ettore lo Gatto et Giovanni Maver*. Firenze: Sansoni, 1962. Pp. 417-441.

Nodier's *Jean Sbogar* was not translated into Russian because of the rebelliousness of the hero, but it circulated in the original and may have been in Pushkin's library along with his other volumes of Nodier. It is proposed here that it was a source for certain portions of *Evgenij Onegin*. Nodier's passages on the nocturnal Adriatic and the panoramic view of Venice were, in particular, drawn upon by Pushkin. But the elegant character, in general, of Nodier's descriptions may have influenced Pushkin in describing Petersburg.

251. Oliver, A. Richard. "Charles Nodier's Cult of Shakespeare as a Facet of French Romanticism," *Orbis Litterarum, Revue Internationale d'Études Littéraires*, XVII (1962), [154]-165.

Oliver looks at Nodier's youthful and mature criticism and finds that he was a real student of Shakespeare, with a fine appreciation of his genius. By early identification of Shakespeare with French Romanticism, Nodier laid the foundation of one of the principal facets of this movement. But he also used Shakespeare as a weapon to combat the traditional theatre. Oliver holds that it was Brockett's (237) failure to distinguish between Nodier the student and admirer and Nodier the propagandist that led him to the conclusion that Nodier's ideas on Shakespeare were similar to those of his contemporaries and that he put Shakespeare's plays and French melodrama in the same category.

252. Richer, Jean. *Autour de "L'Histoire du roi de Bohême," Charles Nodier "dériseur sensé"; suivi de "La Plus Petite des pantoufles," par Charles Nodier*. Archives des Lettres Modernes, 1962 (III), no. 42. Paris: Lettres Modernes, 1962.

Incorporates material from two other published sources: "Charles Nodier, dériseur sensé, [suivi de] *Ce Pacte inouï* [et] *La Plus Petite des pantoufles*" (176), omitting from it only *Ce Pacte inouï*; and "*Le Roi de Bohême* ou les tentations du langage," Richer's postface to the reimpression of Nodier's novel (166). Also includes a verbal portrait of Nodier by a contemporary, Cécile L., and three documents: an article by Balzac on the *Histoire du roi de Bohême*; variants in Hugo's letter in verse on this story; and a letter of Nodier to the bookseller Dumont. In this very informative composite publication Richer says that at every opportunity Nodier attacked the idea of progress and perfectibility. As a young man he even went further, believing that society was bad in its essence. An unpublished novel, *Le Voleur,* written around 1805, is especially revealing in this respect. Nodier also had a precocious satiric streak that may be seen in a text that remained long unpublished: *La Plus Petite des pantoufles,* also written around 1805. It is really the sketch for the *Histoire du Roi de Bohême,* though it lacks Nodier's principal idea in the latter of putting himself in the story as three different personages, and though very few lines from the text of *La Plus Petite des pantoufles* are found in *Le Roi de Bohême. Le Roi de Bohême* seems like a series of pastisches inspired by Rabelais, Sterne, Montaigne, Charron, Cervantes, Cyrano, and Swift. But Nodier shows himself here a precursor of Mallarmé, Apollinaire, Jarry, and Joyce.

1963

253. Battista, Piero. "L'Analisi del sogno in *La Fée aux Miettes,*" *Le Lingue Straniere,* XII, no. 6 (nov.-dic. 1963), 9-12

Stresses the difference between Nodier's solution for his torment and the solution of the other Romantics. They found escape in an appeal to ecstasy, which is an abandonment to a different reality. But Nodier sought relief in the marvellous and the "féerique." *La Fée aux Miettes* is both a myth and a dream. All the particulars of this work allude symbolically, but without a necessity of specific explanation, to man's irresolutions and doubts. The Fée aux Miettes and Belkiss are two aspects of the same person, each adding to the other that which is lacking to an ideal conception. The mandrake is a symbol of growing maturity. But in resolving the significance of the story in this way, one risks dispelling its magic. By avoiding any effort at detailed analysis Battista's article seems, rather, an attempt to put back into perspective a story which has elicited various, and sometimes controversial, interpretations. Draws especially from Béguin (96).

254. Castex, Pierre-Georges. *Anthologie du conte fantastique français. Deuxième édition, entièrement refondue, avec des textes nouveaux et des notices inédites.* Paris: José Corti, 1963. 343 pp.

Has same material on Nodier as the 1947 edition (144). See pp. 27-29 for introduction to the excerpt from *Smarra.*

255. Clancier, Georges-Emmanuel. *De Chénier à Baudelaire; panorama critique.* Collection Melior: La Poésie Française. Paris: Éditions Seghers, 1963. 442 pp.

> Presents on pages 211-218 short selections, with introductory comments, from three of Nodier's works: *Smarra, La Fée au Miettes,* and *L'Histoire du roi de Bohême.* Contains more errors of fact than one would normally expect in so few pages.

256. Coco, Antonino. *Miti solari. P. B. Shelley in Italia. Il Profeta di Monte Labbro. Trieste vista da un romantico.* Trieste: Tipografia Triestina, 1963. 55 pp.

> In the last section of this book, "Trieste vista da un romantico," pp. 53-54, Nodier and *Jean Sbogar* are treated. Although the novel is of good workmanship, its special interest for Coco lies in the description of Trieste as it was in the Romantic era. Of minor significance to Nodier studies.

257. Decottignies, Jean. "Variations sur un succube; *Histoire de Thibaud de la Jacquière,*" *Revue des Sciences Humaines,* n. s., no. 111 (1963), pp. [329]-340.

> Finds the source for Nodier's *Aventures de Thibaud de la Jacquière* (one of the tales included in the *Infernaliana*) to be *Les Dix Journées de la vie d'Alphonse van Worden,* 1814, attributed to the Polish nobleman, Jan Potocki, who in turn was indebted to a seventeenth-century tale by François de Rosset. Nodier's story is actually closer in spirit to the eighteenth century than to the Romantic era. "C'est à tort que sa présence dans le recueil de Nodier l'a fait ranger dans la littérature 'frénétique,' à qui elle doit quelques lignes de son dénouement."

258. Frandon, I.-M. "Commedia dell'Arte et imagination poétique," *Cahiers de l'Association Internationale des Études Françaises,* no. 15 (mars 1963), pp. [261]-276.

> Has two brief, but interesting, references to Nodier. On p. 266 there is a mention of his interest in the Pierrot of Deburau. Page 268 refers to his preference for *féerique* pantomime.

> *a.* D. Dalla Valle. *Studi Francesi,* VIII (1964), 195.

259. Gendzier, Stephen J. "Diderot's Impact on the Generation of 1830," *Studies on Voltaire and the Eighteenth Century*, XXIII (1963), 93-103.

Discusses Diderot's rehabilitation, after a temporary eclipse following his death, in the 1830's through the writings of Sainte-Beuve, Nodier, and Janin. Nodier presented Diderot to a wide public in 1830 with his article, "De la Prose française de Diderot," published in the *Revue de Paris*. He emphasized Diderot's significance for contemporary society and took special pleasure in his style, the unity of his subject matter, and his proficiency in execution.

260. Isola, Francesco. "Postille francesi di Alessandro Manzoni a Charles Nodier," *Studi Francesi*, VII (1963), 56-72.

Publishes for the first time Manzoni's forty-three marginal annotations in French on a copy of the 1829 edition of Nodier's *Examen critique des dictionnaires de la langue françoise*. To understand better the significance of the comments, Isola examines what Manzoni knew of Nodier's work and what influence it might have had on his own linguistic studies. Although some influence can be established, Nodier and Manzoni differ greatly in their ideas on language. It is not possible to date Manzoni's comments exactly, but they probably were written between 1829 and 1836. A good article on a previously unnoted area of Nodier's influence. The pertinent sections of Nodier's *Examen* are reproduced alongside Manzoni's comments.

260-A. Masson, André, and Paule Salvan. *Les Bibliothèques*. 2ᵉ éd. Que Sais-je?, No. 944. Paris: Presses Universitaires de France, 1963. 128 pp.

Makes the same observation on Nodier as that made in the first edition (241-A).

261. Metastasio, Arthur Paul. "Vico and French Romanticism." Ann Arbor, Mich.: University Microfilms, 1963. 251 pp.

This Boston University dissertation seeks to establish the Italian philosopher, Vico, as an initiator of French Romanticism, especially through the 1744 edition of his *Scienza nuova*, translated by Michelet in 1823. The author compares Vico's ideas with those of the more important French

Romanticists, including Nodier, in an attempt to associate him directly with their theories. Although he finds numerous parallels in thought, he concludes that there is apparently no way to prove that the authors in question had direct knowledge of Vico's work. But at least his ideas appeared at a time when they could provide a unifying influence for the French Romantic movement. For Nodier, see, in particular, pp. 115, 133, 182, 183, 188-198, 200-201, 202-206, 224-225, 231-236.

262. Moreau, Pierre. *Amours romantiques.* L'Amour et l'Histoire. Paris: Hachette, 1963. 320 pp.

This book is concerned with the love affairs of the major Romantics and the traces of these affairs in their works. There are only side glances at Nodier, as he was not noted for any liaison. But these are revealing. On p. 35 Nodier and "quelques autres folkloristes de l'amour" are cited as believing that the provinces are the last stronghold of innocent and sincere love. Page 227 gives a new picture of the society of Nodier's salon. "Que les contredanses du salon de l'Arsenal ne fassent pas illusion! Ces jeunes étourdis sont souvent des vaincus de la vie, de la vie des lettres comme de celle du cœur. Leurs pâles visages ne disent pas seulement la passion et le byronisme, mais plus souvent les gênes matérielles et la maladie." On p. 288 the author speaks of the "attendrissement" in the pages of Nodier's *De l'Amour et de son influence.*

263. Richer, Jean. *Nerval, expérience et création.* Paris: Hachette, 1963. 708 pp.

Numerous good references to the parallels in Nodier and Nerval have to be located through the index. Some of Nerval's borrowings here were pointed out by Richer in his 1950 article (165). For other material on the same subject see Juin (249).

1964

264. Barineau, Elizabeth. "La *Tribune Romantique* et le romantisme de 1830," *Modern Philology,* LXII (1964-65), 302-324.

Describes the contents of the first three numbers (perhaps the only ones published) of the extremely rare *Tribune Romantique* and relates them to their time—1830. The first number (21 mars) has a flattering *compte rendu* by Victor

Pavie of Nodier's *Histoire du roi de Bohême*. This review is described on p. 305 and mentioned again on p. 319.

265. Bays, Gwendolyn. "The Seer in French Romanticism: Voyance in the Unsophisticated Characters of Charles Nodier," in her *Orphic Vision: Seer Poets from Novalis to Rimbaud*. Lincoln: University of Nebraska Press, 1964. Pp. 77-80.

Points out the evolution in Nodier's subject matter from black magic and nightmare, as in *Smarra,* to white magic and innocent seers. Finds four of these simple, instinctive characters in Nodier's contes: Soeur Françoise in *Hélène Gillet,* Jean-François les Bas-Bleus, Baptiste Montauban, and Lydie in the stories of the same names. These characters present a sharp contrast with Balzac's sophisticated seers, Louis Lambert and Séraphita.

265-A. Bousquet, Jacques. *Les Thèmes du rêve dans la littérature romantique (France, Angleterre, Allemagne); essai sur la naissance et l'évolution des images.* Études de Littérature Étrangère et Comparée, 47. Paris: Didier, 1964. 656 pp.

Numerous references, well-indexed, relate the themes Nodier used in fictional dreams to those of other writers (primarily but not exclusively Romantic) using dream in literature.

 a. J.-B. Barrère. *Revue Belge de Philologie et d'Histoire,* XLV (1967), 155-157.

266. Dédéyan, Charles. *Victor Hugo et l'Allemagne.* Vol. I. *La Formation.* Bibliothèque de Littérature et d'Histoire, no. 3. Paris: M. J. Minard, 1964. 265 pp.

Important for its recognition of the large debt Hugo owed to Nodier, with emphasis on the Germanic and Anglo-Saxon influence which can be seen in Hugo's poetry, novels, and plays. Hugo did not wait for Nodier's prompting to read German works, but Nodier's exemple helped him. The *Odes* and especially the *Ballades* best show the union of the two currents of Germanic inspiration: the one coming through Nodier and the other directly from German literature. Many specific instances of influence are given. See pp. 63-64, 117-139, 140-147, 194, 197, 212. See also Charles (73), Bauer (89), and Wilson (289).

267. Duhamel, Roger. "De Nouveaux Noms, des œuvres nouvelles," *Revue de l'Université d'Ottawa*, XXXIV (1964), 191-220.

> Pages 191-198 constitute a general essay on Nodier that adds little, if anything, to Nodier studies, except the emphases of the author's somewhat unusual negative atittude. Even in the salon at the Arsenal he does not allow Nodier the pre-eminence usually accorded him. He does, however, recognize Nodier's charm and his position as a precursor in the knowledge of foreign literatures. This article also appears as Chapter VII of Duhamel's *Aux Sources du romantisme français* (267-A).

267-A. Duhamel, Roger. "De Nouveau Noms, des œuvres nouvelles," in his *Aux Sources du romantisme français*. Ottawa. Université. Publications Sériées, No. 74. Ottawa: Éditions de l'Université d'Ottawa, 1964. Pp. [159]-188.

> Treats Nodier pp. 159-166. Same material as in no. 267.

268. Easton, Malcolm. *Artists and Writers in Paris; the Bohemian Idea, 1803-1867*. New York: St. Martin's Press, 1964. viii, 205 pp.

> Considers Nodier's youthful relations in Paris with the young painters, Maurice Quaï and Lucile Franque and their group of friends, and then the artist as seen in Nodier's early work: *Le Peintre de Salzbourg;* the *Méditations du cloître,* published with the *Peintre;* and the *Essais d'un jeune barde,* which contains eulogistic obituary notices for Lucile and Quaï. See pp. 12-18. Pages 41-42 comment on the early relations of Hugo and Nodier at the Arsenal, and the large number of artists in the salon.

269. George, Albert J. *Short Fiction in France 1800-1850*. Syracuse, N. Y.: Syracuse University Press, 1964. ix, 245 pp.

> Because George is dealing with the whole spectrum of brief fiction during the first half of the nineteenth century, he does not become deeply involved with any one author, and can therefore see each in relation to his whole period. Recognizes the weakness of much of Nodier's work but also his importance. "In the development of the forms of short prose fiction, Nodier's is a name to be reckoned with, historically,

as one of the first to dedicate a major part of his literary life to the brief narrative." But he is not of historical significance only. Some of his writing still sparkles. George places unusual emphasis on two aspects of Nodier: the strong influence of the eighteenth century in his work, and his didacticism. Sees Nodier as a writer for the people. Also advances a refreshing explanation of *La Fée aux Miettes:* it is truly a fairy tale, though a difficult one and liberally dotted with didacticism, in which in the customary manner of the fairy tale the hero is placed in jeopardy three times. All of George's opinions will not be accepted, but he does give a thought-provoking treatment of Nodier. See pp. 29-46.

    a. M. Guggenheim. *The French Review,* XL (1966-67), 294-295.

269-A. Letessier, Fernand. "La Romancière Louise d'Estournelles de Constant (1792-1860) et ses amis," *Bulletin de l'Association Guillaume Budé,* Sér. 4 (1964), pp. 464-478.

Shows the friendly relations existing between Louise de Constant and her compatriots Charles Nodier and his daughter, Marie.

270. Locker, Malka. *Les Romantiques: Allemagne, Angleterre, France.* Paris: Presses du Temps Présent, 1964. 308 pp.

This reference work (published first in Yiddish in 1958 under the title *Romantiker,* rewritten in French, and enlarged from that version to the present one) devotes a page and a half of little significance to Nodier. One interesting reference, however, mentions an apparently little-known poem of Nodier, "Les Fous de Pirieu" (Author presumably means "Le Fou du Pirée.), in which he tries to show "que la folie est sans doute l'état le plus heureux pour l'homme." Ses pp. 281-282.

270-A. Menemencioglu, Mme Melahat. "Un Aspect surréaliste de Charles Nodier," *Procès-Verbaux et Mémoires de l'Académie des Sciences, Belles-Lettres et Arts de Besançon,* 1964-65, pp. [99]-108.

Demonstrates more specifically than heretofore shown that "entre Nodier et les surréalistes les parentés dépassent les coïncidences accidentelles et proviennent d'une communauté radicale de pensée."

271. Oliver, A. Richard. *Charles Nodier, Pilot of Romanticism.* Syracuse, N. Y.: Syracuse University Press, 1964. xi, 276 pp.

A solidly documented biography that gives a good account of Nodier's life, literary production, and place in the Romantic movement, and an objective picture of his changeable, and not always admirable, character. Oliver is especially enlightening in chapter V on the relations between Nodier and Hugo. However, there is little effort at literary criticism, and the useful bibliography is scattered through the "Notes to Chapters" and therefore difficult to use. Though Nodier's elusive personality does not come through, for the reader seeking an up-to-date, factual treatment the book has much to offer.

 a. R. C. Dale. *L'Esprit Créateur,* V (1965), 249-250.

 b. J. B. Sanders. *The French Review,* XXXIX (1965-66), 172-73.

 c. V. Brombert. *The Romanic Review,* LVII (1966), 305-307.

 d. J. Decottignies. *Revue d'Histoire Littéraire de la France,* LXVI (1966), 728-729.

 e. J. W. Montgomery. *The Library Quarterly,* XXXVI (1966), 58-60.

 f. S. Raphael. *French Studies,* XX (1966), 82-83.

 g. D. P. Scales. *A. U. M. L. A. Journal of the Australasian Universities Language and Literature Association,* XXV (1966), 148-149.

272. Pichois, Claude. "Surnaturalisme français et romantisme allemand: simple esquisse," in *Connaissance de l'étranger. Mélanges offerts à la mémoire de Jean-Marie Carré.* Études de Littérature Étrangère et Comparée, 50. Paris: Marcel Didier, 1964. Pp. [385]-396.

 Mentions Nodier a few times in contexts in which he has often been placed.

273. Raitt, A. W. "Introduction: Balzac and the Short Story," in [Honoré de] Balzac, *Short Stories Selected and Edited with*

Introduction and Notes by A. W. Raitt. Clarendon French Series. Oxford: Oxford University Press, 1964. Pp. [7]-19.

> Compares Balzac as a short story writer with Nodier and Mérimée. "Nodier, by then the elderly *éminence grise* of Romanticism, exploited two veins in the short story: the sentimental and the fantastic, both in an urbane and discursive style; whereas Mérimée was in the process of creating what one may call the 'modern' short story—laconic, direct, and compressed." Balzac has resemblances to both, but where he is superior to either "is in his combination of Nodier's gifts of imagination with Mérimée's mastery of form; he is as remote from the rambling emotionalism of the one as from the cynical dexterity of the other." See p. 17.

274. Ryner, Han. "Charles Nodier," *Cahiers des Amis de Han Ryner*, n. s., no. 74 (sept. 1964), pp. 20-22.

> Of little significance to Nodier studies. Considers briefly Nodier's life and work.

275. Schneider, Marcel. *La Littérature fantastique en France.* Les Grandes Études Littéraires. Paris: Fayard, 1964. 425 pp.

> For this author, Nodier's fantastic work is mainly that which came after 1830 and was written under the influence of Hoffmann. He analyses *La Fée aux Miettes* at length, adding some entirely new ideas, pointing out resemblances between Nodier's story and A.-V. C. Berbiguier's *Les Farfadets,* and calling attention to a rapprochement between the "C'est moi, c'est moi, c'est moi" of Nodier's song and "Je vous tiens, je vous y tiens" in Berbiguier's. He also mentions ties of *La Fée aux Miettes* with Hoffmann's *La Princesse de Brambilla.* See pp. 126-129 for a discussion of Nodier's work in the frenetic vein; pp. 146-147 for a discussion of *Du Fantastique en littérature,* and pp. 163-172 for consideration of the fantastic works.

276. Stowe, Richard Scribner. "Alfred de Musset and His Contemporaries: a Study of the Man and the Artist as He Appeared in His Day," *Dissertation Abstracts,* XXIV (1964), 3760-61 (Wisconsin).

> A University of Wisconsin dissertation. Not seen. The dissertation abstract indicates a limited amount of material on Nodier: "Musset's relations with other romantic writers

confirm the impression that he had no close friends among literary figures. Charles Nodier, like Vigny, enjoyed a warm but semipaternal connection."

1965

276-A. Blanco, Louise S. "Origin and History of the Plot of *Marianela*," *Hispania, a Journal Devoted to the Interests of the Teaching of Spanish and Portuguese*, XLVIII (1965), 463-467.

> Sees the probability of the direct influence of Nodier's *Les Aveugles de Chamouny* on Pérez Galdós' novel, *Marianela*.

277. Citron, Pierre. "Aux Sources d'*Une Fille d'Ève*," in *L'Année balzacienne, 1965*. Paris: Éditions Garnier Frères, 1965. Pp. [201]-215.

> Disagrees with those Balzac scholars who have proposed Nodier as a model for the character of Nathan in *Une Fille d'Ève*. See p. 203.

278. Engler, Winfried. *Der französische Roman von 1800 bis zur Gegenwart*. Sammlung Dalp, Bd. 97. Bern: Francke, 1965. 299 pp.

> This survey of the large literary currents from 1800 to the present deals with Nodier only cursorily, on pp. 84-85. A more interesting reference occurs on p. 159, where Engler suggests that the young people's lack of development in Alain-Fournier's work and their growing sense of loss came from Nodier.
>
> > a. W. Drost. *Rivista di Letterature Moderne e Comparate*, XIX (1966), 246-247.

279. Engstrom, Alfred G. "The Voices of Plants and Flowers and the Changing Cry of the Mandrake," in *Medieval Studies in Honor of Urban Tigner Holmes, Jr.* Edited by John Mahoney and John Esten Keller. University of North Carolina Studies in the Romance Languages and Literatures, No. 56. Chapel Hill, N. C.: University of North Carolina Press, 1965. Pp. [43]-52.

> A paper of unusual interest in which Nodier's *La Fée aux Miettes* is said to be possibly the first literary work where the mandrake sings. Here "the voice of the mandrake has

changed from the lethal cry of Philippe de Thaün's 12th-century bestiary, and from the later *shrieks, shrikes, groans* and *howles* to a lovely music. It seems to have acquired meaning in common with the wild flower of Blake and with the Blue Flower of Novalis, and it joins the other singing plants and flowers of myth and folklore and literature with a song that is all its own."

280. Guyon, Bernard. "Balzac et Stendhal, romanciers de l'évasion," *Sthendhal Club*, VIII (1965-66), [25]-31.

This article points out the similarity between Fabrice's escape in Stendhal's *La Chartreuse de Parme* and the escape of the Chevalier de Beauvoir in Balzac's *La Muse du département*, and examines who influenced whom. Concludes that, as Balzac's narration came first, it must have been the influence, but proposes that both men may have heard Nodier relate the incident originally.

281. Jensen, C. "The 'Romanticism' of the *Annales de la Littérature et des Arts*," *French Studies*, XIX (1965), 341-357.

Investigates the role of the *Annales de la Littérature et des Arts*, which was published from 1820-1829, in the evolution of the Romantic movement and finds that: "With the exception of the early articles of Nodier, rarely do the *Annales* show anything except a rigidly reactionary spirit." And even the Romanticism shown by Nodier is subdued. No articles by him appeared after 1823, possibly implying a difference of opinion with the editors. But his new duties at the Arsenal were more probably the reason.

282. Lemaître, Henri. *La Poésie depuis Baudelaire*. Collection U: Série "Lettres Françaises." Paris: Armand Colin, 1965. 371 pp.

A ten-line text from Nodier's *Mélanges de littérature et de critique* is cited as leading toward a "poétique de l'insolite." See pp. 79-80.

    a. R. R. Nunn. *The French Review*, XL (1967), 700-701.

283. Maixner, Rudolf. "Un Aspect de Philarète Chasles," *Revue de Littérature Comparée*, XXXIX (1965), [396]-405.

The first paragraph calls Nodier, along with Mérimée, one of the most famous of the Romantic literary "mystificateurs." Page 403 shows, in connection with their Dalmatian works, the "filière suivie par la forme *gusla (guzla)* chez les écrivains français: Nodier-Mérimée-Chasles."

284. Maixner, Rudolf. "Sur Certains Pseudo-bardes du XVIIIe et du XIXe siècle," in *Actes du Sixième Congrès National de la Société Française de Littérature Comparée. Littérature savante et littérature populaire. Bardes, conteurs, écrivains. Rennes, 23-25 mai, 1963*. Études de Littérature Étrangère et Comparée, 49. Paris: Didier, 1965. Pp. [106]-111.

> Shows how Alberto Fortis' *Viaggio in Dalmazia*, written in 1774 and translated into French in 1778, served as a source for a vogue in pseudo-popular literature. Countess Orsini-Rosenberg, Nodier, and Mérimée were all indebted to this work; but this indebtedness is not discussed at length here. For fuller treatment of Nodier's obligation see Maixner's *Charles Nodier et l'Illyrie* (231).
>
> a. J.-P. Leroy. *Revue de Littérature Comparée*, XL (1966), 162-170.

285. Maples, Robert J. B. "Technique and Vision in the Fiction of Charles Nodier." Ann Arbor, Mich.: University Microfilms, 1965. 255 pp.

> A Yale University Ph. D. dissertation, fall, 1964. An original attempt to remedy the lack of "a textually oriented aesthetic analysis of the value of the short stories [of Nodier] as literature and for an examination of their unity and originality as creations of a single mind." Successfully demonstrates a unity in the characters of Nodier and in his plot treatments, but is much less convincing in the effort at the construction of a unified vision of life for Nodier in which various characters in his stories evidence one or more stages of "maturation" toward "individuation" and "psychic wholeness" through rebellion against the rational and mechanistic. "Thus love, imagination, religious and cosmic vision are fused into one principle of life, which offers man redemption in the face of trial, accident, and death." Presentation marred by the irritating use of pretentious language.

286. Monchoux, André. *L'Allemagne devant les lettres françaises de 1814 à 1835.* Seconde édition. Paris: Armand Colin, 1965. 526 pp.

Has exactly the same material on Nodier as the first edition (179).

287. Orlando, Francesco. "Charles Nodier memoralista: una infanzia sotto la Rivoluzione," *Critica Storica,* IV (1965), 279-298.

In his middle years Nodier wrote two sets of memoirs, "uno ufficiale ed offerto alla storia, l'altro personale": *Souvenirs, épisodes et portraits pour servir à l'histoire de la Révolution et de l'Empire* and *Souvenirs de jeunesse.* "Da una parte ... le memorie tendono a farsi storia romanzata, dall'altra novella a sfondo vagamente storico ...." Orlando examines the "official" *Souvenirs* at some length and finds that though it lacks authenticity and political passion, it has something which to a certain extent takes their place: "un senso profondo, vissuto, della crudeltà dell'epoca, della sua spietata febbre morale, del suo incubo di supplizi fisici fattosi collettivo e quotidiano." He selects one section, *Séraphine,* from the *Souvenirs de jeunesse* and finds that, "aurorale e primitivo da un lato, magico dall'altro," it has a measure of autobiographical genuineness in the impressions of youth that it renders. A nice apology for these two often-criticized works of Nodier. See also Orlando (291-A) and Dargand (170).

287-A. Pichois, Claude. *Philarète Chasles et la vie littéraire au temps du romantisme.* 2 vols. Paris: Librairie José Corti, 1965.

Scattered quotations from Chasles, well-indexed, show his high esteem for Nodier and especially Nodier's translation of *The Vicar of Wakefield.*

287-B. Porter, Laurence Minot. "Le Style et l'art narratif de Charles Nodier dans les Contes." Unpub. Diss., Harvard Univ., May, 1965. viii, 378 pp.

A good study of Nodier's style and the way in which it relates to his cosmology. Examines his metaphysical thought, stylistic doctrines, choice of a *genre,* techniques used to create *vraisemblance,* changes in style to intensify the visionary experiences of his characters, and the opposition between the spiritual and the material in Nodier. Concludes that, in the main, Nodier's thought is clear and coherent.

288. Richer, Jean. "Textes rares ou inédits: un autoportrait fantaisiste et douze lettres de Charles Nodier," *Revue des Sciences Humaines,* n. s., no. 120 (1965), pp. [553]-572.

Richer presents Nodier's self-portrait and twelve letters, which he believes to be previously unpublished, and places them in their historical background where necessary and possible. These letters are:

- a. Letter of December, 1812, to Tamisier, a lawyer of Lons-le-Saunier, asking him to forward to Milan anything concerning Nodier, who was on his way to Laybach.
- b. Letter of Nov. 18, 1816, to Abel Rémusat presenting his qualifications for election to the Académie des Inscriptions et Belles-Lettres.
- c. Letter of July 8, 1825, to the comte de Corbière, asking reimbursement for his trip to the coronation at Reims.
- d. A follow-up letter to the preceding one, dated Paris, July 10, 1825.
- e. Another, dated Paris, July 27, 1825.
- f. Another, dated July 29, 1825.
- g. A final letter to the comte, dated July 30, 1825, thanking him for his services.
- h. A letter of May 29, 1829, to a German bookseller about the sale of a part of his library, and the publication of his *Variétés littéraires et philologiques.*
- i. Letter dated May 3, 1830, to Abel Rémusat, again seeking his support for election to the Académie des Inscriptions.
- j. Letter dated Paris, Dec. 3, 1833, to the editors of the "Musée des Familles" concerning an article he is sending to them for publication.

k. Letter from Lille, June 16, 1835, to Fred. Hennebert, Archiviste de la ville de Tournay, thanking him for his letter and regretting the abridgment of his trip to Belgium.

l. Letter of Nov. 28, 1836, to Louis Babeuf, thanking him for a gift.

289. Wilson, N. "Charles Nodier, Victor Hugo and *Les Feuilles d'automne,*" *The Modern Language Review,* LX (1965), [21]-31.

> The author believes that "some of the ambiguities, hesitations, awkward half-silences, contradictions in tone and spirit to be found in the *Feuilles d'automne,* are intimately related to Hugo's friendship with Charles Nodier." The friendship, which started as a warm one, was gradually weakened by growing differences in political and aesthetic opinions. Wilson sees *Les Feuilles d'automne* as evidence of an effort by Hugo to mend the rift. On two important issues, art separated from politics and respect for the monarchy, Hugo made great concessions to Nodier. But there are inconsistencies and conflicts in the volume, for Hugo was trying to steer the difficult path between "le père de l'église romantique-royaliste" and the militant new group of Romantics. Nodier praised the volume, not for what he actually found, but rather, appreciative of Hugo's effort, for what he would have liked to find. See also Charles (73), Bauer (89), and Dédéyan (266).

1966

289-A. Keller, Luzius. "Piranèse et les poètes romantiques," *Cahiers de l'Association Internationale des Études Françaises,* no. 18 (1966), pp. [179]-188.

> Very brief presentation of a theme fully developed in Keller's book (290). Calls Nodier, in his literary use of the Piranesian spiral staircase, once again "un précurseur des grands poètes romantiques."

290. Keller, Luzius. *Piranèse et les romantiques français, le mythe des escaliers en spirale.* Paris: José Corti, 1966. 255 pp.

> This highly interesting book shows that the Piranesian visions that multiplied in French literature around 1830 go

back, rather than to Piranesi's work itself, to a description of one of his plates included in Thomas de Quincey's *Confessions of an English Opium Eater,* translated into French by Musset in 1828. Nodier's *Piranèse* appeared in 1833. *Inès de las Sierras* (1837) also seems to have Piranesian elements in the description of the castle. "Cependant c'est moins par le côté pittoresque que Nodier se sent attiré vers l'artiste italien que par la foi que celui-ci accorde aux visions de la fantaisie humaine." As *Piranèse* appeared before any of the other Romantics (Balzac, Gautier, and Hugo) and later Baudelaire and Mallarmé had used de Quincey's Piranesian text, Nodier once again appears as a literary precursor of those who are better known to us today. See pp. 60-66.

    a. P. Georgel. *Revue d'Histoire Littéraire de la France,* LXVII (1967), 847-848.

291. Mauriac, Claude. "La vie des lettres: les chers fantômes d'Alexandre Dumas et de Charles Nodier," *Le Figaro,* 14 mars 1966, p. 18.

The recent text of Dumas père's *Mille et un fantômes,* presented by Hubert Juin in the collection "Marabout-Géant," serves as the point of departure for Mauriac to write about not only what Dumas, but also the contemporary scholars, Richer (288) and Schneider (275), have said of Nodier. Apparently takes seriously Schneider's bantering opening remarks to his treatment of the fantastic in Nodier.

291-A. Orlando, Francesco. *Infanzia, memoria e storia da Rousseau ai romantici.* Padova: Liviana Editrice, 1966. 253 pp.

Part I, Chapter 7, "L'Esilio nella natura," concerns Nodier as memorialist: his intentions in writing two sets of memoirs, reasons for their omissions and fragmentary character, and Nodier's own apology for them. Looks at the *Souvenirs, épisodes et portraits pour servir à l'histoire de la Révolution et de l'Empire* with particular reference to the elements of horror and violence to be found in them. Sees in the idyllic description of Novilars in the *Souvenirs de Jeunesse* an effort to create a terrestrial paradise merely in order that it might be possible to lose it and lament it eternally. For other references to the idea of the earthly paradise in Nodier, see Béguin (156) and Engler (247). For other work on Nodier as memorialist, see Orlando (287) and Dargaud (170).

292. Poulet, Georges, "Piranèse et les poètes romantiques français," *La Nouvelle Revue Française*, XIV, no. 160 (1er avril 1966), [660]-671; no. 161 (1er mai 1966), [849]-862.

Treats the Piranesian staircase as found in Nodier, Gautier, Hugo, Baudelaire, and Mallarmé. Draws on Keller (290), with, as far as Nodier is concerned, a few personal insights. See pp. 670-671.

293. Poulet, Georges. "Piranèse et les poètes romantiques français," in his *Trois Essais de mythologie romantique*. Paris: José Corti, 1966. Pp. 135-187.

Contains the same material on Nodier as 292.

 a. M. Romano. *Studi Francesi*, XI (1967), 162.
 b. *The Times* [London] *Literary Supplement*, no. 3406, June 8, 1967, pp. [497]-498.

294. Willard, Charity Cannon. "The Remarkable Case of Clotilde de Surville," *L'Esprit Créateur*, VI (1966), 108-116.

Mentions the 1826 edition of the *Poésies inédites de Clotilde de Surville* by Nodier and Roujoux and suggests that their motive in producing it may have been amusement in continuing the hoax started by others.

1967[2]

295. Kies, Albert. "Lettres inédites de Charles Nodier à Émile Buloz," *Bulletin de l'Académie Royale de Langue et de Littérature Françaises*, XLV (1967), [213]-223.

Publishes ten previously unpublished letters of Nodier to Émile Buloz dating from March, 1836, to December, 1843, consisting largely of requests for advances on material he is writing and reports of progress on his work.

296. Mönch, Walter. *Charles Nodier und die deutsche und englische Literatur, eine Studie zur romantischen Denkform in*

---

[2] Since this material went to the printer's, several other items for 1967 have been noted. They will be included in a future supplement planned to keep the bibliography of Nodier studies current.

Frankreich. Romanische Studien, Vol. XXIV. Berlin: Emil Ebering, 1931. Denkform und Jugendreihe, No. 1. Nendeln, Liechtenstein: Kraus, 1967. 128 pp.

> A reprint of no. 64. Not seen.

297. Schenk, H[ans] G[eorg]. *The Mind of the European Romantics: an Essay in Cultural History,* with a Preface by Isaiah Berlin. New York: Frederick Ungar Publishing Co., 1967 [c. 1966]. xxiv, 303 pp.

> Includes a few scattered references to Nodier.

298. Schulze, J. *Enttäuschung und Wahnwelt. Studien zu Nodiers Erzählungen.* Beihefte zu Poetica, 1. München: Allach, 1967. Ca. 190 pp.

> Not seen.

299. Storzer, Gerald H. "The Fictional Confession of Adolescent Love: a Study of Seven Romantic Novels." Ann Arbor, Mich.: University Microfilms, 1967. iv, 255 pp.

> A University of Wisconsin Ph. D. dissertaion. Chapter VI, pp. 122-149, concerns Nodier's *La Fée aux Miettes.* This novel shows that the idea that Romantic literature treats the particular and the unusual rather than the general and universal is only partially true. Michel is "a truly representative hero, incarnating the fundamental need of all men to transcend their condition." See also other pages, especially pp. 77, 180, 181-183.

300. Thompson, Antoinette F. "Charles Nodier's Translation of *The Vicar of Wakefield.*" Unpub. Master's Thesis, Univ. of Florida, August, 1967. iii, 48 pp.

> Examines Nodier's translation technique in *The Vicar of Wakefield,* compares it with two other translations of the same novel, and comes to the conclusion that, though there are good things to be said for Nodier's, it "does not faithfully reproduce Goldsmith's work and is not justified in the immoderate alterations of style and tone".

1968[3]

301. Bender, Edmund John. "Charting French Romanticism: the Criticism of Charles Nodier." Ann Arbor, Mich.: University Microfilms, Inc., 1968. 289 pp.

> Doctoral dissertation at Indiana University, 1968. The only comprehensive investigation of Nodier's literary criticism as it relates to the French Romantic movement. Shows the significance of his work to the movement but reckons that his importance has not yet been fully ascertained. If his criticism "does not represent the type... to which we have since become accustomed," it is an improvement over that which preceded it. An extensive appendix, which is intended to correct and bring up-to-date Larat (3), contains a catalogue of the works, letters, and manuscripts of Nodier and selected bibliographies of studies concerning him from 1840 to 1967. Appendiz published separately in 1969. See footnote 2 of the Preface.

302. Horchler, D. Henriette. "Dream and Reality in the Works of Charles Nodier." Diss., Univ. of Pennsylvania, 1968.

> Studies the role of the real and the dream worlds in Nodier's work, showing that the two fuse in his settings, his characters, and his treatment of historical and social problems. Concludes that Nodier shared many of the ideas of the Surrealists but did not have the ability necessary to realize his vision. Not seen, but the author has supplied pertinent information. See also *Dissertation Abstracts,* XXIX (1969), 2264-A.

303. Morse, J. Mitchell. "Charles Nodier and *Finnegans Wake,*" *Comparative Literature Studies,* V, no. 2 (1968), 195-201.

> Sees no influence of Nodier on Joyce but finds the similarities between their theories, especially in regard to dream in literature, so remarkable that the two must have discovered independently the same literary truth. However, Nodier, unlike Joyce, lacked the skill to demonstrate his theory fully.

---

[3] This bibliography was intended to comprehend Nodier studies only through 1967. The few items which were at hand for 1968 have been included, but do not represent full coverage for that year.

MISCELLANEOUS REFERENCES IN OTHER LANGUAGES

304. Maixner, Rudolf. *Charles Nodier i Illirija.* Rad Jugoslav, Akademije, 229. Zagreb, 1924.

[Not seen.]

305. *La Llegenda del llibreter assassí de Barcelona,* per R. Miquel y Planas. Barcelona: Prempses de la Casa Miquel-Rius, 1928. xxvii, 281 pp.

[According to L. S. T., "Charles Nodier and the Don Vicente Legend" (142), contains a sound investigation as to the original author of this story, with the editor inclining toward Nodier.]

306. Tobarina, Josip. "Ranjina, Boškovič, Nodier, Grenville," *Prilozi za Knjizevnost, Jezik i Folklor.* Belgrade, livre VIII (1928).

[Not seen.]

307. Tavzes, Janko. "Slovenski preporod pod Francozi." Ljubljana, 1929.

[Dobrovoljc (19a) says that Tavzes "donna la bibliographie la plus exacte [of Nodier's articles for the *Télégraphe Officiel*] jusqu'aujourd'hui dans sa thèse ...; cependant l'auteur y omet deux articles et attribue à Nodier le premier article des 'Observations sur le sol de Laybach et de ses environs' qui ne provient pas de la plume de celui-ci." Superseded, of course, by Dobrovoljc. Not seen.]

308. Frieiro, Eduardo. "O Verdadeiro bibliófilo," *Revista do Livro,* Orgão do Instituto Nacional do Livro, V (1957), 183-186.

[The "verdadeiro bibliófilo" is Lowrich in Nodier's *Franciscus Columna.*]

Part II

A TENTATIVE BIBLIOGRAPHY OF THE WORKS OF
CHARLES NODIER, 1923-1967

Complete Works

1a. *Œuvres complètes.* 12 vols. in 8. Genève: 1967. (Réimpression de la seule édition collective des œuvres de Charles Nodier parue à Paris de 1832 à 1837.)

Not seen.

Selected Works

2a. *Contes de la veillée.* Paris: Bibliothèque-Charpentier, E. Fasquelle, Éditeur, 1923.

A four-page "Avertissement" recalls Nodier's charm as a person and a raconteur.

3a. *Contes de la veillée.* Paris: Plon-Nourrit, 1923. 191 pp.

An edition adapted for "la jeunesse," with a short "Notice biographique" by Mme Carette also intended for young readers.

4a. *Contes de la veillée.* Notice et annotations par Gauthier-Ferrières. Bibliothèque Larousse. Paris: Larousse, 1923. 176 pp.

Not seen.

5a. *Œuvres choisies de Charles Nodier; romans, nouvelles, souvenirs, contes, légendes, fantaisies, œuvres en vers, correspon-*

dance. Préface et notices par Albert Cazes. 2ᵉ éd. Paris: Delagrave, 1923. 464 pp.

> A good edition to have where Nodier resources are limited. Preceded by a long, well-documented biography of Nodier and a sane appreciation of his talent and influence. Collection includes novels, *nouvelles, contes,* memoirs, 15 poems, a large selection of correspondence, and Nodier's discourse before the Académie Française. A serious drawback for some purposes, however, is that in many cases excerpts rather than entire works are presented.

6a. *Contes fantastiques.* Notice et annotations par Gauthier-Ferrières. Bibliothèque Larousse. Paris: Larousse, 1924. 200 pp.

> For Gauthier-Ferrières's introduction, "Charles Nodier (1780-1844)," see 8.

7a. *Le Chien de Brisquet; La Combe de l'homme mort; Paul ou la ressemblance.* Nelson, 1925.

> Not seen.

8a. *Trésor des Fèves, Fleur des Pois. Le Génie Bonhomme. Histoire du chien de Brisquet.* Vignettes par Tony Johannot. Petite Bibliothèque Blanche. Paris: Hachette, 1925. 123 pp.

> An edition for children. A preface by P. J. Stahl is apparently reproduced from a nineteenth-century edition.

9a. *Trois contes: Le Chien de Brisquet, La Combe de l'homme mort, Paul ou la ressemblance.* Edited by H. L. Hutton and A. M. Savage. Oxford: Clarendon Press, 1925. 64 pp.

> Not seen.

10a. *Contes et nouvelles de Charles Nodier;* publiés avec une introduction d'Edmond Jaloux. Paris: Payot, 1927. xxi, 297 pp.

> For "Charles Nodier" by Jaloux (pp. vii-xxi) see 31.

11a. *Contes de la veillée;* avec introduction et notes par Ad. Duch. Milano: Signorelli, 1928. 113 pp.

Not seen.

12a. *Trésor des Fèves et Fleur des Pois. Le Génie Bonhomme.* Paris: Gedalge, 1928. 96 pp.

Not seen.

13a. *Nouvelles.* Paris: F. Lanore, 1929. 128 pp.

Not seen.

14a. *Inès de las Sierras. La Fée aux Miettes.* Paris: Nilsson, 1930.

Not seen.

15a. *Contes de la veillée.* Avec introduction et notes par Ad. Duch. Milano: Signorelli, 1933. 116 pp.

Not seen.

16a. *Contes et nouvelles.* La Bibliothèque Précieuse. Paris: Nilsson, 1933. 256 pp.

17a. *Deux Contes de la veillée.* Hrsg. v. Christoph Beck. 2 Aufl. Bamberg: Buchners Verl., 1933. 40 pp.

Not seen.

18a. *Histoire du chien de Brisquet. Suivie de Trésor des Fèves et Fleur des Pois.* Illustrations d'Adrianne Ségur. Paris: Société Universitaire d'Éditions et de Librairie, 1933. 95 pp.

19a. *Statistique illyrienne. Articles complets du "Télégraphe Officiel" de l'année 1813,* rédigés et annotés par France Dobrovoljc. Introduction par Janko Tavzes. Ljubljana: Édition "Satura," 1933. xvi, 160 pp.

> Publishes for the first time Nodier's articles for the *Télégraphe Officiel.* In his introduction Tavzes describes the new milieu of Laybach into which Nodier came, indicates the improvement in the journal under Nodier's editorship, and discusses the wide variety of articles on Illyrian subjects

written by Nodier and his collaborators. Ends with an expression of gratitude to Nodier on the part of the Yugoslavs for his contribution to their country. In the introduction to his annotations Dobrovoljc gives an evaluation of the various bibliographies of Nodier's articles for the *Télégraphe Officiel* and lists for the first time those which were translated for the German edition of the paper. A valuable edition.

20a. *Contes fantastiques.* La Bibliothèque Préciuse. Paris: Nilsson, 1934.

Not seen.

21a. *Contes de Nodier.* Adaptation Gisèle Vallerey. Paris: Fernand Nathan, 1935. 192 pp.

An adaptation for young people.

22a. *Contes et nouvelles.* La Bibliothèque Précieuse. Paris: Nilsson, 1935. 256 pp.

Not seen.

23a. *Contes et nouvelles.* Paris: Gründ, 1936. 256 pp.

24a. *Trilby ou le lutin d'Argail. Trésor des Fèves et Fleur des Pois. Histoire du chien de Brisquet.* Illustrations de A. Ballet. Paris: Delagrave, 1936. 93 pp.

25a. *Contes et nouvelles.* French Classics. London: Imperia Book Co., 1940.

Not seen.

26a. *Contes choisis.* Introduction, choix et notes de R.-N. Raimbault. Collection Les Lettres et la Vie Française, 1re Sér., 6. Angers: Jacques Petit, 1941. 301 pp.

For the introduction, "Charles Nodier et son temps," see 108.

27a. *Iñès* [sic] *de las Sierras. ... [La Combe de l'homme mort. Jean-François les Bas-Bleus].* Paris: Éditions Littéraires de France, 1943. 180 pp.

28a. *Trilby, La Fée aux Miettes.* Les Trésors de la Littérature Française, collection dirigée par Edmond Jaloux. Gèneve: Albert Skira, 1944. 315 pp.

29a. *Contes à ma sœur.* Ill. par P. Rousseau. Lausanne: Imprimerie Populaire Coopérative, 1945.

Not seen.

30a. *Les Contes fantastiques.* Illustrations de Mario Prassinos. Paris: Calmann-Lévy, 1945. 439 pp.

31a. *Inès de las Sierras et autres contes.* Illustrations de Yliane Labaudt. Paris: M. Gasnier, 1945. 191 pp.

32a. *Smarra ou les démons de la nuit. Suivi de Trilby et de Une Heure ou la vision.* Coll. "Les Maîtres du Fantastique." Paris: Éditions des Quatre Vents, 1945.

Not seen.

33a. *Contes.* Ill. de Mario Prassinos. Paris: Calmann-Lévy, 1946.

Not seen.

34a. *Les contes fantastiques.* Ill. de Mario Prassinos. Paris: Calmann-Lévy, 1946-48. 439 pp.

Not seen.

35a. *Deux contes de la veillée.* Gráf. Hispanoitaliana. Barcelona: Rauter, 1946. 32 pp.

Not seen.

36a. *Smarra ou les démons de la nuit, suivi de Trilby ou le lutin d'Argail, et de Une Heure ou la vision.* Les Maîtres du Fantastique. Paris: Éditions des Quatre Vents, 1946. 214 pp.

37a. *Contes.* Frontispice de Jacques Ferrière. Paris: Les Compagnons du Livre, 1948. 279 pp.

38a. *Iñès* [sic] *de las Sierras, roman. Lydie ou la résurrection.* Illustrations de Henri Crosnier. Paris: Librairie Gründ, 1948. 190 pp.

39a. *Contes choisis.* Collezione d'Autori Stranieri Annotati per le Scuole Italiane. Roma: Albrighi et Segati, 1949-50. 103 pp.

Not seen.

40a. *Contes choisis.* Frontispice de Jacques Ferrière. (S. I.) Lille: Les Compagnons du Livre, 1949. 287 pp.

Same as the Paris edition, 1948 (37a).

41a. *Trésor des Fèves et Fleur des Pois, et autres contes.* Poitiers: Société Française d'Imprimerie et de Librairie et Impr. M. Texier Réunies, 1950. 125 pp.

42a. *Histoire du chien de Brisquet, suivie de Trésor des Fèves et Fleur des Pois.* Illustrations d'Adrienne Ségur. Paris: Société Universitaire d'Éditions et de Librairie, 1951. 94 pp.

43a. *Contes et nouvelles, œuvres choisis.* Préface et notes de Robert Mauzi. Paris: Delmas, 1953. 331 pp.

Preface contains a short sketch of Nodier's life, which is suspect because of inaccuracies, followed by a brief general appreciation of the *contes*, which is unreliable for its judgments. Notes helpful factually but not for interpretation.

44a. *Contes.* Front. de Jacques Ferrière. Les Compagnons du Livre, 1953. 279 pp.

Not seen.

45a. *La Fée aux Miettes ... L'Homme et la fourmi.* Bibliothèque Mondiale, no. 8, 7 mai 1953. Paris: Éditions de la Bibliothèque Mondiale, 1954. 200 pp.

Includes three introductory articles for the general reader on Nodier and *La Fée aux Miettes:* "Charles Nodier," by Pierre Descaves (184); "*La Fée aux Miettes,*" by Francis de Miomandre (188); and "Nodier et sa multiple figure," by Henri Clouard (182). An edition without date (46a) contains the same articles. A 1956 edition (75a) contains the one by Descaves. (Listed in the Bibliothèque Nationale catalogue, under the title, as follows: "Charles Nodier," par Pierre Descaves. "*La Fée aux Miettes*," par Francis de Miomandre. *La Fée aux Miettes ... L'Homme et la fourmi*, par Charles Nodier. "Nodier et sa multiple figure," par Henri Clouard.)

46a. *La Fée aux Miettes ... suivi de L'Homme et la fourmi, apologue primitif.* Paris: Le Livre Mondiale, s. d. [Entre 1936-1959]. 192 pp.

Contains the same material as the 1954 edition (45a).

47a. *Contes choisis.* Adaptation de J.-P. Bayard. Aquarelles de M. Sommer. Paris: Bias, 1956. 92 pp.

An adaptation for young people.

48a. *Trésor des Fèves et Fleur des Pois. Trilby ou le lutin d'Argail. Histoire du chien de Brisquet.* Illustrations de Pierre Rousseau. Paris: Delagrave, [Lagny: Impr. de E. Grévin et Fils], 1956. 80 pp.

49a. *Contes du pays des rêves.* Saverne: Club des Libraires de France, 1957. 451 pp.

> An attractively produced selection of *contes*, including some that are seldom published. Notes negligible, but accompanied by a good postface, "Nodier et ses rêves," reprinted, without footnotes and bibliography, from Pierre-Georges Castex' *Le Conte fantastique en France de Nodier à Maupassant* (167).
>> *a.* A. Wurmser. "Alors, dans la Grande Boutique romantique," *Les Lettres Françaises,* 13 mars 1958, p. 2.

50a. *Contes fantastiques.* Présentés par Michel Laclos. 2 vols. Paris: Jean-Jacques Pauvert, 1957.

> One of the more important editions of Nodier's *contes*. Volume I contains an Introduction (pp. 7-14) which aims to incline the reader toward an exceptional *conteur;* Sainte-Beuve's "Notice sur Charles Nodier et ses ouvrages" pp. 15-59); a "Bio-bibliographie sommaire de Charles Nodier"

(pp. 60-73), which is a very useful chronological presentation of the essential events of his life, together with the publication dates of his principal works; and a selected bibliography of old and recent works concerning Nodier. Reflects current efforts to establish more securely Nodier's reputation as a man of letters.

    a. C. Bourniquel, *Esprit,* XXVI (janv.-juin 1958), 167-169.

51a. *Contes choisis.* Préface et notes de A. Nigri. Roma: Società Editrice Dante Alighieri [s. d. 1959?].

Not seen.

52a. *Contes fantastiques.* 2 vols. Coll. "Classiques Illustrées." Paris: Pauvert, 1959.

Not seen.

53a. *Deux contes de la veillée.* Biblioteca Linguistica. Serie A. Textos franceses, Vol. 2, pp. 44-88. (Colección Oasis, 84.) Barcelona: Rauter, 1959.

Not seen.

54a. *Contes choisis;* extraits avec une notice biographique, une notice historique et littéraire, des notes explicatives, des jugements, un questionnaire et des sujets de devoirs, par Bernard Lalande. Classiques Larousse. Paris: Larousse, 1960. 133 pp.

Notices and notes give a balanced, competent treatment of Nodier for the student.

55a. *La Fée aux Miettes* [et autres contes]. Préface de Jean Vagne. Lausanne: Éditions Rencontre, 1960. 381 pp.

The preface is a good introduction for the general reader to Nodier's life and character.

56a. *Contes,* annotés par Pierre-Georges Castex. Ill. de 32 reprod. Coll. "Selecta." Paris: Garnier, 1961. 1,032 pp.

Not seen.

57a. *Contes, avec des textes et des documents inédits.* [Sommaire biographique, introduction, notices, notes, bibliographie et appendice critique par Pierre-Georges Castex.] Classiques Garnier. Paris: Éditions Garnier, 1961. xxiii, 944 pp.

> The best, and by far the most complete edition of the *contes* available, and the only one that might be called scholarly. A biographical summary and perceptive introduction precede the collection. Equally good "Notices" introduce each of the seven cycles of *contes* that Castex distinguishes. Abundant notes clarify the texts. A good selective bibliography is included, as well as an appendix describing the manuscripts discovered since Larat (3) published his bibliography. One of the manuscripts, *Le Songe d'or*, is published beside the text generally used.
>
> a. *Studi Francesi,* VI (1962), 166.
>
> b. J. Morel. *Revue des Sciences Humaines,* n. s., no. 106 (1962), pp. 293-294.
>
> c. A. W. Raitt. *French Studies,* XVII (1963), 268-270.

58a. *Contes choisis;* adaptation de J. P. Bayard. Aquarelles de M. Sommer. Paris: Bias, 1961. 91 pp.

An adaptation for young people.

59a. *Trésor des Fèves et Fleur des Pois. Le Génie Bonhomme.* Paris: Club Français du Livre, 1963.

60a. *Contes.* Coll. "Jeunesse sélection. Minimes," no. 4. St.-Germain-en-Laye: Édit. Maison des Instituteurs, 1964.

Not seen.

61a. *Trésor des Fèves et Fleur des Pois. Le Génie Bonhomme.* Vignettes de Tony Johannot. Reproductions en fac-similé d'un extrait du tome II du *Nouveau Magasin des Enfants,* publié par Hetzel en 1860. Paris: Club Français du Livre, 1964. 94 pp.

Not seen.

62a. *Trésor des Fèves et Fleur des Pois.* Aquarelles de W. P. Les Albums de l'Âge d'Or. Tournai, Belgique: Casterman, 1965. 32 pp.

Contains also *Le Chien de Brisquet.* An edition for children.

62a-A. *Infernaliana.* Préface de Hubert Juin. Poche-Club Fantastique, 42. Paris: Pierre Belfond, 1966. 189 pp.

> The preface traces the Rousseau-Nodier-Nerval relationship. Examines the reasons for and against the contention that Nodier wrote the *Infernaliana*, siding with those who believe that he did.

Individual Works

Les Aveugles de Chamouny

63a. *Les Aveugles de Chamouny.* Kempten, München, Verl. f. zeitgemäss. Sprachmethodik, 1923. 54 pp.

> Not seen.

Le Bibliomane

64a. *Le Bibliomane, conte fantastique.* Maestricht: A. A. M. Stolz, 1926. 34 pp.

65a. *Le Bibliomane,* publié avec préface et annotations par Ejnar Munksgaard. 24 Illus. par Maurice Leloir. Paris: H. Champion, 1928. 83 pp.

> For the preface, "Charles Nodier et son cercle," by Munksgaard, see 42.

Bonaventure Despériers. Cirano de Bergerac

65a-A. *Bonaventure Despériers. Cirano de Bergerac.* Genève: Slatkine Reprints, 1967. 112 pp.

> A photographic reproduction.

"De Quelques Livres satyriques"

66a. "De Quelques Livres satyriques et de leurs clefs," *Bulletin du Bibliophile et du Bibliothécaire,* 1940-45, pp. [169]-178.

Dictionnaire onomatopéique des oiseaux

67a. "*Dictionnaire onomatopéique des oiseaux.* Extraits suivis de la traduction de *Philomèle.*" *Saisons, Almanach des Lettres et des Arts,* no. 3 (hiver 1946-47), pp. 179-194.

La Fée Aux Miettes

68a. *La Fée aux Miettes, conte fantastique.* Poitiers: Société Française d'Imprimerie et de Librairie, 1936. 223 pp.

An adaptation for young people. Preceded by a condensed, accurate biography of Nodier and an *aperçu* of his work.

69a. *La Fée aux Miettes.* Illustrations de Pierre Gandon. Paris: La Tradition, 1938. 233 pp.

A lovely edition with excellent illustrations.

70a. *La Fée aux Miettes.* Ill. de Jacques Ferrand. Paris: José Corti, 1945.

Not seen.

71a. *La Fée aux Miettes.* Coll. "Jeunesse de France." Paris: Gasnier, 1946. 191 pp.

72a. *La Fée aux Miettes.* Poitiers: Société Française d'Imprimerie et de Librairie, 1946-1948.

Not seen.

73a. *La Fée aux Miettes.* Illustrations de Jacques Ferrand. Paris: J. Corti, 1947. 187 pp.

74a. *La Fée aux Miettes.* Ill. par aquar. de J. Ferrant. Paris: J. Corti, 1952.

Not seen.

75a. *La Fée aux Miettes*, présentée par Pierre Descaves. Paris: Éditions de la Bibliothèque Mondiale, 1956. 202 pp.

The presentation, "Charles Nodier," is the same as in the 1954 edition (45a) and the undated edition (46a). However, the two other essays to be found there are lacking here.

76a. *La Fée aux Miettes.* Introduction et notes par Auguste Viatte. Roma: Signorelli, 1962. 179 pp.

Viatte does not present a critical edition but has tried to rectify the numerous misprints which have crept into previous editions. A fine introduction sees *La Fée aux Miettes* as a "roman initiatique" and considers, in particular, the role of the themes of the Orient and the Queen of Sheba, and of the technique of the dream in this work. Notes are helpful.

 a. Studi Francesi, VII (1963), 173.

Franciscus Columna

 77a. *Franciscus Columna.* Prélection de Clément Janin. Le Rayon du Mandarin, No. 4. Paris: La Connaissance, 1927. 56 pp.

The good seven-page "Prélection" discusses Nodier as a bibliophile, the two sales of his library effected during his lifetime, and the sale after his death. Concludes that *Franciscus Columna* could have been written only by a bibliophile and bibliographer.

 78a. *Franciscus Columna, la dernière nouvelle de Charles Nodier,* précédée d'une étude bibliographique et littéraire de Mario Roques sur *Le Songe de Poliphile* et illustrée de gravures sur bois choisis dans l'édition italienne du *Songe* de 1499 et l'édition française de 1546. Brie-Comte-Robert: Les Bibliolâtres de France; Paris: Impr. de E. Baudelot, 1949. 91 pp.

Except for one short paragraph on Nodier's story, the study by Roque is concerned with the interpretation of the *Songe de Poliphile* and its 1499 and 1546 editions.

Le Génie Bonhomme

 79a. *Le Génie Bonhomme.* Illustrations de R. Coucheney. Marcq-en-Barœul (Nord): M. Dervaux et fils, 1935. 43 pp.

 80a. *Le Génie Bonhomme.* Illustrations de R. Coucheney. Marcq-en-Barœul (Nord): M. Dervaux et fils, 1938. 44 pp.

 81a. *Le Génie Bonhomme.* Illustrations de R. Coucheney. Marcq-en-Barœul (Nord): Dervaux, 1954. 43 pp.

Histoire du chien de Brisquet

 82a. *Le Chien de Brisquet.* Imagerie Française sur des Thèmes Français. Paris: H. Laurens, 1926. 30 pp.

Not seen.

83a. *Le Chien de Brisquet.* Città di Castello: Giacomini, 1929. 20 pp.

Not seen.

84a. *Histoire du chien de Brisquet.* Paris: Ferroud, 1929.

Not seen.

85a. *Histoire du chien de Brisquet.* Illustrations de E. Dot. Tours: A. Mame et fils, 1933. 32 pp.

Not seen.

86a. *Le Chien de Brisquet.* S. U. D. E. L., 1934.

Not seen.

87a. *Histoire du chien de Brisquet;* illustrations de E. Dot. Tours: Alfred Mame et fils, 1934.

Not seen.

88a. *Histoire du chien de Brisquet.* Illus. de A. Uriet. Tours: Mame, 1942. 22 pp.

89a. *Histoire du chien de Brisquet.* Illustrations de F. Rojanskovsky. Paris: Flammarion, 1942. [18 pp.]

90a. *Le Chien de Brisquet.* Bois gravés de Camille Berg. [Préface de Raymond Lecuyer.] Paris: Compagnie Française des Arts Graphiques, 1945. 11 pp.

Preface intended for the casual reader.

91a. *Le Chien de Brisquet.* In: René de Chateaubriand et Charles Nodier, *Avenir du monde, lettre portugaise. Le Chien de Brisquet.* Compagnie Française des Arts Graphiques, 1946.

Not seen.

92a. *Histoire du chien de Brisquet.* Ill. d'Albert Uriet. Coll. M. Tours: Mame, 1947. 24 pp.

Not seen.

93a. *Histoire du chien de Brisquet.* Illus. d'Albert Uriet. Tours: Mame, 1949. 24 pp.

94a. *Le Chien de Brisquet.* Illustrations de A. Jourcin. Paris: Bias, 1954. 24 pp.

Histoire du roi de Bohême et de ses sept châteaux

95a. *Histoire du roi de Bohême et de ses sept châteaux.* Paris: Delangle Frères, 1830. [Réimpression en fac-similé faite à Paris, par le Club Français du Livre (impr. de P. Dupont), 1950, dans la collection Le Club Français du Livre, Classiques, Vol. XV.—Suivi d'une postface de Jean Richer, intitulée: "*Le Roi de Bohême,* ou les tentations du langage."] 398 pp.

> A much-needed reprinting of one of the rarest of Nodier's works. For Richer's postface, see 166.

Inès de las Sierras

96a. *Inès de las Sierras.* Edited by J. A. Groves, etc. Blackie's Longer French Texts. London: Blackie, 1926. 88 pp.

> Not seen.

97a. *Inès de las Sierras.* Paris: Grande Librairie Universelle, 1927. 240 pp.

> Not seen.

La Légende de Sœur Béatrix

98a. *Légende de Sœur Béatrix.* Paris: M. Glomeau, 1924. 59 pp.

> Not seen.

Mademoiselle de Marsan

99a. *Mademoiselle de Marsan.* [Charles Nodier et le salon de l'Arsenal, par Alexandre Dumas. Préface de Jacques Suffel.] Paris: Éditions de Montsouris, 1944. 96 pp.

> Preface for the general reader. Excerpts from the *Mémoires* of Dumas père describing the soirées at the Arsenal.

Les Quatre Talismans

100a. *Les Talismans.* Illustrations de E. Dot. Paris: 6 rue Madame, 1931. 52 pp.

Not seen.

101a. *Les Talismans.* Illustrations de E. Dot. Tours: Mame, 1934. 61 pp.

Le Songe d'or

102a. *Le Songe d'or.* [Préface de M. Faure-Cousin.] Illustrations de Marcel Depré. Paris: Éditions I. P. C., 1945. 127 pp.

Preface of no significance.

Thérèse Aubert

103a. *Thérèse Aubert,* avec une préface d'Edmond Pilon. Bibliothèque Plon, no. 41. Paris: Plon-Nourrit, s. d. [1923?]. 206 pp.

For the preface, "Charles Nodier," by Edmond Pilon, see 5.

104a. *Thérèse Aubert.* Hrsg. v. August Ewald. Paderborn: F. Schöningh, 1928. 78 pp.

Not seen.

Trésor des Fèves et Fleur des Pois

105a. *Trésor des Fèves et Fleur des Pois.* Tours: A. Mame et Fils, 1926. 70 pp.

Not seen.

106a. *Trésor des Fèves et Fleur des Pois.* Tours: A. Mame et Fils, 1930. 70 pp.

Not seen.

107a. *Trésor des Fèves et Fleur des Pois.* Marcq-en-Barœul (Nord): M. Dervaux et Fils, 1939. 59 pp.

108a. *Trésor des Fèves et Fleur des Pois, conte de fées,* adapté et simplifié par H. Canac ... Illustré par K. Charlemagne. Collection d'Antan et de Toujours, 2ᵉ degré, no. 1. Paris: H. Didier, 1939. 56 pp.

109a. *Trésor des Fèves et Fleur des Pois, conte de fées,* adapté et simplifié par H. Canac ... Illustré par K. Piralian. Paris: Didier, 1951. 56 pp.

110a. *Trésor des Fèves et Fleur des Pois.* Marcq-en-Barœul (Nord): Dervaux, 1953. 60 pp.

Trilby ou le lutin d'Argail

111a. *Trilby.* Bibl. de la Plume de Paon. Neuchâtel et Paris: Delachaux et Niestlé, 1923. 101 pp.

Not seen.

Le Voleur

112a. *Le Voleur, roman inédit* précédé d'une introduction historique et littéraire par Jean Richer. Thèse Secondaire Inédite de l'Université de Paris, 1964. 242 pp.

> A critical edition established from the manuscript in the collection of M. Jean Mennessier-Nodier, accompanied by a choice of variants and with "Notes et Éclaircissements," pertinent documents, and bibliographies. The 95-page introduction discusses the manuscript, its date, the themes in the story, German and English influences, and the relationship of this work to later works of Nodier. A scholarly study.

TRANSLATIONS - ENGLISH

L'Amateur de livres

113a. *The Book Collector.* Cambridge, Mass.: 1951.

> Beautifully printed and illustrated with reproductions of Daumier lithographs. Handpainted covers. A tribute to Nodier, the bibliophile, who "would not be happy to leave

the precious volume that has so enthralled him clad in the drab habiliments of poverty, when it is in his power to clothe it luxuriously in watered silk and morocco."

Franciscus Columna

114a. *Francesco Colonna: a fanciful tale of the writing of the Hypnerotomachia.* Translated by Theodore Wesley Koch. Chicago: Privately Printed, 1929. 62 pp.

A book beautifully printed and illustrated with facsimiles of the wood-engravings in the Aldus Manutius edition of the *Hypnerotomachia* and of the frescoes from the walls of the seminary where Francesco Colonna lived and wrote. The Foreword by Theodore Wesley Koch describes the Aldine edition of the *Hypnerotomachia*, mentions some of its early French editions, and gives valuable bibliographical information about editions of Nodier's story derived from the acrostic contained in it. Also has information on Nodier's love for books and the care he lavished on his personal library. Reproduces some of the information included in the catalog of the exhibition at the Arsenal commemorating the Romantic centenary in May and June, 1927, and translates into English Dumas's description in his *Memoirs* of Nodier's soirées at the Arsenal.

Nausicaa

115a. *Nausicaa. Golden Book Magazine of Fiction and True Stories That Will Live*, XIII, no. 74 (Feb., 1931), 30-33.

Trésor des Fèves et Fleur des Pois

116a. *The Luck of the Bean-Rows. A Fairy Tale Translated from the French.* Illustrated by Claud Lovat Fraser. London: O'Connor, 1924. 60 pp.

An edition for children.

117a. *The Luck of the Bean-Rows...* Illustrated by Claud Lovat Fraser. London: O'Connor, 1927. 60 pp.

Not seen.

TRANSLATIONS - SPANISH

Selected Works

118a. *Lydia y Francisco Columna. Dos cuentos.* La Traducción del francés ha sido hecha por J. J. Morato. Colección Universal, núm. 835. Madrid: Espasa-Calpe, 1923. 88 pp.

Not seen.

119a. *Franciscus Columna, novela bibliográfica de Carlos Nodier, precedida de El Bibliómano del mismo autor.* Traducción de Rafael V. Silvari. Pequeña Colección del Bibliófilo, dirigida por R. Miquel y Planas, Vol. III. Madrid: Librería de los Bibliófilos Españoles, 1924. clxxxiv, 101 pp.

For Miquel y Planas' introduction, "Una Vida de bibliófilo Nodier," see 12.

120a. *Inés de las Sierras* [conteniendo, además, *Sor Beatriz*]. Bibliotecas Populares Cervantes, Ser. 2. Las Cien Mejores Obras de la Literatura Universal, Vol. 58. Madrid: Compañía General de Artes Gráficas. Compañía Iberoamericana de Publicaciones, 1930. 141 pp.

Not seen.

121a. *Trilby y Franciscus Columna.* Traducción de Manuel Vallvé. Biblioteca Selección, 23. Barcelona: Montaner y Simón, 1945. 213 pp.

Not seen.

Le Bibliomane

122a. *El Bibliómano y Subasta de mi biblioteca de Octavio Uzanne.* Traducido por María Brey; prólogo de A. Rodríguez Moñino. Valencia: Editorial Castalia, 1948. 76 pp.

Prologue of no significance.

La Combe de l'homme mort

123a. *La Vall de l'home mort. Novella.* Quadernis Literaris. Any II, vol. 84. Barcelona: 1935. 67 pp.

Not seen.

Inès de las Sierras

124a. *Inés de las Sierras.* [Traducida del francés por J. J. Morato.] Madrid: Imp. y Edit. Espasa-Calpe, 1923. 93 pp.

Not seen.

125a. *Inés de las Sierras.* Traducción de José Janés y Olivé. Quadernis Literaris. Any II, numéro 60. Barcelona: 1935. 75 pp.

Not seen.

126a. *Inés de las Sierras.* Traducción de Manuel Vallvé. Barcelona: Montaner y Simón, 1946. xv, 187 pp.

Not seen.

La Légende de Soeur Béatrix

127a. *Sor Beatriz.* Gráf. Industrial, E. Granados, núm. 70. Grano de Arena. Barcelona: Edit. J. Janés, 1942. 60 pp.

Not seen.

Mademoiselle de Marsan

128a. *La Señorita de Marsán.* Traducida del francés por Paulino Masip. Madrid: Imp. y Edit. Espasa-Calpe, 1924. 142 pp.

Not seen.

La Neuvaine de la Chandeleur

129a. *La Novena de la Candelaria.* Traducida por Paulino Masip. Colección Universal, núm. 964. Madrid: Espasa-Calpe, 1924. 62 pp.

Not seen.

Souvenirs de jeunesse

130a. *Recuerdos de juventud.* La traducción del francés ha sido hecha por Paulino Masip. Colección Universal, números 946-948. Madrid: Talleres y Editorial Calpe, 1924. 272 pp.

Not seen.

131a. *Recuerdos de juventud.* Versión de C. Pérez Armisán. Colección Oasis, 84. Barcelona: Ediciones Reguera, Imp. Favencia, 1947. 95 pp.

Not seen.

132a. *Recuerdos de juventud.* [Traducido del francés por Paulino Masip.] Colección Austral. Buenos Aires, Argentina: Espasa-Calpe, 1950.

132a-A. *Recuerdos de juventud.* Novelas y Cuentos. Madrid: Dédalo, 1965. 40 pp.

Not seen.

Trilby ou le lutin d'Argail

133a. *Trilby o el duendecillo de Argail.* Traducción de J. J. Morato. Colección Universal, núm. 774. Madrid: Talleres Calpe, 1923. 80 pp.

Not seen.

134a. *Trilby o el duendecillo de Argail.* Traducción de María Francisca Gil. Colección Atlántida, Azul, 1. Barcelona: Edit. Atlántida, Imp. Simpar, 1945. 79 pp.

Not seen.

TRANSLATIONS - ITALIAN

Mademoiselle de Marsan, see *La Torre maledetta.*

La Torre maledetta

135a. *La Torre maledetta: romanzo storico.* Vers di Mario Frattini. Torino: Taurinia ed., 1937. 64 pp.

Not seen. Presumably a translation of *Mademoiselle de Marsan*. The title of the third episode of this work is "La Torre maledetta."

Trésor des Fèves et Fleur des Pois

136a. *Baccellino e Fior di Pisello.* Firenze: Salani, 1929. 191 pp.

Not seen.

137a. *Tesor di Fave e Fior di Pisello.* Traduz. di L. Fiorentino, con illustraz. di U. Fontana. Firenze: Marzocco, 1949. 52 pp.

Not seen.

TRANSLATIONS - GERMAN

Le Bibliomane

138a. *Der Büchernarr.* Mit Vorw. u Erl. von Ejnar Munksgaard. Übers. von Inga Junghanns. Leipzig: Heilingsche Verlagsanstalt, 1926. 46 pp.

Not seen.

MISCELLANEOUS TRANSLATIONS IN OTHER LANGUAGES

139a. *Janez Zbogar. Zgodovinski roman.* Poslovenil Fr. Robar. Gorizia: izdala knjiž. založba Sigma, 1932. 115 pp.

[Not seen.]

140a. De droom van het goud en andere vertellingen, uit het Fransch vertaald door Leo Roelants, met teekeningen van Jan Waterschoot. Hoogstraten: Moderne Uitgeverij, 1943. 89 pp.

[A Dutch translation of *Le Songe d'or* and other tales. Not seen.]

141a. *Bibliomanen.* Med indledning og noter av Ejnar Munksgaard samt illustrationer av Ebbe Sadolin. [Översattning av Carl Sam Åsberg.] Stockholm: Norstedt, 1947. 98 pp.

[A Swedish translation of *Le Bibliomane*. Not seen.]

APPENDIX

BIBLIOGRAPHY, BY AUTHOR, OF NODIER STUDIES, 1923-1967

Adhémar, Jean. "Le Livre romantique," *Le Portique*, no. 5 (1947), [93]-110.
Amadou, Robert, and Robert Kanters, eds. *Anthologie littéraire de l'occultisme*. Paris: R. Juliard, 1950. 365 pp.
Ancelot, Mme. "Le Salon de Charles Nodier; souvenirs," *Les Annales Politiques et Littéraires*, LXXXVII (1926), 597-598.
Archer, E. A. "The Prose Poem in French Literature from 1800 up to and Including the Publication of Baudelaire's 'Petits Poèmes en prose,' in 1869, with Special Reference to Ch. Nodier, Aloysius Bertrand, Maurice de Guérin and Gérard de Nerval." Diss., London, Westfield College, 1957-58.
Aubert, R. "Le Centenaire de la mort de Charles Nodier a été commémoré à Lons-le-Saunier," *Le Nouvelliste* (de Lyon), 8 févr. 1944.
―――. "Le Centenaire de la mort de Charles Nodier; conférence et théâtre; la journée de dimanche," *Le Nouvelliste* (de Lyon), 10 févr. 1944.
―――. "Le Centenaire de la mort de Charles Nodier. Une Voix du terroir," *Le Nouvelliste* (de Lyon), 9 févr. 1944.
Aymonnier, Camille. "Charles Nodier linguiste," *Le Pays Comtois*, CVII (août 1937), 227-233.
Aynard, Joseph. "Les Idées et les livres: Charles Nodier," *Journal des Débats*, Édition Hebdomadaire, 26 janv. 1924, pp. 185-187.
Bain, Margaret I. *Les Voyageurs français en Écosse, 1770-1830, et leurs curiosités intellectuelles*. Bibliothèque de la Revue de

Littérature Comparée, Vol. 79. Paris: Honoré Champion, 1931. 226 pp.

Baldensperger, F[ernand]. "Les Années 1827-1828 en France et au dehors: I. [Introduction]," *Revue des Cours et Conférences*, XXIX, sér. 1, (1927-28), [405]-420; "II. Les Nouveaux Contacts de société," XXIX, sér. 1, (1927-28), [494]-511; "V. L'Appel au romantisme des provinces," XXIX, sér. 2, (1928), [227]-240; "VII. Les 'Moyennes' romantiques de 1827-1828," XXX, sér. 1, (1928-29), [177]-192; "IX. Les Représentations anglaises à Paris en 1827-28," XXX, sér. 1, (1928-29), [629]-645.

——. *La Critique et l'histoire littéraires en France au dix-neuvième et au début du vingtième siècles*, en collaboration avec H. S. Craig, Jr. Bibliothèque Brentano's, Études d'Histoire et de Critique Littéraires. New York: Brentano's, 1945. 244 pp.

Banachévitch, N. "Les Romantiques français et la Serbie," *La Revue des Lettres Modernes*, no. 10 (nov. 1954), pp. 9-15.

Barineau, Elizabeth. "La *Tribune Romantique* et le romantisme de 1830," *Modern Philology*, LXII (1964-65), 302-324.

Battista, Piero. "L'Analisi del sogno in *La Fée aux Miettes*," *Le Lingue Straniere*, XII, no. 6 (nov.-dic. 1963), 9-12.

Bauer, Henri François. *Les "Ballades" de Victor Hugo*. Paris: Les Presses Modernes, 1935. xlv, 199 pp.

Bays, Gwendolyn. "The Seer in French Romanticism: Voyance in the Unsophisticated Characters of Charles Nodier," in her *Orphic Vision: Seer Poets from Novalis to Rimbaud*. Lincoln: University of Nebraska Press, 1964. Pp. 77-80.

Bazziconi, Michèle. "Le Rêve dans l'œuvre de Charles Nodier. Diplôme d'études supérieures." [s. d. 1961?]

Béguin, Albert. *L'Âme romantique et le rêve; essai sur le romantisme allemand et la poésie française*. 2 vols. Marseille: Éditions des Cahiers du Sud, 1937.

——. *L'Âme romantique et le rêve; essai sur le romantisme allemand et la poésie française*. Nouv. éd. Paris: José Corti, 1939. xvii, 413 pp.

——. "Charles Nodier ou l'enfance restaurée," *Cahiers du Sud*, no. 304 (1950), pp. [353]-357.

Béguin, Albert. "Charles Nodier ou l'enfance restaurée," in his *Poésie de la présence. De Chrétien de Troyes à Pierre Emmanuel*. Les Cahiers du Rhône, 95. Sér. Blanche, 29. Neuchâtel: La Baconnière; Paris: Éditions du Seuil, 1957. Pp. [169]-175.

———. "Nodier et Nerval," *Labyrinthe*, no. 1 (1944).

Benassis, Docteur. "Essais de clinique romantique: Charles Nodier ou l'onirique," *Revue Thérapeutique des Alcaloïdes; Recueil d'Études Physiologiques et Cliniques sur les Alcaloïdes et Autres Principes Actifs Retirés du Règne Végétal*, 4e sér., 48e année (1940), pp. 70-76, 94-101, 118-126; 5e sér., 49e année (1941), pp. 8-15, 30-38, 54-65.

Bender, Edmund John. "Charting French Romanticism: the Criticism of Charles Nodier." Ann Arbor, Mich.: University Microfilms, Inc., 1968. 289 pp. [Diss. from Indiana University, 1968.]

Bérence, Fred. "Charles Nodier ou les sources de la poésie (1780-1844)," in his *Grandeur spirituelle du XIXe siècle français. I. Les Aînés*. Paris: La Colombe, 1958. Pp. [153]-176.

Bernard, Jean-Jacques. *Le Camp de la mort lente (Compiègne, 1941-42)*. Paris: Éditions Albin Michel, 1944. 246 pp.

Billey, Maurice. "Un Magistrat révolutionnaire: le père de Charles Nodier," *Bulletin de la Fédération des Sociétés Savantes de Franche-Comté*, no. 2 (1955), pp. 116-164.

Blanco, Louise S. "Origin and History of the Plot of *Marianela*," *Hispania, a Journal Devoted to the Interests of the Teaching of Spanish and Portuguese*, XLVIII (1965), 463-467.

Blaser, Edouard. "Um Charles Nodier," *Neue Schweizer Rundschau*, XX (1927), 599-605.

Bousquet, Jacques. *Les Thèmes du rêve dans la littérature romantique (France, Angleterre, Allemagne); essai sur la naissance et l'évolution des images*. Études de Littérature Étrangère et Comparée, 47. Paris: Didier, 1964. 656 pp.

Brandicourt, Virgile. "Charles Nodier naturaliste," *La Nature*, LXII, pt. 1 (1934), 369-371.

Bray, René. *Chronologie du Romantisme (1804-1830)*. Bibliothèque de la Revue des Cours et Conférences. Paris: Boivin, 1932. vii, 238 pp.

Brockett, O. G. "Charles Nodier's Estimate of Shakespeare," *Shakespeare Quarterly*, XII (1961), 345-348.

Broyer, Ch. "Charles Nodier, cryptogamiste," *Bulletin de la Société Botanique de France*, LXXX (1933), 30-31.

———. "La Jeunesse agitée de Charles Nodier en Franche-Comté," *Bulletin de la Société des Naturalistes et Archéologues de l'Ain*, no. 50 (1936), pp. 271-285.

Brunot, Ferdinand. *Histoire de la langue française des origines à nos jours*. Vol. XII: *L'Époque romantique*, by Charles Bruneau. Paris: Armand Colin, 1948. xix, 593 pp.

C., G. "Le Centenaire de la réception de Nodier à l'Académie," *Journal des Débats* [Édition Hebdomadaire?], 5 janv. 1934, p. 36.

Cailliet, Émile. *The Themes of Magic in Nineteenth Century French Fiction*. English Translation by Lorraine Havens. Paris: Les Presses Universitaires de France, 1932. xii, 228 pp.

Caillois, Roger. "Puissances du rêve," *Tel Quel*, no. 8 (hiver 1962), pp. [14]-25.

Callet, Albert. "Une Audience de Charles Nodier à l'Arsenal," *Rev. Franche-Comté et Monts Jura*, avril 1923, p. 156.

C[alot], Fr[antz]. "En 1844 Charles Nodier mourait," *Bulletin du Bibliophile et du Bibliothécaire*, 1940-45, pp. [157]-168.

———. " 'Le Salon de Charles Nodier et les romantiques,' exposition à la Bibliothèque de l'Arsenal (16 mai-16 juin 1927)," *Bulletin du Bibliophile et du Bibliothécaire*, n. s., VI (1927), [266]-272.

Castex, Pierre-Georges. *Anthologie du conte fantastique français*. Paris: José Corti, 1947. 326 pp.

———. *Anthologie du conte fantastique français. Deuxième édition, entièrement refondue, avec des textes nouveaux et des notices inédites*. Paris: José Corti, 1963. 343 pp.

———. "Balzac et Charles Nodier," in *L'Année balzacienne, 1962*. Paris: Éditions Garnier Frères, 1962. Pp. [197]-212.

———. "Un Inédit de Charles Nodier: 'Ferry Barbis,' " *Annales Publiées par la Faculté des Lettres de Toulouse. Littératures*, IV, fasc. 1-2 (1956), 7-19.

———. "Nodier et ses rêves," in *Le Conte fantastique en France de Nodier à Maupassant*. Paris: José Corti, 1951. Pp. [121]-167.

Castex, Pierre-Georges. "Nodier et ses rêves," in Charles Nodier, *Contes du pays des rêves*. Saverne: Club des Libraires de France, 1957. Pp. [391]-443.

―――. "Nodier et ses rêves," in *Le Conte fantastique en France de Nodier à Maupassant*. Nouvelle ed. Paris: José Corti, 1962. Pp. [121]-167.

―――. "Une Source de *La Fée aux Miettes*," *Revue des Sciences Humaines*, n. s., 1950, pp. [205]-208.

Charles, Paul-A. "Charles Nodier et Victor Hugo," *Revue d'Histoire Littéraire de la France*, XXXIX (1932), 568-586.

Charlier, Gustave. *Le Mouvement romantique en Belgique (1815-1850)*. 2 vols. Bruxelles: Palais des Académies, 1948-59.

―――. "Sœur Béatrice et Béatrijs," in *Mélanges publiés en l'honneur de M. le professeur Vaclav Tille à l'occasion de son 60ème anniversaire, 1867-1927*. Prague: Éditions Orbis, 1927. Pp. 26-30.

Chouan's Geneviève. "Ceux du Cénacle, vus par les frères Pavie, d'Angers," *La Revue Moderne des Arts et de la Vie*, 1er juil. 1958, pp. 28-29; 1er août 1958, pp. 28-29.

Citron, Pierre. "Aux Sources d'*Une Fille d'Ève*," in *L'Année balzacienne, 1965*. Paris: Éditions Garnier Frères, 1965. Pp. [201]-215.

Clancier, Georges-Emmanuel. *De Chénier à Baudelaire; panorama critique*. Collection Melior: La Poésie Française. Paris: Éditions Seghers, 1963. 442 pp.

Clarac, Pierre. "Onze Lettres adressées à Chateaubriand (1819-1825)," *Societé Chateaubriand Bulletin*, n. s., no. 3 (1959), pp. 19-30.

Clouard, Henri. "Nodier et sa multiple figure," in Charles Nodier, *La Fée Aux Miettes ... L'Homme et la fourmi*. Bibliothèque Mondiale, no. 8, 7 mai 1953. Paris: Éditions de la Bibliothèque Mondiale, 1954. Pp. 185-192.

―――. "Nodier et sa multiple figure," in Charles Nodier, *La Fée aux Miettes ... suivi de L'Homme et la fourmi, apologue primitif*. Paris: Le Livre Mondiale, s. d. [Entre 1936-1959.]

Cluzel, Étienne. "Une Édition fantôme des 'Petits Châteaux de Bohême,'" *Bulletin du Bibliophile et du Bibliothécaire*, n. s., 1956, pp. [80]-86.

Coco, Antonio. *Miti solari. P. B. Shelley in Italia. Il Profeta di Monte Labbro. Trieste vista da un romantico.* Trieste: Tipografia Triestina, 1963. 55 pp.

Coindre, Gaston. *Mon Vieux Besançon; histoire pittoresque et intime d'une ville.* Éd. abrégée avec la collaboration de Guy Chassagnard et Jean Ledoux. Besançon: Imprimerie Jacques & Demontrond, 1960. 525 pp.

Cuentos de bibliófilo; originales de C. Nodier [et al.], precedidos de un prólogo de R. Miguel y Planas. Ilus. de Triadó [et al.] con ornamentaciones de J. Figuerola. Barcelona: Instituto Catalán de las Artes del Libro, 1951. 101, 349 pp.

Cummings, Edith Katharine. *The Literary Development of the Romantic Fairy Tale in France.* Bryn Mawr, Pa., 1934. 100 pp.

Dargaud, Marius. "Les Amis jurassiens de Charles Nodier vont célébrer le centenaire de sa mort," *Journal des Débats,* 29-30 janv. 1944.

―――. "Autour de Charles Nodier. Antoine de Mailly de Châteaurenaud, curieuse figure de la Révolution, et la famille Charve," *Le Nouvelliste* (de Lyon), 12 janv. 1944.

―――. "Autour d'un Centenaire. Charles Nodier au *Journal des Débats,*" *Journal des Débats,* 24 janv. 1944.

―――. "Autour d'un Centenaire. Charles Nodier, jurassien," *Le Nouvelliste* (de Lyon), 7 janv. 1944.

―――. "Autour d'une Exposition littéraire. Le Douzième Fauteuil académique, de Charles Nodier à Marcel Pagnol (1833-1947)," *L'Espoir* (Saint-Étienne), 7 et 8 avril 1947.

―――. "Le Centenaire de la mort de Charles Nodier," *Chroniques* (Vichy), no. 38. [1944?]

―――. "Le Centenaire de la mort de Charles Nodier," *Lyon Républicain,* 25 janv. 1944.

―――. "Le Centenaire de la mort de Charles Nodier," *Le Mois à Lyon.* [ca. 1944?]

―――. "Le Centenaire de la mort de Charles Nodier," *La Page* (Lyon), 4 févr. 1944.

―――. *Centenaire de la mort de Charles Nodier (1780-1844), Lons-le-Saunier, 5 et 6 février, 1944. Théâtre Municipal. Représentations littéraires et artistiques avec le concours du Cercle Artistique Lédonien. Programme.* Lons-le-Saunier: M. Declume, 1944. 4 pp.

Dargaud, Marius. "Charles Nodier dans ses horizons," *Journal des Débats*, 6 juil. 1944.

———. "Charles Nodier et le marquis de Moustier," *La République de Franche-Comté et du Territoire de Belfort* (Besançon), 12 sept. 1945.

———. "Charles Nodier, jurassien," *Le Mois à Lyon*. [ca. 1944?]

———. "Charles Nodier poète et l'épopée napoléonienne (1833)," *Bulletin du Bibliophile et du Bibliothécaire*, n. s., 1951, pp. [211]-217.

———."Charles Nodier (1780-1844). La Commémoration du centenaire de sa mort sous l'oppression," *Bulletin du Bibliophile et du Bibliothécaire*, n. s., 1946, pp. [216]-223.

———. "Une Correspondance familiale inédite de Marie Nodier (1833-1868)," *Bulletin du Bibliophile et du Bibliothécaire*, n. s., 1949, pp. [371]-399.

———. "Deux Lettres de jeunesse de Marie Nodier (1827)," *Bulletin du Bibliophile et du Bibliothécaire*, n. s., 1948, pp. [560]-569.

———. "L'Édition originale du *Génie Bonhomme* de Charles Nodier (1836)," *Bulletin du Bibliophile et du Bibliothécaire*, n. s., 1950, pp. [42]-50.

———. "L'Étrange Nuit de Ghismondo," *La Liberté* (Lyon), 24 déc. 1945.

———. *Exposition organisée à la Chambre de Commerce de Lons-le-Saunier par le Comité des Amis Jurassiens de Charles Nodier à l'occasion du centenaire de sa mort, 5-6 février, 1944. Autour de Charles Nodier*. Catalogue établi par M. Marius Dargaud. Lons-le-Saunier: M. Declume, 1944. 39 pp.

———. "Une Filleule de Madame Nodier à l'Arsenal (d'après des documents inédits)," in *Mélanges d'histoire du livre et des bibliothèques offerts à Monsieur Frantz Calot*, conservateur en chef honoraire de la Bibliothèque de l'Arsenal. Paris: Librairie d'Argences, 1960. Pp. [337]-368.

———. "Une Lettre inédite de Charles Nodier," *Journal des Débats*, 17 juil. 1944.

———. "Une Lettre retrouvée de Charles Nodier," *Bulletin du Bibliophile et du Bibliothécaire*, n. s., 1946, pp. [102]-110.

Dargaud, Marius. "Nodier mémorialiste: *Suites d'un mandat d'arrêt* (fragment inédit)," *Revue des Sciences Humaines,* n. s., 1951, pp. [273]-281.

———. "Une Pseudo-Édition du *Livre de beauté* (1846)," *Bulletin du Bibliophile et du Bibliothécaire,* n. s., 1950, pp. [298]-302.

Decottignies, Jean. "Variations sur un succube; Histoire de Thibaud de la Jacquière," *Revue des Sciences Humaines,* n. s., no. 111 (1963), pp. [329]-340.

Dédéyan, Charles. *Victor Hugo et l'Allemagne.* Vol. I. *La Formation.* Bibliothèque de Littérature et d'Histoire, no. 3. Paris: M. J. Minard, 1964. 265 pp.

Dédéyan, Christian. "Charles Nodier annociateur du rêve," *Points et Contrepoints,* no. 62-63 (déc. 1962), pp. 28-32.

Deharme, Lise. "Charles Nodier," in Francis Dumont, ed., *Les Petits Romantiques français.* Liguge: Les Cahiers du Sud, 1949. Pp. 189-205.

Delétang-Tardif, Yanette. "Je visite les soleils ...," *Cahiers du Sud,* no. 304 (1950), pp. [358]-363.

———. "Souvenir de Nodier; cheval pâle," *Paris, les Arts et les Lettres,* 2e année, no. 6 (9 janv. 1946), 1.

Descaves, Pierre. "Charles Nodier," in Charles Nodier, *La Fee aux Miettes ... L'Homme et la fourmi.* Bibliothèque Mondiale, no. 8, 7 mai 1953. Paris: Éditions de la Bibliothèque Mondiale, 1954. Pp. 1-5.

———. "Charles Nodier," in Charles Nodier, *La Fée aux Miettes,* présentée par Pierre Descaves. Paris: Éditions de la Bibliothèque Mondiale, 1956.

———. "Charles Nodier," in Charles Nodier, *La Fée aux Miettes ... suivi de L'Homme et la fourmi, apologue primitif.* Paris: Le Livre Mondiale, s. d. [Entre 1936-1959.]

Deslandres, Paul. "La Bibliothèque de l'Arsenal, berceau du romantisme et sanctuaire du théâtre," *Le Correspondant,* CCCVII (1927), 737-743.

Dollot, René. "Les Romans illyriens de Charles Nodier," *Revue de Littérature Comparée,* XI (1931), 285-314.

———."Trieste et la France. Histoire d'un consulat. La Révolution et l'Empire (Suite et fin)," *Revue d'Histoire Diplomatique,* LXXIII (1959), [137]-164.

Dollot, René. *Trieste et la France (1702-1958); histoire d'un consulat.* Paris: A. Pedone, 1961. 259 pp.

Duban, Edmund. "Charles Weiss, un ami de Charles Nodier." Thèse compl. Lettres, Paris, 1952.

———. "La Jeunesse de Charles Nodier." Thèse. Lettres, Paris, 1952.

Duhamel, Georges, ed. *Anthologie de la poésie lyrique en France de la fin du XVe siècle à la fin du XIXe siècle.* Paris: Flammarion, 1946. xxxix, 532 pp.

Duhamel, Roger. "De Nouveaux Noms, des œuvres nouvelles," *Revue de l'Université d'Ottawa,* XXXIV (1964), 191-220.

———. "De Nouveau Noms, des œuvres nouvelles," in his *Aux Sources du romantisme français.* Ottawa. Université. Publications Sériées, No. 74. Ottawa: Éditions de l'Université d'Ottawa, 1964. Pp. [159]-188.

Durry, Marie-Jeanne, *see* Morlanwelz, Belgium. Musée de Mariemont.

Easton, Malcolm. *Artists and Writers in Paris; the Bohemian Idea, 1803-1867.* New York: St. Martin's Press, 1964. viii, 205 pp.

Eggli, Edmond. *Schiller et le romantisme français.* 2 vols. Paris: J. Gamber, 1927.

———, and Pierre Martino. *Le Débat romantique en France, 1813-1830. Pamphlets. Manifestes. Polémiques de presse.* Publications de la Faculté des Lettres d'Alger, IIe sér., Vol. VI. Paris: Société d'Édition "Les Belles Lettres," 1933—. 498 pp.

Engler, Winfried. *Der französische Roman von 1800 bis zur Gegenwart.* Sammlung Dalp, Bd. 97. Bern: Francke, 1965. 299 pp.

———. "Der Mythos vom verlorenen Paradies bei Charles Nodier," *Antaios,* IV (1962-63), 521-535.

Engstrom, Alfred G. "The Formal Short Story in France and Its Development before 1850," *Studies in Philology,* XLII (1945), 627-639.

———. "The French Artistic Short Story before Maupassant." Unpub. Diss., Univ. of North Carolina, 1941. v, 331 pp.

———. "The Voices of Plants and Flowers and the Changing Cry of the Mandrake," in *Medieval Studies in Honor of Urban Tigner Holmes, Jr.* Edited by John Mahoney and John Esten Keller. University of North Carolina Studies in the Romance

Languages and Literatures, No. 56. Chapel Hill, N. C.: University of North Carolina Press, 1965. Pp. [43]-52.

Evans, Serge. "La Jeunesse d'un conteur comtois," *Le Pays Comtois*, 20 août 1933, pp. 573-576.

Festgabe für Eduard Berend zum 75. Geburtstag am 5. Dezember 1958. Weimar: Hermann Böhlaus Nachfolger, 1959. xi, 479 pp.

Fongaro, Antoine. "A-t-on lu la *Fée aux Miettes?*" *Revue des Sciences Humaines*, n. s., no. 107 (1962), pp. [439]-452.

Fontana, Luigi. "L'Arte di Charles Nodier," *Annali della Scuola Friulana*, 1949-50, pp. 21-64.

Frandon, I.-M. "Commedia dell'Arte et imagination poétique," *Cahiers de l'Association Internationale des Études Françaises*, no. 15 (mars 1963), pp. [261]-276.

Freymann, Hella-Henriette. "Aspects littéraires des tendances platoniciennes dans la France du XIXe siècle (Literary Aspects of Platonic Tendencies in XIXth Century France)." Ann Arbor, Mich.: University Microfilms, 1956. 321 pp. [Diss. from Columbia University, 1956.]

Frieiro, Eduardo. "O Verdadeiro bibliófilo," *Revista do Livro*, Orgão do Instituto Nacional do Livro, V (1957), 183-186.

Gaiffe, Félix. "Quand Nodier pense à la petite patrie," *Le Pays Comtois*, 20 juil. 1934, pp. 453-455.

Gaulmier, Jean. "Nodier manqua d'être Nerval! En Tout Cas l'auteur d'*Aurélia* et des *Filles du feu* reconnaît en celui de *La Fée aux Miettes* son 'tuteur littéraire,'" *Le Figaro Littéraire*, 13e année (4 janv. 1958), 3.

Gauthier-Ferrières. "Charles Nodier (1780-1844)," in Charles Nodier, *Contes fantastiques*. Notice et annotations par Gauthier-Ferrières. Bibliothèque Larousse. Paris: Larousse, 1924. Pp. 5-20.

Gazier, Georges. "Un Centenaire romantique: le mariage de Marie Nodier," *Mémoires de la Société d'Émulation du Doubs*, 1930, pp. [11]-30.

———. "Nodier à l'Arsenal, d'après les carnets de voyage de son ami Ch. Weiss," *Revue d'Histoire Littéraire de la France*, XXXI (1924), 419-433.

———. "Une Œuvre de jeunesse inédite de Charles Nodier," *Procès-Verbaux et Mémoires de l'Académie des Sciences, Belles-Lettres et Arts de Besançon*, 1928, pp. [95]-102.

Gendzier, Stephen J. "Diderot's Impact on the Generation of 1830," *Studies on Voltaire and the Eighteenth Century*, XXIII (1963), 93-103.

George, Albert J. "Nodier: 'Le Vieux Marinier,'" *Modern Language Notes*, LXXV (1960), 139-143.

———. *Short Fiction in France 1800-1850*. Syracuse, N. Y.: Syracuse University Press, 1964. ix, 245 pp.

Gordon, R. K. "Le Voyage d'Abbotsford," *Proceedings and Transactions of the Royal Society of Canada*, 3d. sér., XXXIV, Sec. II (1940), 71-85.

Grillet, Claudius. *Le Diable dans la littérature au XIXe siècle*. Paris: Desclée de Brouwer, 1935. 226 pp.

Guischard, John A. *Le Conte fantastique au XIXe siècle*. Les Publications de l'Université Laval. Montréal: Fides, [1945?]. 181 pp.

Guyon, Bernard. "Balzac et Stendhal, romanciers de l'évasion," *Stendhal Club*, VIII (1965-66), [25]-31.

Guyot, Charly. *Voyageurs romantiques en pays neuchâtelois*. Neuchâtel, Paris: Delachaux et Niestlé, 1933. 181 pp.

Hartland, Reginald W. *Walter Scott et le roman frénétique, contribution à l'étude de leur fortune en France*. Bibliothèque de la Revue de Littérature Comparée, Vol. LII. Paris: Honoré Champion, 1928. 266 pp.

Hartmann, Georges. "Charles Nodier et la Garde Nationale à l'Arsenal pendant les journées de juillet 1830," *La Cité*, janv. 1931, pp. [253]-262.

Hawkins, Richmond-Laurin. "Lettres inédites de romantiques français [Nodier]," *Le Figaro*, 16 mai 1931, p. 6, and 22 août 1931, p. 5.

Held, Mariette. *Charles Nodier et le romantisme*. Thèse présentée à la Faculté des Lettres de l'Université de Berne pour obtenir le grade de docteur. Bienne: Éditions du Chandelier, 1949. 100 pp.

Henriot, Émile. "Charles Nodier ou le mythomane," in his *Courrier littéraire. XIXe siècle*. Vol. I: *Autour de Chateaubriand*. Paris: Marcel Dauban, 1948. Pp. [311]-318.

———. "Courrier littéraire: Charles Nodier ou le mythomane," *Le Temps*, 21 juil. 1931, p. 3.

Henriot, Émile. *Courrier littéraire, XIXe siècle.* Paris: Plon, Nourrit, 1925.

———. "Le Salon de Charles Nodier; la jeunesse des romantiques; pastels français du XVIIe et du XVIIIe siècles," *Revue Universelle,* XXIX (1927), 743-748.

Henry-Rosier, Mme Marguerite. "Autour du Romantisme. Deux Épisodes de la vie de Charles Nodier. I. Marie," *Le Figaro,* 18 oct. 1930, p. 6; and "II. Illyria," 25 oct. 1930, p. 6.

———. "Autour du Romantisme. La Jeunesse de Charles Nodier," *La Revue de France,* 10e année, III (1930), [304]-333.

———. "Un Chapitre inédit de la vie de Charles Nodier," *Franche-Comté, Monts-Jura et Haute Alsace,* avril 1931.

———. "Charles Nodier à Dole," *Le Pays Jurassien,* 5e année, no. 40 (oct. à déc. 1950), pp. 99-103.

———. "Un Pamphlet de Charles Nodier," *Le Figaro,* 5 sept. 1931, p. 5.

———. "Quand M. de Lamennais s'inspire de Charles Nodier," *Procès-Verbaux et Mémoires de l'Académie des Sciences, Belles-Lettres et Arts de Besançon,* 1937, pp. [16]-23.

———. "Une Satire de Charles Nodier, ou la surprise de M. Geoffroy," *Procès-Verbaux et Mémoires de l'Académie des Sciences, Belles-Lettres et Arts de Besançon,* 1935, pp. [120]-129.

———. *La Vie de Charles Nodier.* Vies des Hommes Illustres, No, 73. Paris: Gallimard, 1931. 258 pp.

Hoffmann, Léon-François. *Romantique Espagne; l'image de l'Espagne en France entre 1800 et 1850.* Publications du Département de Langues Romanes de l'Université de Princeton. [Princeton], N. J.: Université de Princeton, Dépt. de Langues Romanes; Paris: Presses Universitaires de France, 1961. 202 pp.

Horchler, D. Henriette. "Dream and Reality in the Works of Charles Nodier." Diss., Univ. of Pennsylvania, 1968. See also *Dissertation Abstracts,* XXIX (1969), 2264-A.

Iknayan, Marguerite. *The Idea of the Novel in France: the Critical Reaction, 1815-1848.* Genève: E. Droz; Paris: Minard, 1961. 199 pp.

Isola, Francesco. "Postille francesi di Alessandro Manzoni a Charles Nodier," *Studi Francesi,* VII (1963), 56-72.

Jaloux, Edmond. "Charles Nodier," in Charles Nodier, *Contes et nouvelles;* publiés avec une introduction d'Edmond Jaloux. Paris: Payot, 1927. Pp. vii-xxi.

―――. *Visages français.* Avant-propos par Henri Mondor. Paris: Albin Michel, 1954. 254 pp.

Jensen, C. "The 'Romanticism' of the *Annales de la Littérature et des Arts,*" *French Studies,* XIX (1965), 341-357.

Juin, Hubert. *Chroniques sentimentales.* Paris: Mercure de France, 1962. 232 pp.

Keller, Luzius. "Piranèse et les poètes romantiques," *Cahiers de l'Association Internationale des Études Françaises,* no. 18 (1966), pp. [179]-188.

―――. *Piranèse et les romantiques français, le mythe des escaliers en spirale.* Paris: José Corti, 1966. 255 pp.

Kies, Albert. "À propos d'un exemplaire de *Trilby* ayant appartenu à Victor Hugo," *Bulletin du Bibliophile et du Bibliothécaire,* n. s., 1957, pp. [91]-93.

―――. "Charles Nodier et Sir Herbert Croft d'après des documents inédits," *Bulletin du Bibliophile et du Bibliothécaire,* n. s., 1957, pp. [53]-56.

―――. "Deux Inédits de Charles Nodier ['Description d'une nuit orageuse dans le style des anciens bardes'; 'Le Mariage d'un faune']," *Bulletin de l'Académie Royale de Langue et de Littérature Françaises,* XXXVII (1959), 146-154.

―――. "Imitation et pastiche dans l'œuvre de Charles Nodier," *Cahiers de l'Association Internationale des Études Françaises,* no. 12 (juin 1960), pp. [67]-77.

―――. "Lettres inédites de Charles Nodier à Émile Buloz," *Bulletin de l'Académie Royale de Langue et de Littérature Françaises,* XLV (1967), [213]-223.

Killen, Alice M. *Le Roman terrifiant ou roman noir de Walpole à Anne Radcliffe et son influence sur la littérature française jusqu'en 1840.* Bibliothèque de la Revue de Littérature Comparée, Vol. IV. Paris: Édouard Champion, 1923. xvi, 255 pp.

Koch, Theodore W., ed. and tr. *Tales for Bibliophiles; Translated from the French.* Chicago: The Caxton Club, 1929. 212 pp.

Kos, Milko. "*Télégraphe Officiel* in njegove izdaje. (Le *Télégraphe Officiel* et ses éditions.)," *Muzejsko društvo za Slovenijo,*

Ljubljana. *Glasnik. Bulletin de l'Association du Musée de Slovénie*, VII-VIII, Cahier 1-4, (1926-27), 5-12.

Larat, Jean. *Bibliographie critique des œuvres de Charles Nodier, suivie de documents inédits*. Bibliothèque de la Revue de Littérature Comparée, Vol. X. Paris: Édouard Champion, 1923. 144 pp.

———. "Charles Nodier en Alsace," *L'Alsace Française, Revue Hebdomadaire d'Action Nationale*, 10ᵉ année, XX (1930), 417-422.

———. "Une première esquisse inédite des *Proscrits* de Nodier," *Revue de Littérature Comparée*, IV (1924), 111-120.

———. *La Tradition et l'exotisme dans l'œuvre de Charles Nodier (1780-1844): étude sur les origines du romantisme français*. Bibliothèque de la Revue de Littérature Comparée, Vol. IX. Paris: Édouard Champion, 1923. vi, 450 pp.

Le Yaouanc, Moïse. "Autour de *Louis Lambert*," *Revue d'Histoire Littéraire de la France*, LVI (1956), [516]-534.

Lebois, André. *Un Bréviaire du compagnonnage: "La Fée aux Miettes" de Charles Nodier*. Archives des Lettres Modernes, 1961 (III), no. 40. Paris: Lettres Modernes, 1961. 40 pp.

Lemaître, Henri. *La Poésie depuis Baudelaire*. Collection U: Série "Lettres Françaises." Paris: Armand Colin, 1965. 371 pp.

Lenôtre, G., pseud. of Louis Léon Gosselin. *La Compagnie de Jéhu; épisodes de la réaction lyonnaise, 1794-1800*. Paris: Perrin, 1931. 296 pp.

Letessier, Fernand. "La Romancière Louise d'Estournelles de Constant (1792-1860) et ses amis," *Bulletin de l'Association Guillaume Budé*, Sér. 4 (1964), pp. 464-478.

"Une Lettre inédite de Charles Nodier," *Le Figaro*, 28 mai 1927, *Supplément Littéraire*, p. 2.

"Lettre [inédite] de Charles Nodier [1ᵉʳ juillet 1828]," *Le Vieux Papier. Bulletin de la Société Archéologique, Historique et Artistique*, XX (1950-53), 354.

Lévy, Paul. "Les Romantiques français et la langue allemande," *Revue Germanique: Allemagne.—Autriche.—Pays-Bas.—Scandinavie*, XXIX (1938), [225]-252.

La Llegenda del llibreter assassí de Barcelona, per R. Miquel y Planas. Barcelona: Prempses de la Casa Miquel-Rius, 1928. xxvii, 281 pp.

Locker, Malka. *Les Romantiques: Allemagne, Angleterre, France.* Paris: Presses du Temps Présent, 1964. 308 pp.

Lods, Armand, C. M. R., and R. B. "Charles Nodier," *L'Intermédiaire des Chercheurs et Curieux,* XCIII (1930), 776-777.

Luporini, Maria Bianca. "Un Paesaggio italiano dell' *Evgenij Onegin,* Charles Nodier e 'La superba lira d'Albione,' " in *Studi in onori di Ettore lo Gatto et Giovanni Maver.* Firenze: Sansoni, 1962. Pp. 417-441.

Maingot, Éliane. "Le Baron Taylor (1789-1879)," *Le Bouquiniste Français,* 39ᵉ année, n. s., no. 14 (Noël 1959), 17-24.

———. "Les Voyages pittoresques du baron Taylor," *Le Bouquiniste Français,* n. s., no. 15 (janv. 1960), pp. 7-17.

Maixner, Rudolf. "Un Article 'illyrisant' posthume de Charles Nodier," *Annales de l'Institut Français de Zagreb,* 2ᵉ sér., nos. 2 et 3 (1953-54), pp. 163-171.

———. "Un Aspect de Philarète Chasles," *Revue de Littérature Comparée,* XXXIX (1965), [396]-405.

———. "Charles Nodier en Illyrie," *Revue des Études Slaves,* IV (1924), [252]-263.

———. *Charles Nodier et l'Illyrie.* Études de Littérature Étrangère et Comparée, 37. Paris: Didier, 1960. 132 pp.

———. *Charles Nodier i Illirija.* Rad Jugoslav, Akademije, 229. Zagreb, 1924.

———. "L'Élément illyrien dans *Jean Sbogar* de Charles Nodier," *Annales de l'Institut Français de Zagreb,* no. 20-23 (1942-43), pp. 101-123.

———. "Le Projet de l'édition illyrienne du *Télégraphe,*" *Annales de l'Institut Français de Zagreb,* no. 28-29 (1946-47), pp. [232]-242.

———. "Sur Certains Pseudo-bardes du XVIIIᵉ et du XIXᵉ siècle," in *Actes du Sixième Congrès National de la Société Française de Littérature Comparée. Littérature savante et littérature populaire. Bardes, conteurs, écrivains. Rennes, 23-25 mai, 1963.* Études de Littérature Étrangère et Comparée, 49. Paris: Didier, 1965. Pp. [106]-111.

———. "Voyageurs français en Dalmatie, réels et imaginaires: Xavier Marmier, Albert Dumont et Francis Levasseur," *Annales de l'Institut Français de Zagreb,* 8ᵉ année, nos. 24-25 (1944), pp. 84-119.

Maples, Robert J. B. "Technique and Vision in the Fiction of Charles Nodier." Ann Arbor, Mich.: University Microfilms, 1965. 255 pp. [Diss. from Yale University, 1964.]

Marc, Fernand. "Une lettre inédite de Charles Nodier," *Les Lettres; Poésie, Philosophie, Littérature, Critique*, I (1945-46), 213-216.

Marquardt, Hans. *Französische Liebesgeschichten von Nodier bis Maupassant*. Ubertr. v. Helmut Bartuschek. Ill. v. Max Schwimmer. Leipzig: Reclam, 1957. 637 pp.

Marsan, Jules. *Notes sur Charles Nodier (documents inédits)*. Toulouse: Privat, 1926.

———. "Notes sur Charles Nodier (documents inédits)," in his *Autour du romantisme*. Toulouse: Aux Éditions de l'Archer, 1937. Pp. 33-55.

Martino, Pierre. *L'Époque romantique en France, 1815-1830*. Le Livre de l'Étudiant, coll. dirigée par Paul Hazard, 16. Paris: Boivin, 1945. 186 pp.

Masson, André, and Paule Salvan. *Les Bibliothèques*. Que Sais-je?, No. 944. Paris: Presses Universitaires de France, 1961. 128 pp.

———. *Les Bibliothèques*. 2ᵉ éd. Que Sais-je?, No. 944. Paris: Presses Universitaires de France, 1963. 128 pp.

Mauriac, Claude. "La Vie des lettres: les chers fantômes d'Alexandre Dumas et de Charles Nodier," *Le Figaro*, 14 mars 1966, p. 18.

Menemencioglu, Mme Melahat. "Un Aspect surréaliste de Charles Nodier," *Procès-Verbaux et Mémoires de l'Académie des Sciences, Belles-Lettres et Arts de Besançon*, 1964-65, pp. [99]-108.

Mennessier-Nodier, Jean. "Charles Nodier et l'éducation du peuple, pages inédites," *Revue des Sciences Humaines*, n. s., no. 76 (1954), [393]-401.

Metastasio, Arthur Paul. "Vico and French Romanticism." Ann Arbor, Mich.: University Microfilms, 1963. 251 pp. [Diss. from Boston University, 1963.]

Milner, Max. *Le Diable dans la littérature française de Cazotte à Baudelaire, 1772-1861*. 2 vols. Paris: J. Corti, 1960.

Miomandre, Francis de. "*La Fée aux Miettes*," in Charles Nodier, *La Fée aux Miettes ... L'Homme et la fourmi*. Bibliothèque

Mondiale, no. 8, 7 mai 1953. Paris: Éditions de la Bibliothèque Mondiale, 1954. Pp. 7-12.

Miomandre, Francis de. "*La Fée aux Miettes*," in Charles Nodier, *La Fée aux Miettes ... suivi de L'Homme et la fourmi, apologue primitif.* Paris: Le Livre Mondiale, s. d. [Entre 1936-1959.]

Miquel y Planas, R. [Article on the personal relations of Nodier with the great bibliophile and book seller of Valencia, V. Salvá], *Correo Catalán*, 19 avril 1928.

M[iquel y] P[lanas], R. "Una Vida de bibliófilo Nodier," in Charles Nodier, *Franciscus Columna, novela bibliográfica de Carlos Nodier, precedida de El Bibliómano del mismo autor.* Traducción de Rafael V. Silvari. Pequeña Colección del Bibliófilo, dirigida por R. Miquel y Planas, Vol. III. Madrid: Librería de los Bibliófilos Españoles, 1924. Pp. ix-clxxxiv.

Mönch, Walter. *Charles Nodier und die deutsche und englische Literatur, eine Studie zur romantischen Denkform in Frankreich.* Romanische Studien, Vol. XXIV. Berlin: Emil Ebering, 1931. 128 pp.

―――. *Charles Nodier un die deutsche und englische Literatur, eine Studie zur romantischen Denkform in Frankreich.* Romanische Studien, Vol. XXIV. Berlin: Emil Ebering, 1931. Denkform und Jugendreihe, No. 1. Nendeln, Liechtenstein: Kraus, 1967. 128 pp.

―――. *Charles Nodier. Zusammenhang von Erlebnisübertragung und Denkform in der Wesensbestimmung des literarischen Einflusses.* (Teildruck). Inaugural-Dissertation zur Erlangung der Doktorwürde genehmigt von der Philosophischen Fakultät der Friedrich-Wilhelms-Universität zu Berlin. Tag der münlichen Prüfung: 16.1.1930. Tag der Promotion: 24:2.1931. Berlin: Ebering, 1931. 50 pp.

Monchoux, André. *L'Allemagne devant les lettres françaises de 1814 à 1835.* Paris: Armand Colin, [1953?]. 526 pp.

―――. *L'Allemagne devant les lettres françaises de 1814 à 1835.* Seconde édition. Paris: Armand Colin, 1965. 526 pp.

Mongland, André. "Éditeurs romantiques: Nicolas Delangle et Charles Nodier," in *Mélanges d'histoire littéraire et de bibliographie offerts à Jean Bonnerot*, conservateur en chef honoraire de la Bibliothèque de la Sorbonne, par ses amis et ses collègues. Paris: Nizet, 1954. Pp. [317]-326.

Monnot, Abel. "La Slovénie et Charles Nodier," *Bulletin Trimestriel de l'Académie des Sciences, Belles-Lettres et Arts de Besançon,* 1924, pp. 195-211.

———. "La Slovénie et Charles Nodier," in his *Études comtoises.* Besançon: Imprimerie de l'Est, 1946. Pp. 51-69.

Moraud, Marcel. *Le Romantisme français en Angleterre de 1814 à 1848; contributions à l'étude des relations littéraires entre la France et l'Angleterre dans la première moitié du XIXe siècle.* Bibliothèque de la Revue de Littérature Comparée, Vol. 90. Paris: Honoré Champion, 1933. 479 pp.

Moreau, Pierre. *Amours romantiques.* L'Amour et l'Histoire. Paris: Hachette, 1963. 320 pp.

———. "Les Faux Jours de Charles Nodier," *Droit et Liberté; Revue Bimestrielle de l'Union Chrétienne des Professeurs de l'Enseignement Officiel de Belgique,* VI (1954-55), 112-124.

———. "Les Origines du réalisme franc-comtois," *Procès-Verbaux et Mémoires de l'Académie des Sciences, Belles-Lettres et Arts de Besançon,* 1936, pp. [22]-43.

———. *Le Romantisme.* Histoire de la Littérature Française, pub. sous la direction de J. Calvet, Vol. VIII. Paris: J. de Gigord, 1932. 546 pp.

———. *Le Romantisme.* In Jean Calvet, ed., Histoire de la Littérature Française, Vol. VIII. Paris: Del Duca, 1957. 470 pp.

———. *La Tradition française du poème en prose avant Baudelaire.* Archives des Lettres Modernes, 1959 (III), no. 19-20. Paris: Lettres Modernes, 1959. 52 pp.

Morlanwelz, Belgium. Musée de Mariemont. *Autographes de Mariemont.* By Marie-Jeanne Durry. Deuxième partie, Vol. II: *De Marchangy à Victor Hugo.* Paris: Nizet, 1959.

Mornand, Pierre. "Des Physiologies en général, de celles des bouquinistes et bouquineurs en particulier," *Le Bouquiniste Français,* n. s., no. 5 (févr. 1959), pp. 11-14.

Morrow, Christine. *Le Roman irréaliste dans les littératures contemporaines de langues française et anglaise.* Paris: Didier, 1941. 332 pp.

Morse, J. Mitchell. "Charles Nodier and *Finnegans Wake*," *Comparative Literature Studies*, V, no. 2 (1968), 195-201.

Munksgaard, Ejnar. "Charles Nodier et son cercle," in Charles Nodier, *Le Bibliomane*, publié avec préface et annotations par Ejnar Munksgaard. 24 Illus. par Maurice Leloir. Paris: H. Champion, 1928. Pp. 13-28.

Nodier, Charles. "Textes de Charles Nodier: 'Jugement dernier' [présenté par J. Richer]; 'Lettre sur les origines de l'alphabet' [présentée] par Marius Dargaud; 'Piranèse. Contes psychologiques à propos de la monomanie réflective,'" *Cahiers du Sud*, no. 304 (1950), pp. [372]-386.

Oliver, A. Richard. "Charles Nodier and the Marquis de Sade," *Modern Language Notes*, LXXV (1960), 497-502.

―――. *Charles Nodier, Pilot of Romanticism*. Syracuse, N. Y.: Syracuse University Press, 1964. xi, 276 pp.

―――. "Charles Nodier's Cult of Shakespeare as a Facet of French Romanticism," *Orbis Litterarum, Revue Internationale d'Études Littéraires*, XVII (1962), [154]-165.

―――. "Nodier as Bibliographer and Bibliophile," *The Library Quarterly*, XXVI (1956), 23-30.

―――. "Nodier at the Newberry," *The Newberry Library Bulletin*, n. s., III (1952-55), 237-241.

―――. "Nodier's Criticism of the *Dictionnaire de l'Académie Française*," *The Modern Language Journal*, XLI (1957), 20-25.

―――. "An Unpublished Analysis of Some Fine Editions by the Young Bibliophile Charles Nodier," *The Library Quarterly*, XXX (1960), 140-143.

―――. "An Unpublished Letter of Charles Nodier," *Modern Language Notes*, LXXII (1957), 578-579.

Orlando, Francesco. "Charles Nodier memoralista: una infanzia sotto la Rivoluzione," *Critica Storica*, IV (1965), 279-298.

―――. *Infanzia, memoria e storia da Rousseau ai romantici*. Padova: Liviana Editrice, 1966. 253 pp.

P., J. G. "Bibliographie de Charles Nodier et de Noël et Chapsal," *Mercure de France*, CCLIV (1934), 666-667.

Palfrey, Thomas R. "Charles Nodier et l'*Europe Littéraire*," *Revue de Littérature Comparée*, VI (1926), 130-131.

Paris. Bibliothèque de l'Arsenal. *Le Salon de Charles Nodier et les romantiques, exposition à la Bibliothèque de l'Arsenal, rue de Sully, mai-juin 1927.* Paris: Albert Morancé [1927?]. 22 pp.

Partridge, Eric. *The French Romantics' Knowledge of English Literature (1820-1848) according to Contemporary Memoirs, Letters and Periodicals.* Bibliothèque de la Revue de Littérature Comparée, Vol. 14. Paris: Édouard Champion, 1924. xv, 370 pp.

Patin, Jacques. "Sur un exemplaire de Charles Nodier," *Le Figaro,* 13 déc. 1930, pp. 5-6.

Perret, J. "L'Utilisation littéraire d'un drame judiciaire bressan. Hélène Gillet," *Annales de la Société d'Émulation de l'Agriculture, Sciences, Lettres et Arts de l'Ain,* 1950, pp. [83]-94.

Pichois, Claude. *Philarète Chasles et la vie littéraire au temps du romantisme.* 2 vols. Paris: Librairie José Corti, 1965.

―――. "Surnaturalisme français et romantisme allemand: simple esquisse," in *Connaissance de l'étranger. Mélanges offerts à la mémoire de Jean-Marie Carré.* Études de Littérature Étrangère et Comparée, 50. Paris: Marcel Didier, 1964. Pp. [385]-396.

Picon, Gaëtan. "Le Roman et la prose lyrique au XIXe siècle," in Raymond Queneau, *Histoire des littératures.* Encyclopédie de la Pléiade. 3 vols. Paris: Gallimard, 1955-58. III, [999]-1107.

Pilon, Edmon. "Charles Nodier," in Charles Nodier, *Thérèse Aubert,* avec une préface d'Edmond Pilon. Bibliothèque Plon, no. 41. Paris: Plon-Nourrit, s. d. [1923?]. Pp. 7-24.

Pitollet, Camille. "Charles Nodier," *L'Intermédiaire des Chercheurs et Curieux,* XCIV (1931), 112-115.

Porter, Laurence Minot. "Le Style et l'art narratif de Charles Nodier dans les Contes." Unpub. Diss., Harvard Univ., May, 1965. viii, 378 pp.

Poulet, Georges. "Piranèse et les poètes romantiques français," *La Nouvelle Revue Française,* XIV, no. 160 (1er avril 1966), [660]-671; no. 161 (1er mai 1966), [849]-862.

―――. "Piranèse et les poètes romantiques français," in his *Trois Essais de mythologie romantique.* Paris: José Corti, 1966. Pp. 135-187.

Pourrat, Henri. *La Fontaine au bois dormant.* Les Cahiers de Paris, 2. sér., 1926, Cahier IV. Paris: Les Cahiers de Paris, 1926. 127 pp.

———. "Une imagination de province: Charles Nodier," *Nouvelles Littéraires, Artistiques et Scientifiques; Hebdomadaire d'Information, de Critique et de Bibliographie,* 25 juil. 1931, p. [1].

Prévost, Jean-Laurent. *Le Prêtre, ce héros de roman d'Atala aux Thibault.* Collection Présence du Catholicisme. Paris: P. Téqui, 1953.

Prinet, Gaston. "Charles Nodier," *L'Intermédiaire des Chercheurs et Curieux,* XCIII (1930), 738-739.

Raimbault, R.-N. "Charles Nodier et son temps," in Charles Nodier, *Contes choisis.* Introduction, choix et notes de R.-N. Raimbault. Collection Les Lettres et la Vie Française, 1re Sér., 6. Angers: Jacques Petit, 1941. Pp. vii-lxvi.

Raitt, A. W. "Introduction: Balzac and the Short Story," in [Honoré de] Balzac, *Short Stories Selected and Edited with Introduction and Notes by A. W. Raitt.* Clarendon French Series. Oxford: Oxford University Press, 1964. Pp. [7]-19.

[Recueil de documents concernant la célébration du centenaire de la mort de Charles Nodier—Lons-le-Saunier et Quintigny, 5-6 février 1944.] (Dossier comprenant 1 br. in 8° et 27 ff. in 4°.)

Richer, Jean. *Autour de "L'Histoire du roi de Bohême," Charles Nodier "dériseur sensé"; suivi de "La Plus Petite des pantoufles," par Charles Nodier.* Archives des Lettres Modernes, 1962 (III), no. 42. Paris: Lettres Modernes, 1962.

———. "Charles Nodier, dériseur sensé, [suivi de] 'Ce pacte inouï' *(Le Voleur,* chapitre IV) [et] *La Plus Petite des pantoufles,* par Charles Nodier," *Mercure de France,* CCCXV (1952), [92]-119.

———. "Gérard de Nerval et *Sylvie,*" *La Revue de Paris,* 62e année (oct. 1955), [116]-126.

———. "Le Manuscrit et les premières éditions de *La Fée aux Miettes* de Charles Nodier (matériaux pour une édition critique)," in *Mélanges d'histoire littéraire et de bibliographie offerts à Jean Bonnerot,* conservateur en chef honoraire de la

Bibliothèque de la Sorbonne, par ses amis et ses collègues. Paris: Nizet, 1954. Pp. [365]-371.

Richer, Jean. *Nerval, expérience et création.* Paris: Hachette, 1963. 708 pp.

———. "Nodier et Nerval," *Cahiers du Sud,* no. 304 (1950), pp. [364]-371.

———. "Notes bibliographiques sur Charles Nodier," *Revue des Sciences Humaines,* n. s., 1951, pp. [282]-284.

———. "*Le Roi de Bohême* ou les tentations du langage," in Charles Nodier, *Histoire du roi de Bohême et de ses sept châteaux.* Paris: Delangle Frères, 1830. [Réimpression ... 1950.]

———. "Romantiques français devant les sciences occultes," in *Proceedings of the Sixth Triennial Congress of the International Federation for Modern Languages and Literatures. Literature and Science. Oxford, 1954.* Oxford: Basil Blackwell, 1955. Pp. 242-250.

———. "Textes rares ou inédits: un auto-portrait fantaisiste et douze lettres de Charles Nodier," *Revue des Sciences Humaines,* n. s., no. 120 (1965), pp. [553]-572.

Rosenfeld, Paul. "Nodier After a Century," *The Nation,* CLIX (1944), 18-19.

Rosier, Mme Marguerite Henry-, see Henry-Rosier, Mme Marguerite.

Rudwin, Maximilian J. "The Devil-Compact in Legend and Literature," *The Open Court,* XLIV (1930), [321]-341, [419]-437.

———. *Les Écrivains diaboliques de France.* Paris: Éditions E. Figuière, 1937. 186 pp.

———. "Nodier's Fantasticism," *Open Court,* XXXVIII (1924), 8-15.

———. "Romantisme et Satanisme," *La Grande Revue,* CXXIII (1927), 549-573.

Ruff, Marcel A. "Maturin et les romantiques français," in C. R. Maturin, *Bertram, ou le château de Saint-Aldobrand.* Traduit Librement de l'Anglais par Taylor et Ch. Nodier. Éd. commentée et précédée d'une introduction sur Maturin et les romantiques français par Marcel A. Ruff. Paris: José Corti, 1956. Pp. [7]-66.

Ryner, Han. "Charles Nodier," *Cahiers des Amis de Han Ryner*, n. s., no. 74 (sept. 1964), pp. 20-22.

Sauvage, R. N. "Nodier et les Vaudevires," *Normannia, Revue Bibliographique et Critique d'Histoire de Normandie*, déc. 1931, pp. [166]-169.

Schenk, H[ans] G[eorg]. *The Mind of the European Romantics: an Essay in Cultural History*, with a Preface by Isaiah Berlin. New York: Frederick Ungar Publishing Co., 1967 [c. 1966]. xxiv, 303 pp.

Schneider, Marcel. *La Littérature fantastique en France*. Les Grandes Études Littéraires. Paris: Fayard, 1964. 425 pp.

Schulze, J. *Enttäuschung und Wahnwelt. Studien zu Nodiers Erzählungen*. Beihefte zu Poetica, 1. München: Allach, 1967. Ca. 190 pp.

Schutz, A. H. "The Nature and Influence of Charles Nodier's Philological Activity," *Studies in Philology*, XXIII (1926), 464-472.

Simon, Gustave. "Charles Nodier; lettres inédites à Victor Hugo," *La Revue Mondiale*, CLXXVII (1927), 329-339; and CLXXVIII (1927), 11-17.

Smith, Francis Prescott. "Peter Irving, Translator of *Jean Sbogar*," *Franco-American Review*, I (1937), 341-346.

Soudain, J., and Georges Goyau. "Charles Nodier," *L'Intermédiaire des Chercheurs et Curieux*, XCIII (1930), 932.

Souday, Paul, ed. *Les Romantiques à l'Académie, suivi des discours de réception de MM. de Lamartine, Charles Nodier, Victor Hugo, Sainte-Beuve, Alfred de Vigny, Alfred de Musset, et des réponses de MM. le baron Cuvier, de Jouy, de Salvandy, Victor Hugo, le comte Molé, Nisard*. Paris: Ernest Flammarion, 1928. xiii, 284 pp.

Souriau, Maurice. *Histoire du romantisme en France*. 2 vols. in 3. Paris: "Éditions Spes," 1927.

Souza, Robert de. "À Propos du phonographe.—Il faut remonter à Charles Nodier et pour l'idée et pour le mot," *Mercure de France*, CCXLVI (1933), 462-466.

Stadelmann, Josef. *Charles Nodier im Urteil seiner Zeitgenossen*. Inaugural-Dissertation, zur Erlangung der Doktorwürde der philosophischen Fakultät (I. Sektion) der Ludwig-Maximilians-Universität zu München. [Tag der mündlichen Prüfung: 19 Dezember 1929] 1929.

Stambak, Dinko. "La Complainte de la noble femme d'Asan-Aga ou l'invitation romantique au voyage illyrien," *Revue de Littérature Comparée*, 22ᵉ année (1948), 296-303.

Steib, Charles. *Les Secrets d'un conte populaire (Le Chien de Brisquet, de Charles Nosier* [sic]). Thann, 1935. 16 pp.

Storzer, Gerald H. "The Fictional Confession of Adolescent Love: a Study of Seven Romantic Novels." Ann Arbor, Mich.: University Microfilms, 1967. iv, 255 pp. [Diss. from the University of Wisconsin, 1967.]

Stowe, Richard Scribner. "Alfred de Musset and His Contemporaires: a Study of the Man and the Artist as He Appeared in His Day," *Dissertation Abstracts*, XXIV (1964), 3760-61 (Wisconsin).

Switzer, Richard. "Charles Nodier: A Re-examination," *The French Review*, XXVIII (1954-55), 224-232.

T., L. S. "Charles Nodier and the Don Vicente Legend," *American Notes and Queries, a Journal for the Curious*, VI (1946-47), 134-135.

Tavzes, Janko. "Slovenski preporod pod Francozi." Ljubljana, 1929.

Teichmann, Elizabeth. *La Fortune d'Hoffmann en France*. Genève: E. Droz; Paris: Minard, 1961. 288 pp.

Thérive, André. "La Cité des plumes—Nodier précurseur," *Aujourd'hui (Paris)*, Nº des 1ᵉʳ-2 juil. 1944, p. 2.

Thiébaut, Marcel. "À Propos de Charles Nodier," *La Revue de Paris*, 38ᵉ année, V (1931), [209]-229.

Thompson, Antoinette F. "Charles Nodier's Translation of *The Vicar of Wakefield*. Unpub. Master's Thesis, Univ. of Florida, August, 1967. iii, 48 pp.

Tisseau, Paul. "Deux lettres de Charles Nodier," *Revue d'Histoire Littéraire de la France*, XXXIX (1932), 260-262.

Tobarina, Josip. "Ranjina, Bošković, Nodier, Grenville," *Prilozi za Knjizevnost, Jezik i Folklor*," Belgrade, livre VIII (1928).

Trahard, Pierre. *Prosper Mérimée et l'art de la nouvelle*. Paris: Les Presses Universitaires de France, 1923. 28 pp.

———. *Prosper Mérimée et l'art de la nouvelle*. 2ᵉ éd. Paris: Jean-Renard, 1941.

———. *Prosper Mérimée et l'art de la nouvelle. Troisième édition avec un fac-simile*. Paris: Nizet, 1952. 53 pp.

Vial, Francisque, and Louis Denise. *Idées et doctrines littéraires du XIXᵉ siècle (extraits des préfaces, traités et autres écrits théoriques)*. Paris: Delagrave, 1931. iv, 344 pp.

Viatte, Auguste. *Les Sources occultes du romantisme: illuminisme—théosophie, 1770-1820*. Bibliothèque de la Revue de Littérature Comparée, Vols. XLVI-XLVII. 2 vols. Paris: Honoré Champion, 1928.

Visan, Tancrède de. "Ce Bon Nodier," *Le Nouvelliste* [de Lyon], 5 janv. 1944, p. 1.

Vivier, Michel. "Charles Nodier, romantique et royaliste," *Aspects de la France*, V, no. 158 (1951), 3.

———. "Victor Hugo et Charles Nodier collaborateurs de *L'Oriflamme* (1823-1824)," *Revue d'Histoire Littéraire de la France*, LVIII (1958), [297]-323.

Vodoz, Jules. *"La Fée aux Miettes." Essai sur le rôle du subconscient dans l'œuvre de Charles Nodier*. Paris: Honoré Champion, 1925. xvi, 321 pp.

———. "Zu Charles Nodier's *Moi-même*," *Jahrbuch für Philologie*, II (1927), 35-[61].

Vuillame, Camille. "Nodier journaliste," *Journal des Débats*, Édition Hebdomadaire, mai 22 1927, pp. 853-854.

Warnier, R. "Contribution à la biographie intellectuelle de Ch. Nodier," *Revue de Littérature Comparée*, XIV (1934), 191-208.

Whyte, Lancelot Law. *The Unconscious before Freud*. New York: Basic Books, 1960. xi, 219 pp.

Willard, Charity Cannon. "The Remarkable Case of Clotilde de Surville," *L'Esprit Créateur*, VI (1966), 108-116.

Wilson, N. "Charles Nodier, Victor Hugo and *Les Feuilles d'automne*," *The Modern Language Review*, LX (1965), [21]-31.

Wood, Kathryn L. *Criticism of French Romantic Literature in the "Gazette de France," 1830-1848*. Philadelphia, 1934. ix, 139 pp.

INDEX*

The numeral references are to entry numbers in the bibliography.

Académie Française: 43, 83, 144-A, 212.
Alain-Fournier: 107, 247, 278.
Amateur de livres, L': 225.
Amélie: 79, 209.
Amour et le grimoire, L': 53-A.
Amyot: 166.
Andromaque: 77.
Angélique: 216.
Annales de la Littérature et des Arts: 281.
Annales ecclésiastiques: 27.
Antigone: 77.
Apocalypse du solitaire, L': 97.
Apollinaire: 128, 160.
Apuleius: 160.
Arsenal: 1, 9, 28, 57.
Arsenal, Salon at: 8, 18, 24, 26, 30, 31, 33, 34, 36, 108, 115, 184, 186, 222, 267, 99a, 114a.
Arvers, Félix: 123.
Asselin: 68.
Athalie: 77.
Aurélia: 114, 165, 216.
Aventures de Thibaud de la Jacquière: 257.
Aveugles de Chamouny, Les: 276-A.

Ballades, Les: 89, 266.
Ballanche: 77, 229.
Balzac: 90, 132, 197, 202, 244, 252, 265, 273, 277, 280, 290.
Baronius: 27.
Barthélemy, Auguste-Marseille: 58.
Baudelaire: 201, 205, 246, 290, 292.
Beaumarchais: 77.
Belgium, Nodier and: 146.
Belkiss. See "Queen of Sheba."
Berbiguier, A.-V. C.: 275.
Bernard, Jean-Jacques: 123.
Bernardin de Saint-Pierre: 229.
Bertram, ou le château de Saint-Aldobrand: 2, 204, 222.
Bertram, ou le pirate: 204.
Bertrand, Aloysius: 205, 223.
Bibliographer, Nodier as: 203.
Bibliography: 3, 167, 231, 271, 301, 307, 50a, 57a, 112a.
Bibliomane, Le: 45, 168.
Bibliophile, Nodier as: 12, 41, 42, 45, 203, 234, 241-A, 77a, 113a, 114a.
"Billet à Charles Nodier": 35.
Biography, Nodier's: 8, 22, 31, 36, 48, 49, 60, 62, 78, 98, 103, 108, 174, 184, 185, 186, 200, 271, 5a, 55a, 68a.
Blake: 279.
Breton, André: 144.
Bulletin du Bibliophile: 130, 203.

---

* Nodier's correspondence has been indexed under "Correspondence, Nodier's." The names of individual correspondents are not, for the most part, included here.

Buloz, Émile: 295.
Byron: 70.
Bzovius: 27.

Cabell, James Branch: 107.
Cailleux: 55, 143.
Calligrammes: 160.
Capote, Truman: 247.
Centenary anniversary of Nodier's death: 104, 111, 112, 113, 116, 117, 118, 119, 120, 120-A, 121, 122, 123, 124, 125, 127, 128, 129, 130, 136.
Centenary commemorations of Romanticism. See "Romanticism, Centenary commemorations of."
Cervantes: 252.
Charron: 252.
Chartreuse de Parme, La: 280.
Charve, Louise-Désirée-Victoire: 227.
Chasles, Philarète: 283, 287-A.
Chateaubriand: 61, 90, 217-A, 229.
Châteaurenaud, Antoine de Mailly de: 117, 127.
Chien de Brisquet, Le: 92.
Combe de l'homme mort, La: 53-A.
Comédie humaine, La: 202.
Compagnie de Jéhu: 63.
Compagnons de Jéhu: 63.
Confessions of an English Opium Eater: 290.
"Conscrit, Le": 169.
Constant: 229.
Constant, Louise de: 269-A.
Conte: 106, 132.
Conte de fées: 6, 84.
Contes philosophiques: 244.
Conteur féerique: 123.
Correspondence, Nodier's: 32, 35, 58, 75, 98, 125-A, 134, 137, 147, 162, 163, 171, 209, 213, 217-A, 224, 252, 288, 295, 5a.
Cosmology, Nodier's: 287-B.
Cours de littérature dramatique: 77.
Croft, Sir Herbert: 58, 209.
Cummings, E. E.: 128.
Cyrano: 252.

Dalmatie ancienne et moderne, La: 126.
D'Angers, David: 215.
Dargaud, Marius: 123.

Daumier: 113a.
De la Palingénésie humaine: 155.
De l'Amour et de son influence: 262.
"De Quelques Logomachies classiques": 135.
De Quincey, Thomas: 290.
Deburau: 258.
Delangle, Nicolas: 190.
Denise: 5.
Descendants, Nodier's: 53.
Deschamps, Émile: 217.
"Description d'une nuit orageuse dans le style des anciens bardes": 221.
Despériers, Bonaventure: 166.
Diabolism and Satanism: 15, 34, 53-A, 90, 99, 232.
Dialogus miraculorum: 27.
Dictionnaire de l'Académie Française: 212.
Diderot: 259.
Dix Journées de la vie d'Alphonse van Worden, Les: 257.
Don Vicente legend: 142, 305.
Dream, Nodier and: 25, 96, 102, 167, 197, 207, 211, 236, 245, 246, 253, 265A, 302, 303, 76a.
Drouet, Juliette: 52, 208.
Du Fantastique en littérature: 70, 275.
Ducis: 77.
Dumas père: 33, 45, 63, 291, 99a, 114a.
Dumont, Albert: 126.

Eighteenth century, Nodier and: 7, 191, 257, 269.
"Elle était bien jolie": 139.
England, Nodier and: 80.
English literature, Nodier and: 2, 14, 40, 64, 65, 153, 296.
English theatre at Paris: 24.
Esotericism and occultism: 44, 155, 197.
Essais d'un jeune barde: 2, 268.
Eugénie: 77.
Europe Littéraire, L': 21.
Evjenij Onegin: 250.
Examen critique des dictionnaires de la langue françoise: 260.
Exoticism, Nodier's: 4, 22.
Expédition des portes de fer: 35.

Fantastic, The: 5, 15, 34, 44, 72, 74, 90, 99, 133, 152, 167, 207, 245, 246, 275.
Farfadets, Les: 275.
Fée aux Miettes, La: 17, 25, 37, 72, 84, 96, 114, 153, 156, 157, 188, 189, 192, 195, 216, 241, 248, 253, 255, 269, 275, 279, 299, 76a.
"Femme d'Asan": 126.
Femme d'Hassan-Aga, La: 126, 149.
"Ferry Barbis": 198.
Feuilles d'automne, Les: 289.
Fille d'Ève, Une: 277.
Filles du feu, Les: 216.
Finnegans Wake: 303.
Folklore and popular legends and literatures, Nodier and: 68, 74.
Fortis, Alberto: 126, 231, 284.
"Fous de Pirieu, Les": 270.
"Fou du Pirée, Le": 270.
France, Anatole: 164.
Franciscus Columna: 12, 168, 180, 308, 77a.
Franque, Lucile: 268.
Freemasonry: 241.

Gaspard de la nuit: 223.
Galdós, Pérez: 276-A.
Gaule poétique, La: 70.
Gautier: 90, 290, 292.
Genealogy, Nodier's: 194.
Génie Bonhomme, Le: 84, 158.
German literature and language, Nodier and: 64, 65, 101, 152, 153, 179, 286, 296.
Giraudoux: 107.
Goethe: 90.
Gourmont: 160.
Green, Julien: 107.
Guérin, Maurice de: 205.

Hamlet: 77.
Hasanaghinitsa. See "Femme d'Hassan-Aga."
Heisterbach, Césaire de: 27.
Heredia: 129.
Histoire des califats: 171.
Histoire d'Hélène Gillet: 164, 265.
Histoire du roi de Bohême: 35, 128, 138, 160, 165, 166, 176, 190, 193, 244, 252, 255, 264.

Hoffmann: 90, 242, 275.
Hugo: 30, 35, 52, 73, 89, 99, 197, 208, 217, 252, 266, 268, 289, 290, 292.
Hypnerotomachia. See "Songe de Poliphile."

Ideal woman, Theme of: 153.
Illuminism: 44, 165.
Illyria, Nodier and: 11, 13, 19, 48, 56, 58, 87, 110, 141, 178, 218, 231, 238, 284, 304, 307.
Inès de las Sierras: 2, 53-A, 106, 132, 165, 167, 239, 290.
Infernaliana: 257.
Irving, Peter: 100.
Irving, Washington: 100.
Isabey: 55.

Janin: 259.
Jarry: 160.
Jean-François les Bas-Bleus: 265.
Jean Sbogar: 56, 100, 110, 128, 165, 231, 250, 256.
Johannot, Tony: 143.
Journal des Débats: 83, 118.
Journalist, Nodier as: 19, 21, 38, 77, 118, 217, 19a.
Jouy, de: 83.
Joyce: 303.

La Bruyère: 229.
La Fontaine: 229.
Laforgue: 160.
Lamennais: 90, 97.
Lautréamont: 211.
Levasseur, Francis: 126.
Lewis, Matthew Gregory: 53-A.
Lezeverne: 55.
Librarian, Nodier as: 28, 57, 130, 241-A, 260-A.
Linguistics, Nodier and: 23, 81, 95, 145.
Literary criticism, Nodier's: 29, 70, 73, 77, 131, 153, 240, 282, 301.
Livre de beauté, Le: 159.
Louis Lambert: 202.
Lydie ou la résurrection: 265.

Mademoiselle de Marsan: 2, 56, 231, 249.

Madness: 144, 211, 270, 298.
Maeterlinck: 27.
Magic. See "Fantastic, The."
Mallarmé: 128, 290, 292.
Manutius, Aldus: 114a.
Manzoni: 260.
Marchangy: 70.
Maréchal, Sylvain: 229.
"Mariage d'un faune, Le": 221.
Marianela: 276-A.
Marion Delorme: 73.
Marmier, Xavier: 126.
Marot: 166.
Marvellous, The. See "Fantastic, The."
Mateo Falcone: 6.
Maturin: 204.
Méditations du cloître: 268.
Mélanges de littérature et de critique: 282.
Memorialist, Nodier as: 170, 287, 291-A.
Mennessier-Nodier, Marie. See "Nodier, Marie."
Mérimée: 6, 46, 109, 132, 177, 273, 283, 284.
Mes Mémoires: 33, 45, 99a, 114a.
Mille et un fantômes: 291.
Millevoye: 89.
Moi-même: 37.
Montaigne: 166, 252.
Monténégrins, Les: 165.
Moustier, marquis de: 131-A.
Muse du département, La: 280.
Music, Nodier and: 213.
Musset: 33, 276.
Mythomaniac, Nodier as: 59, 148.

Napoleon: 39, 93, 161.
Napoléone, La: 169.
Naturalist, Nodier as: 76, 82.
Nerval: 31, 114, 129, 153, 165, 172, 197, 199, 201, 205, 216, 246, 249, 263.
Neuvaine de la Chandeleur, La: 128, 249.
Nodier, Désirée (Mme): 17, 227.
Nodier, Marie: 17, 35, 47, 48, 96, 123, 147, 150, 198, 269-A.
Nouvelle: 6.
Novalis: 279.

Occultism. See "Esotericism and occultism."
Odes: 266.
Opinions de Jérôme Coignard, Les: 164.
Orientales, Les: 135.
Oriflamme, L': 217.
Orsini-Rosenberg, Countess: 284.
Ossian, ou les bardes: 77.

Paradise, Idea of in Nodier: 156, 206, 247, 291-A.
Parnasse du jour, Le: 61.
Paroles d'un croyant: 97.
Paul, Jean: 220.
Pavie, Théodore: 215.
Pavie, Victor: 215, 264.
Peintre de Salzbourg, Le: 268.
Pensées de Joseph Delorme: 135.
Perrault: 84.
Petits Châteaux de Bohême, Les: 165, 199.
Petits Poèmes en prose: 205.
Philippe de Thaün: 279.
Pierrot: 258.
Piranèse: 163, 290.
Piranesi: 289-A, 290, 292, 293.
Platonic tendencies in Nodier: 201.
Plus Petite des pantoufles, La: 176, 252.
Poetry, Nodier's: 8, 139, 228, 5a.
Pons, Gaspard de: 217.
Potocki, Jan: 257.
Princesse de Brambilla, La: 275.
Promenade de Dieppe aux montagnes d'Écosse: 55, 76.
Proscrits, Les: 10.
Pushkin: 250.

Quaï, Maurice: 268.
Queen of Sheba: 17, 165, 76a.
Quintigny: 123-A.

Rabelais: 166, 252.
Radcliffe, Ann: 2.
Rançon de Duguesclin, La: 77.
Realism, Nodier's: 94, 153.
"Recherches sur l'éloquence révolutionnaire": 131.
Regionalism, Nodier's: 22, 24, 55, 67, 191.

Renduel: 32, 171.
Revue de Paris: 69.
Rimbaud: 201.
Roman: 6.
Roman noir ou frénétique: 2, 40.
Romanticism, Centenary commemorations of: 26, 30, 33, 43, 47, 83.
Romanticism, Nodier and: 4, 23, 24, 36, 71, 74, 153, 271, 301.
Rosset, François de: 257.
Roujoux: 294.
Rousseau: 64, 145.

Sade, Marquis de: 233.
Sainte-Beuve: 101, 135, 242, 259, 50a.
Saint-Valry, Adolphe de: 217.
Sand, George: 247.
Satanism. See "Diabolism and Satanism."
Schiller: 29.
Schlegel: 77.
Schneider, Euloge: 50.
Scienza nuova: 261.
Scotland, Nodier and: 55, 105.
Scott: 40, 55, 90, 105.
Secret d'Arvers, Le: 123.
Sénancour: 229.
Séraphine: 287.
Shakespeare: 237, 251.
Slovenia. See "Illyria."
Smarra: 144, 165, 167, 193, 231, 242, 243, 254, 255, 265.
Sœur Béatrice: 27.
Songe de Poliphile: 12, 78a, 114a.
Songe d'or, Le: 57a.
Souvenirs: 63, 79, 170, 233, 249, 287, 291-A.
Statistique illyrienne: 87, 140.
Stendhal: 46, 280.
Stephens, James: 107.
Sterne: 160, 166, 229, 252.
Style, Nodier's: 287-B.
Subconscious, The: 17.

Suites d'un mandat d'arrêt: 170.
Surrealism and Surrealists: 211, 246, 270-A, 302.
Surville, Clotilde de: 294.
Swift: 160, 166, 252.
Switzerland, Nodier and: 79.
Sylvie: 196.
Symbolism and Symbolists: 193, 201, 246.

Taylor, Baron: 55, 143, 222, 230.
Télégraphe Officiel: 19, 140, 178, 19a.
Thérèse Aubert: 180, 196.
Tradition in Nodier's work: 4, 7.
Translator, Nodier as: 204, 300.
Travels, Nodier's: 50, 55, 79, 105, 146, 218, 231, 239.
Trésor des Fèves et Fleur des Pois: 84.
Tribune Romantique: 264.
Trilby: 44, 52, 72, 84, 156, 167, 195, 208.
"Triste Ballade de la noble épouse d'Asan-Aga": 126.
Turquéty: 88.

Vampire, Le: 2.
Vampire, The: 70.
Vaudevires: 68.
Viaggio in Dalmazia: 284.
Vicar of Wakefield, The: 287-A, 300.
Vico: 261.
"Vieux Marinier, Le": 228.
Vigny: 276.
Villiers de l'Isle-Adam: 201.
Villon: 229.
Voleur, Le: 163, 176, 252.
Voyages pittoresques et romantiques dans l'ancienne France: 143, 230.

Walpole: 2.
Weiss, Charles: 47, 173.
Woolf, Virginia: 107.

ADDENDUM

To Part II

A TENTATIVE BIBLIOGRAPHY OF THE WORKS OF
CHARLES NODIER, 1923-1967

Nodier's Translations of Works from Other Languages

142a. Goldsmith, Oliver. *Le Vicaire de Wakefield*. Traducción de Charles Nodier. Paris: Librairie Commerciale et Artistique, 1966. 252 pp.

143a. Maturin, C. R. *Bertram, ou le chateau de Saint-Aldobrand*. Traduit librement de l'anglais par Taylor et Ch. Nodier. Edition commentée et précedée d'une introduction sur Maturin et les romantiques français par Marcel A. Ruff. Paris: José Corti, 1956. 158 pp.

For the introduction by Ruff see 204.

www.ingramcontent.com/pod-product-compliance
Lightning Source LLC
Chambersburg PA
CBHW022022220426
43663CB00007B/1177